THE
PROTES
FAIT

THE PROTESTANT FAITH

by
George Wolfgang Forell

FORTRESS PRESS

Philadelphia

Second printing 1977
Third printing 1979

Copyright © 1960 by George W. Forell

First published by Prentice-Hall, Inc. Fortress
Press edition, with revisions, printed in 1975

Biblical quotations, unless otherwise noted, are from the Revised Standard
Version of the Bible; Old Testament Section, Copyrighted 1952; New Testa-
ment Section, First Edition, Copyrighted 1946; New Testament Section,
Second Edition, © 1972 by the Division of Christian Education of the
National Council of Churches of Christ in the U.S.A.

Library of Congress Catalog Card Number 74-26341

ISBN 0-8006-1095-4

8078J79   Printed in the United States of America   1-1095

To my students
Protestant, Catholic, Jewish, Agnostic
at the University of Iowa

TABLE OF CONTENTS

CONTENTS

PREFACE

For some years it was my privilege to teach a course on the Protestant faith in one of our state universities. My students came from the most diverse backgrounds. Every shade of belief and unbelief was represented. But one characteristic was shared by almost all of them: they knew very little about the Protestant faith. The effort to explain to them the common faith of this great Christian tradition eventually produced this book. While assuming very little previous knowledge, it tries to cover the basic teachings of the mainstream of Protestantism. The emphasis is upon the great central Christian assertions and upon the essential unity of classical Protestantism. The apparent diversity of the multitude of denominations should not blind us to the common witness of Protestant Christianity. Denominational differences are real, and some are very important; yet it is apparent that the vital theological discussions of the day are not carried on along denominational lines. Today as in the past, classical Protestantism has found eloquent spokesmen in many of its different branches. That I am indebted to them all, the informed reader will easily perceive. The writing of this book is an effort to express my gratitude to all the Christian thinkers here and abroad whose work has made classical Protestantism a live option for modern America.

1960   G. W. F.

PREFACE TO THE
NEW EDITION

When approached about a new edition of this short summary
of the Christian faith, which first appeared in 1960 just before the
election of John F. Kennedy and two years before the first meeting
of Vatican II, I was aware of how much had changed. Some friends
suggested that the very title of the book, *The Protestant Faith,*
seemed now unnecessarily exclusive. For much of what is here
presented does indeed constitute the catholic Christian faith. This
was stressed particularly by some of the Roman Catholic readers of
the book. Nevertheless I have retained the original title, since the
Protestant emphasis *within* the catholic Christian tradition is
stressed. The careful reader will note, however, that some of the
polemical observations have disappeared. John XXIII and Vatican
II made them obsolete. The same reader will also observe that a
valiant effort has been made to avoid language that might be construed as sexist, a development which is the result of the universal
broadening of consciousness in recent years. However, I ask the
reader to understand with me that I intend the meaning of the
generic word *man* and its relative pronoun *he* to mean human
being.

I have ignored the so-called radical developments in theology since
1960 because they appear to be as evanescent as the pop songs of yesterday. They were never radical in the sense of looking at the roots
of the Christian reality but rather fleeting forms of culture-religion
attempting to make the Christian faith acceptable to its cultured

despisers by removing the "stumbling block" and the "foolishness" at the center of the Christian experience.

The book has remained an effort to acquaint the reader with the faith that undergirds the Christian movement. I hope that in this new edition it will continue to help readers to understand the classic Protestant faith as one of the options available to women and men called to life in our rapidly changing pluralistic world.

1975   GEORGE W. FORELL

Chapter 1

FAITH AND ITS CONSEQUENCES

There are always people who would like to divide mankind into two groups, the believers and the unbelievers. But this is an arbitrary division indeed, for strictly speaking there are no "unbelievers." Faith is universal. Everybody believes in something or somebody. This does not mean that all people go to some church or synagogue. That is obviously not the case. But all people have some God, at least a god with a small *g*.

There are the men who believe in money. They are convinced that money is the answer to all problems. Friends are people we buy with money, happiness is the result of having lots of money, and the purpose of life is to accumulate as much money as possible.

Then there are the believers in education, who hold that all the world's problems can be solved by education. If we are stupid, reading the right books will make us intelligent. If we are ugly, there is a book that can teach us how to become beautiful. If we are worried, there are many books that can teach us peace of mind or how to rearrange our whole life. Even if we weigh only 92 pounds and have trouble *lifting* a book, we can buy one (written by some muscular superman) which will teach us to be six feet six and weigh 250 pounds. Those who believe in the absolute power of education know of no obstacle that cannot be overcome by reading the right book. This widespread faith in education helps to explain the "do-it-yourself" craze. If we want to become an Albert Schweitzer, we can buy a book called *How to Play the Organ*, with

1

a double-your-money-back guarantee. If we want to build a dream house or make money on the stock market, there is a book to teach us how.

There are those who believe in the innate goodness of human beings. A person is by nature good, they say. We do evil things because of the pressures of society, because of faulty training in childhood, because of private property or the lack of it, but hidden within every person is a saint. This would be the best of all possible worlds if we would only remove the outward circumstances that bring in the evil. This is the attitude that Voltaire ridiculed so violently in his book *Candide*. It is as popular today as in Voltaire's time and long before; there have always been people who believe with all their hearts in the basic goodness of humanity.

Others, again, believe firmly in the basic goodness of only a few people, perhaps the Germans, or the Americans, or only the white Americans. I remember a man who was convinced of the innate and indestructible goodness of the Scots. There are no criminals among the Scots, he told me. And if ever a Scotsman is accused of a crime in a newspaper, he is either innocent or a member of some other nationality who has changed his name. The man was completely sincere in this assertion; he had absolute faith in the Scots.

Some believe in the absolute goodness of their own motives and actions. Whatever others might say, these good people are convinced of their own infallibility. They have absolute faith in themselves. There is at least one person like this in every college class. He may have a D average, but he will explain that this is not a reliable indicator of his true worth. He is not trying just now. Or the faculty has joined in some evil conspiracy to keep the world from knowing that such a superior intelligence exists among them.

These examples may suffice to illustrate the assertion that everybody believes in something or somebody. The interesting question is not *whether* we believe, but *what* we believe. "Belief" in the sense in which we have been using this word so far is the description of that certainty that undergirds life. This is the kind of belief that we call faith. There are certain data that seem absolutely reliable, the axioms from which we proceed. They are self-evident truths and not really debatable. They are verified in life, but we do not believe them because they are verified; we believed them before they were ever verified. We confront such basic faith, which represents the key to all sorts of human behavior, everyday. We have learned that we will have trouble understanding a person's actions unless we know the axiom from which he or she proceeds. Let us take a man who is in love with a certain woman, or a woman who is in love with a certain man. This is the basic fact. The basic fact may be verified by the observation that he travels three hundred miles every weekend in order to see her for a few hours. Or by the fact that she isn't interested in having a date with anybody else and that other men bore her. But note—it isn't because he travels three hundred miles every weekend that he is in love with her—rather, it is because he is in love with her that he is willing to travel three hundred miles. Or it isn't because she is bored with all other men that she is in love with him (this would be a serious maladjustment); rather, it is because she is in love with him that she is bored by the others.

This is what we mean when we say that faith is axiomatic; it is the fundamental assertion that gives meaning to all other assertions. Belief in the sense in which we are going to talk about what Protestants believe is primarily of this axiomatic nature.

It is of course true that the word *believe* has many meanings. Often, it denotes uncertainty. We say, "I believe it is going to rain tomorrow," or, "I believe he likes apple pie." This means that it may not rain tomorrow or that perhaps he likes cherry pie. But we are using "believe" in the way we would use it when we are not talking about the weather or pies but about another person.

Suppose you have a good friend by the name of Paul. Somebody comes to you and says, "Paul has stolen my watch." If you answer, "No—I believe in Paul!" you are saying a lot more than, "He didn't steal your watch," or, "He doesn't steal"; you are making a commitment to Paul, for you believe in him.

This is the way in which we are going to use "believe" and "faith" in this book. In describing the Protestant faith we will deal with the statements Protestants make to explain all other statements, the axiomatic hidden or open assertions which are the key to the life of the Protestant people. The great medieval theologian

3

Anselm of Canterbury said, *"Credo ut intelligam,"* or, "I believe in order to understand." Actually all people believe in order to understand. The question is, what do they believe?

Let us look for a moment at some of the axioms from which we can choose. These are all possible alternatives to the basic axiom from which Protestants and Christians in general proceed. We might say, "I believe in nature." We can look around and try to discover the pattern of nature and conform to it. We can start with the axiom that a person is merely a part of nature, a complicated part, to be sure, but in no way more than nature. He or she therefore should conform to the pattern that nature reveals. What is this pattern? People do not all agree, but the great German philosopher Friedrich Nietzsche suggested that the pattern of nature showed that man is merely a bridge to the superman of tomorrow. He is a bridge that has to be crossed. "Man," he said, "is a rope stretched between the animal and the Superman—a rope over an abyss." Man of today has to be sacrificed to the superman of tomorrow.

To apply this axiom to the life we have to live from day to day means the abolition of all those sentimental feelings which would slow up the coming of the superman. For example, we seem to think that it is kind to protect the sick, even those who will never get well. A consistent believer in the survival of the fittest as the axiom of life would say that this is bad. To care for the sick and the senile takes money and time which should be devoted to the development of the superman. Nature does not protect the weak and the sick. In nature the weak and the sick are destroyed by the strong and the healthy. The effort to protect the weak and the sick is therefore unnatural. It is foolish and dangerous. "The sick are the greatest danger for the healthy," Nietzsche claimed. How many millions do we spend to prolong life unnaturally, to preserve life which contributes nothing to the superman of tomorrow? We should quit all this nonsense. Nietzsche believed that Christianity was an invention of the weak to keep the strong from doing the natural thing, namely, destroying the weak.

Similarly, what nonsense it is, once we have adopted this axiom, to spend much money and effort to teach people who will never be very bright anyway. Let us use all our resources to do a great deal for those who will have the best chance to produce the superman of tomorrow. Nietzsche disdained the masses, the common man. Democracy seemed to him the unfortunate offspring of Christianity. He was logical and consistent in his belief that what is natural is good, that nature supplies us with the proper axioms for living. Survival of the fittest is the universal law.

This is a faith; it is an alternative by which we can pattern our lives. It may be somewhat shocking or even revolting to some of us, but at least it is logical. If you grant the axiom that nature supplies us with our standards of life, this attitude makes a great deal of sense. Most of us just do not accept this axiom.

There are, of course, many other equally possible axioms. For example, the pragmatic axiom: good is whatever works or whatever produces socially useful consequences. Or the existentialist axiom: to act is good, to vegetate is subhuman. The humanist axiom: man is the measure of all things. The Marxist axiom: history operates according to the laws of dialectical materialism as discovered by Karl Marx and his disciples.

Obviously, such basic faiths are all around us. Let us ask as we observe ourselves and the people around us, "What are the axioms by which we live?" This can be very interesting, because such axioms are like eyeglasses which help us to see a certain way but have a tendency to make us forget that we are wearing them. We can see them on other people but it takes some effort to notice them on ourselves. Some of the people who have the most fun with other people's faith-axioms are completely and amusingly oblivious to their own. For example, when somebody tells us, "I have no prejudices, I am absolutely objective," we can be pretty sure that what he really means is, "I haven't been able to discover my prejudices and you had better not call them to my attention or I'll get angry."

Often a person proclaims one set of axioms, and even thinks that he adheres to them, but really lives by another set of axioms altogether. What counts is not what he says he believes but what he really believes, not the axioms which he proclaims but the axioms by which he lives. Although they can be most evasive, they are always present. Every person has some faith.

So far we have claimed that every human being has a faith which is descriptive of the axioms which undergird his life. Perhaps we are now ready to ask, "What is the Christian axiom that underlies the Protestant faith?"

This Christian axiom can be put very simply in a sentence from the New Testament: "God was in Christ reconciling the world to himself" (2 Cor. 5:19). Of course this sentence may seem quite obscure at this point, but so are the other axioms when we try to reduce them to one sentence. This would be as true of a naturalistic, a pragmatic, an existentialist, or a humanist axiom as of the Christian axiom. Therefore we must try to discover what this sentence means, if it is the clue to the faith upon which Christians are willing to build their lives. The pattern for man and the world is not found in nature as we observe it all about us. It is not found in the agreement of the group, in the opinion of the majority, and it is not found in man, at the very center of his being. It is not existentialist and it is not materialist—although it says a great deal about existence and matter. Christians claim that the meaning of life has been revealed in Jesus, the Christ. Not the superman of Nietzsche, not the successful man, the well-adjusted man, the proletarian, the capitalist, or the American—but Christ is the true man. He is the God-man, the translation of God into human language. This is the axiom, and what it means to Protestants is the subject of this book.

But let us make it very clear that we are discussing real alternatives. Some people think we can reconcile all these various faiths and come up with some sort of superfaith. But this cannot be done honestly. If we want Nietzsche's superman, we must be as honest as Nietzsche was and say, "God is dead!" We cannot say the supreme law of the universe is the survival of the fittest—and also say: "You shall love the Lord your God with all your heart, and with all your soul, and with all your strength, and with all your mind; and your neighbor as yourself" (Luke 10:27). We have to make a choice.

There are many people today who would like to have exchangeable faiths: one for Sunday morning, another for Monday to Friday, and a third for the early part of the weekend. On Sunday morning they are Christians, during the week they are pragmatists,

6

living by the slogan that business is business, and on the weekend they are hedonists only interested in their own pleasure. They want a variety of "gods" to believe in. Just as the people in the Roman Empire of Jesus' time had gods of nature and of the family, of war and love, so these modern men and women seem to need different faiths and "gods" to meet the many needs of contemporary life. This has given rise to speculation concerning a new polytheism for our complex age. While some students of religion have welcomed this trend, we shall see that this development is at odds with some basic assertions of the Protestant faith.

Some would, indeed, like to retain some aspect of the Christian faith without letting it determine their life. It was said of the great Spanish-American philosopher George Santayana that his creed was: "There is no God—and Mary is his mother!" In other words, he wanted the aesthetic aspects of religion—he liked the music and the paintings, the stained-glass windows and the odor of incense— without the faith which produced them. Santayana is not alone in this position. Some have adopted Christianity for its revolutionary possibilities; others again because it may help preserve things as they are or even bring back the "good old days." But here we are not interested in the popular byproducts of Christianity; we want to study the faith which produces the byproducts.

Every faith involves a decision. To believe in man or in God, in money or in education—one must decide. And this brings us to the next question. Once a person has made a decision about these faith-axioms, this decision has consequences. The kind of pattern, the kind of axiom which undergirds our life makes a great deal of difference.

Again, there are many people who put faith into the same class as fox hunting and pinochle playing. These are interesting leisure-time activities which do not really matter. And so they say, "It doesn't really matter what a man believes—what really matters is how much money he has or how smart he is!"

Like so many other notions which are generally accepted, this one is obviously false. Of course, it makes a great deal of difference whether we believe, for example, in a moral law or whether we believe that right is whatever we can get away with.

This is not hard to prove. Let us say two people try to borrow money from you because they are temporarily caught short of cash. One of these borrowers is actually well-to-do, but he is the kind of person who says, "Right is whatever I can get away with." He does not say it openly, but this is one of the axioms by which he lives. The other person has no money at all, but he believes with all his being that a man is honorbound to pay his debts. Now, who is the better risk for your loan? The man with the principles is the better risk, for we know that having money has never yet by itself made a person pay his debts.

This is what is meant when we say that faith has ultimate significance. What a person believes will make a great deal of difference in his life. Please note, not what he *claims* to believe—that's fairly unimportant—but what he *really* believes. The same principle applies to nations. But let us emphasize once again that it is only the genuine faith, not the assumed faith, which is important.

An American nurse who had just returned from India stated recently in an interview that one of the difficulties she encountered among some people in India with whom she and her health team worked was the relative nonchalance about life and death. People simply did not seem to be as much concerned about staying alive as Americans are.

Indeed, in order to go to the kind of trouble we are willing to go to in order to stay alive, we must really believe that life is meaningful, that it is worthwhile, that it is a gift that we have to protect, or that "we will be dead for a long time." Many Hindus don't believe this at all. For them this present life has no final meaning, and death is not a permanent condition. In fact, a rebirth takes place immediately, and the next life may be far better than the present one.

If we believe in reincarnation, it will certainly make a great difference in our attitude toward life and death and in our behavior in general. This is what the American nurse discovered in India. But the fact that faith has consequences can be observed everywhere. It is an important clue to the history of individuals and nations. Without the understanding of the significance of faith for human behavior, behavior remains completely incomprehensible.

When Christians and Moslems were locked in battle in the Middle Ages, the Christian participants in these wars were astonished and shocked by the heroism of the Mohammedan soldiers. Finally they realized that the disdain for death which characterized these enemy soldiers was the direct result of the Moslem faith. These Moslems believed that their life was governed by a divine kismet. God had decided beforehand what would happen to them, and nothing they could do could change this divine design. If they were to die, they would die; if they were to survive, they would survive. Furthermore, they were convinced that death in battle in a holy war would bring the faithful immediately into a paradise far more desirable than this life. While the Christians might not agree with these ideas, knowing them made it possible to understand the mentality of their enemies. Whether true or false, these were the axioms of their life, and these axioms had measurable consequences.

Who would not be reminded in this context of the behavior of the Japanese pilots during World War II who in suicide flights crashed their planes into American vessels. Here again faith, Shinto faith, had observable consequences. Nothing could be less scientific and more obscurantist than to ignore the fact that faith makes a difference. For good or ill, what people really believe is far more important than even their blood pressure, their basal metabolism, or their intelligence quotient.

It took the almost pathological fear of religion that has clouded the minds of so many otherwise highly intelligent people in our time to make the startling claim that religion is a private affair, that one's faith does not matter, that religious convictions are in the same class as hobbies, such as playing cards, or as inconsequential as preferring baseball or football. Thus the serious study of faith as an aid to understanding man and his society has been neglected, and many otherwise intelligent people pride themselves on their religious illiteracy. Wishing that faith were marginal in the life of man, they have persuaded themselves into believing that this is so. Actually, this assertion is so far from the truth as to be almost ridiculous, and this neglect of the study of faith can only be understood as the result of an almost obsessive fear of religion, which

9

has blinded many observers to the facts as they confront us everywhere.

This attitude toward religion may be compared to the attitude toward sex in the nineteenth century. Even then everybody knew that sex was a real force in human life, but until Sigmund Freud came along nobody wanted to admit it. Some piously hoped that, if the fact of sex were persistently ignored or loudly denied, it would quietly disappear. But the Victorian age was quite unsuccessful in its attempt to ignore the reality of sex. Indeed, the very effort to ignore and repress it became the basis for the obsession with sex of a later generation. And we can say the same about religion. All the efforts on the part of twentieth-century man to ignore religion in the hope that it will disappear have proven completely ineffective. At the very moment when some theologians proclaimed the death of God, in America young people everywhere were embracing many different varieties of religion with renewed passion. A person's faith is one of the basic components of life, and ignoring this obvious reality will not change the facts for a moment. One may not like the fact that faith is so important and wish it to be otherwise. But what one likes does not really matter. The only important question is: Has faith ultimate significance? It is our claim that the evidence available shows that it has.

Compare the Jewish people with their pagan neighbors. They lived in an age in which God and the gods were only loosely related to the concepts of right and wrong. They lived in an age in which morality and piety were not at all identified. Then the Jews heard God speak to them—and reveal himself to them as a moral God, a God who was concerned about right and wrong, a God who loved justice and hated injustice. This made a tremendous difference. The difference between the Jews and their Canaanite neighbors was not racial or linguistic, not cultural or economic, but rather a difference in faith, which had striking consequences. It is this unique faith which has maintained the Jewish people while the Assyrians and Babylonians, the Persians and Philistines have all passed away.

If we look at Christianity we find similarly striking results of faith. Nobody who has ever traveled from a Protestant section to a Roman Catholic section in Germany would deny the difference in the understanding of life which exists even among Christians who belong to different major forms of Christianity. The attitude toward work and leisure, the attitude toward church and home are deeply colored by this fact of faith.

One illustration, which comes from a sociologist rather than a theologian, should suffice. Max Weber, in his famous book *The Protestant Ethic and the Spirit of Capitalism*, pointed out that Protestantism in general, and Calvinism in particular, has supplied the faith-axiom which made *modern* capitalism possible. This theory has been modified by R. H. Tawney and others, but it is interesting from our point of view that an observant sociologist or economist, who is not so emotionally involved in his rejection of religion as to be unable to think clearly when the word occurs, should be struck by the sociological and economic fruits of faith.

It is simply not true, and frequent repetition is not able to make it true, that all religions are the same. It is no more true than that all cultures are the same, or all economic systems are the same, or all philosophical systems are the same. Religions differ significantly, creating different attitudes toward life in their believers and vastly different patterns of life. Our axioms make a difference. We ought to know them and be aware of them and use them consciously as well as unconsciously or discard them.

The issue is particularly important in our time when we are confronted not only by the various historical faiths which have dominated mankind for centuries but by some new faiths which have come upon us. One of the reasons we were so dumbfounded by the rise of communism, for example, is that we were unable to see that it is a religion. It has its own faith-axioms, its dogma, and its high priests. It has most of the outward paraphernalia of a bona fide religion, lacking only a god.

Communism is not merely an economic system with which we may disagree. It promotes a police state and establishes slave-labor camps. These conditions certainly exist, but they are only the by-products of certain Communist faith-axioms. The faith-axioms of communism, like all others, are bound to produce fruits in society. Our inability to understand communism has been caused by our unwillingness to take faith seriously, our own faith as well as the faith of others. If we want to understand other people, or even ourselves, we must understand the faiths which undergird all lives.

It is the importance of faith as a key to the understanding of human beings and society which makes the study of religion so very important. And it is this fact that makes the Protestant faith so interesting to us. We live in a culture whose character is profoundly influenced by the Protestant faith. Even those who do not share it are affected by it, because it is part of our tradition and permeates our institutions. For this reason the study of the Protestant faith may help us to a better understanding of our society and of ourselves.

The Nature of Protestantism

A Historical and Statistical Survey. Historically, the name *Protestant* was first used in connection with the so-called II Diet of Speyer (1529). Speyer is a city in southern Germany, and the Diet was an assembly of the leading citizens, the princes, and the representatives of the free cities for the discussion and solution of common problems. Unlike the Congress of the United States the German Diet did not meet regularly but only when some special political situation made a meeting desirable. Not all people were represented but only the princes, the nobility, the clergy, and the wealthy burghers of the free cities. Since most of the political leaders of the church, the archbishops, bishops, and abbots, belonged to the nobility, the common people were hardly represented at all.

The Emperor Charles V had called the II Diet of Speyer in order to get the support of the leaders of the German people for his plans to suppress what he considered the heresy of Luther and his followers, who would not recognize the supremacy of the Church of Rome and the Roman Pope. Luther's movement had begun twelve years earlier on October 31, 1517, when the young professor of theology at the university of Wittenberg had published his *Ninety-five Theses* inviting theologians to debate the propriety of selling indulgences, the remission before God of the temporal punishment due to those sins for which the guilt had been forgiven. Because of Luther's colorful and aggressive language these theses had been

12

widely distributed and had led to criticism of many other aspects of the teaching and practice of the established church, and the demand for thorough reform.

While some princes and many public figures supported these efforts, the Emperor had never been very friendly toward Luther and his followers. After he had met the reformer at the famous Diet of Worms in April, 1521, he had charged the political leaders of Europe to do everything in their power to stamp out the Reformation movement. In 1521 he had said, "I regret having so long delayed to proceed against this Luther and his false doctrine."[1] However, his own political difficulties made it impossible for him to take firm action. Ironically, much of the opposition to Charles V came from the Pope. The very Pope whose religious power the Emperor was trying to uphold conspired against him for political reasons. The result was that the Emperor was forced to defeat the Pope and his allies militarily before he had a free hand to try to reestablish the Pope's religious authority. In 1529 the Emperor was finally in a position to enforce his will against the supporters of Luther, for he had just defeated the Pope in the military campaign which had ended with the famous sack of Rome (1527). Charles V had at the same time defeated his archenemy, the King of France, who had given him a good deal of trouble since he had become German Emperor.

With these enemies taken care of, the Emperor was in a position to deal with the heretics in general and Martin Luther in particular. The II Diet of Speyer was supposed to be the springboard for action looking forward to the complete suppression of the new heresy.

It may seem odd that the Emperor wanted to suppress this movement to overthrow the authority of the Pope after he had defeated the Pope. But this was an odd period of history. Charles V, the German Emperor and King of Spain, was a loyal subject of the Pope as the *spiritual leader* of Christendom. He only failed to get along with the Pope as the *political leader* of Italy. Charles V didn't mind that the same person held both positions. He was willing to use Lutheran soldiers to defeat the Pope militarily and politically and then turn right around and try to reestablish the power of the Pope as spiritual leader of the Western world.

13

In order to understand this reasoning one should compare it with the attitude of a good Democrat toward a Republican President of the United States. This Democrat will do everything in his power to defeat the President as leader of the Republican party, yet at the same time he will do his best to support him as chief executive of the government of the United States.

Although Charles V had defeated the Pope politically, at the II Diet of Speyer he was trying to support and strengthen him as spiritual leader of Western Christendom and thus prevent the breakup of the religious unity of his empire. To most people in the sixteenth century religious uniformity seemed the necessary basis for political unity.

Of the four hundred estates represented at the Diet, only nineteen opposed the decision of the Emperor and the majority of the Diet to work toward the reestablishment of the teachings and practices of the Roman Catholic Church everywhere in Germany and to suppress what they considered "heresy" with all the power at their command. These nineteen estates protested against the use of force to reestablish the Roman Church and said:

> In matters which concern the honor of God and the salvation of our souls, every individual must stand alone before God and give his account. Therefore, nobody can excuse himself in these matters by relying on the decisions of others.[2]

In other words, at Speyer in 1529 these first Protestants (technically speaking) protested that matters of conscience could not be decided by government action. What Luther had said alone at Worms in 1521 was now repeated only eight years later by some of the mighty political leaders of Germany. At Worms Luther had said before Emperor Charles V:

> Unless I shall be convinced by the testimony of Scriptures or by clear reason, I must be bound by those Scriptures which have been brought forward by me. Yes, my conscience has been taken captive by these words of God. I cannot revoke anything, nor do I wish to; since to go against one's conscience is neither safe nor right. Here I stand, I cannot do otherwise. God help me. Amen.[3]

After the II Diet of Speyer this individual protest was now the position of thousands in Germany and all over Europe. And the people who took this position were called "Protestants."

In spite of all opposition the movement grew. It soon embraced two-thirds of Germany, all of Denmark, Sweden, Norway, and Finland, large sections of Poland, Bohemia, and Hungary. Soon other Reformers spread the Protestant understanding of the Christian faith to Switzerland, France, the Netherlands, and the British Isles. From the British Isles Protestantism was carried to the New World, to America and Australia. Finally, through the great missionary movement, particularly of the nineteenth century, Protestantism in its various forms came also to Asia and Africa. Today entire peoples in Asia, for example, the Bataks in Indonesia, are Protestants, and some of the most rapidly growing Protestant churches are in the so-called Third World.

Some statistics might be helpful in order to illustrate this tremendous growth of Protestantism from the sixteenth century to the present.

Of the total population of the world, approximately one-third are Christians. Of the Christians, about one-third are Protestants; the others are Roman Catholics or Eastern Orthodox. This means that approximately 10 per cent of the people in the world are Protestant.[4]

But while a large proportion of these Protestants live in Europe and North America, there are 5.5 million Protestants in South America, approximately 38 million in Asia, and about 10 million in Oceania, and almost 45 million in Africa. Thanks to the missionary movement, Protestantism has come a long way since the nineteen estates at the II Diet of Speyer made their protest on behalf of religious freedom.

What is the relative distribution of Protestants in the United States? Of those Americans who claim church membership about 70 million are Protestants, about 48 million are Roman Catholics, and about 6 million are Jews. Almost 4 million are Eastern Orthodox, and the rest belong to other groups.

The 70 million Protestants in the United States are members of many different church bodies. But if one looks a little more closely

15

one discovers that most of them can be divided into some great denominational families.

Alphabetically and statistically first are the Baptists, who number approximately 27 million. Next come the 13 million Methodists and the 8.8 million Lutherans. The Presbyterians, Reformed, and United Church of Christ belong historically in the Calvinist family with approximately 6 million adherents. Next come the Episcopalians or Anglicans with about 3.4 million members. Finally, there are the historic pacifist groups, such as the Quakers and the Mennonites, with about 120,000 each.

Of course this does not exhaust the hundreds of Protestant groups, but almost all of these groups belong closely or loosely to one of the following families: (1) Baptist family, (2) Episcopal-Anglican family, (3) Lutheran family, (4) Methodist family, (5) Presbyterian-Calvinist family, (6) Quaker-Mennonite family.

These families are by no means completely different from each other. Rather there are firm ties of relationship between them. For example, the Methodists are closely related to the Episcopal-Anglican family. At the same time, the Episcopal-Anglican family is related to Calvinists and Lutherans. But the significant fact is that the 250 or more Protestant denominations can easily be classified into 6 or at most 10 major denominational families. We are not so much concerned with their differences as with their common qualities which enable us to speak meaningfully of "Protestantism" and the "Protestant faith."

The Spirit of Protestantism. While the history and the statistics of a religious movement are important, a faith is more than its history and its statistics. The question arises: What are the particular identifying marks of Protestantism? If it is a spiritual movement, what are its characteristics? How can we best describe the spirit of Protestantism?

In a movement of the scope and diversity of Protestantism there are probably thousands of "marks" which may seem to some observers or members of the movement to express its very essence. There are five, however, which recur with such regularity and consistency that they can be used as basic identifying marks. They are the emphasis upon (1) grace and the sovereignty of God, (2) faith, (3) Scripture as the rule of faith, (4) the church as the fellowship of saints and the priesthood of all believers, and (5) the fallibility of man and all human institutions.

Protestants insist that their church is based on the New Testament, and that these Protestant emphases can be clearly discerned in the apostolic church. But what do these five emphases mean?

The Protestants' stress on God's grace and sovereignty means that in the relationship between God and human beings it is God who takes the initiative. In this respect Protestantism differs from the general definition of religion. Religion has often been defined as man's way to God, the result of human aspirations, human efforts, and human hopes. Religion is for many a way to reach God.

Various methods of finding God have been suggested by religious people through the ages. There are those who say that we become religious, that we come in touch with God, by obeying his law. This method of reaching God is known as legalism. It asserts that God's will for man can be defined as a legal code. If we obey these rules we are true believers, and if we fail to obey them we are irreligious. The rules are of various kinds. They may regulate what the believer may eat and when he may eat it, what he may wear and where he may wear it. There are a thousand and one rules dealing with such varied matters as the amount of hair on the chin or the type of mechanism used to button one's coat; the alcoholic content of beverages and the literary content of books. The religiously significant fact about legalism in all its forms is that it makes our relationship to God dependent upon our obedience to rules and regulations. Legalism always asserts in some manner that we reach God by way of a legal code. Legalism tends to reduce God to a celestial bookkeeper, or the great computer in the sky. He keeps books, computes the input, or perhaps better, merely keeps score. He does not intervene in the game of life. Whether we reach him or not is entirely up to us. He has given us the law; if we obey the law we can reach him, and if we do not obey the law we will fail. To use a theological term, *salvation* is up to us. We are saving ourselves by obeying the law, or we are losing ourselves by disobeying it. The initiative is with human beings.

17

Against this view, so very common in the world's religions, one of the Protestant emphases found in Luther and Calvin as well as in Arminius and Wesley, among Anglicans as well as Baptists, is the conviction that man's salvation is not the result of anything man can do. God is the sovereign Lord of all life. He is not a spectator in the drama of history but the director as well as the most active participant. Only through the participation of God can man be saved. In other words, God through *his* grace saves man. Man is not saved through any of his works, be they ever so splendid, but entirely and solely because God is merciful. It appears that most people know that this is the view of Lutherans and Calvinists. But Wesley was as convinced of justification by faith as any Calvinist or Lutheran. In defending his position and the position of Jacobus Arminius, accused of teaching salvation by human effort, John Wesley wrote:

> No man that ever lived, not John Calvin himself, ever asserted either original sin or justification by faith in more strong, more clear and express terms, than Arminius has done. These two points, therefore, are to be set out of the question; in these both parties agree. In this respect, there is not a hair's breadth difference between Mr. Wesley and Mr. Whitefield.[5]

In the Articles of Religion of the Anglican Communion, the Episcopal Church, we read in Article XI:

> We are accounted righteous before God, only for the merit of our Lord and Savior Jesus Christ by Faith, and not for our own works or deservings. Wherefore, that we are justified by Faith only, is a most wholesome Doctrine, and very full of comfort, as more largely expressed in the Homily of Justification.[6]

Protestants who stand within the stream of classical Protestantism as expressed in the writings of the Reformers and their successors agree unanimously that salvation, that is, release from human misery without God and communion with God in service to him, is not the result of any merits or good works on the part of people. A person cannot save himself. It is God who through his sovereign grace saves man.

Of course, there are considerable differences of opinion among

Protestants as to the manner in which God accomplishes this purpose and as to the degree of human cooperation necessary, but all agree that the initiative is entirely with God, and nothing that man does has any saving value. God's sovereignty, that he is Lord and Savior, is the common faith of all Protestants. *Sola gratia,* through grace alone, is one of the watchwords of classical Protestantism.

There have always been people who have conceived of God as the supreme intelligence of the universe, and they have suggested that he can be reached by the exercise of reason. Others have insisted that God can be reached through certain mystical experiences. This question will be discussed later in another context. Suffice it to say here that the Protestant emphasis on God's sovereign grace rules out all efforts on the part of people to reach God in their own way, be they legalistic, rationalistic, or mystical.

This brings us to the second Protestant emphasis, the stress on faith. In our discussion so far, considerable emphasis has been placed on faith-axioms, the life-sustaining basic affirmations that a person must make and which undergird life. The cardinal doctrine of Protestantism is known as "justification by faith." This means that according to classical Protestantism the character of the faith-axiom makes all the difference. A person is a Christian because he puts his entire trust in Jesus Christ. Justification by faith must be clearly distinguished from its most prevalent distortion, namely, faith in faith. Classical Protestantism asserts that God wants fellowship with man and that if we trust completely in Jesus Christ and his work we will have communion with God. This complete and utter trust in Jesus Christ is faith. It is making the life, death, and resurrection of Christ the foundation of life. It is trust in what God has done through the life of this unique and all-important person.

This point must be stressed because of a number of obvious confusions. For some people faith is the acceptance of propositions about God or the church. For example, somebody might tell you that the average distance between the moon and the earth is 238,-857 miles. You haven't either the time or the inclination to measure the distance yourself, but you "believe" that this is the average distance. This isn't faith in the sense in which we are using it;

19

rather, it is the acceptance of a proposition. Now all of us accept lots of propositions, some that can be easily verified, others that cannot be verified at all. And there are some people who think that the Christian faith consists of the acceptance of propositions about God, about Jesus, about the church. If we accept certain propositions of this kind we are Christians.

But faith in the sense in which it is used in the phrase *justification by faith* means complete trust in Jesus Christ as the revelation of God and the key to the meaning of life. This is not just one proposition among others; justification by faith means that Christ has become the cornerstone of your life. This is a biblical phrase (Eph. 2:20); another biblical phrase is that you have become a member of the body of which he is the head (Col. 1:18); another that you are now his slave (Rom. 1:1; Phil. 1:1, and so forth). If a man becomes the slave of another man, this is not one fact among others, like buying a new car or getting a new job; it is the fact which changes all other facts, which gives new meaning to all his relationships, which explains everything he does and everything he fails to do. The Apostle Paul described himself frequently as *doulos Iesou Christou*, that is, a slave of Jesus Christ; this is the picture that came to his mind to indicate the new relationship which faith in Jesus Christ had created. The fact of faith had changed all other facts radically; it had given his life a completely new direction. Another New Testament word picture describing the new situation which faith creates is used by Jesus himself when he says, "You must be born anew" (John 3:7). While this phrase has often been used merely as a theological platitude, it is actually a highly significant statement, for truly being "born anew" is an accurate description of the ultimate meaning of justification by faith. It points to the fact that everything has changed. All things have become new.

Here we must guard against another misunderstanding. Justification by faith—or *sola fide*, only by faith—does not mean that faith as an emotional attitude is able to save. There are many people especially in our time who proclaim loudly that it doesn't matter *what* we believe so long as we are sincere. Faith is for them a helpful posture. It is a certain approach to life which is valid quite apart from its object. What matters is the strength of the emotion, the profundity of our feeling; *what* we believe doesn't really matter at all. Faith is here something like Emile Coué's "every day in every way I am getting better and better." It is a psychological technique to help you keep your chin up or to keep a stiff upper lip. From the point of view of psychology such autosuggestion may be very effective and at times very helpful. But in the context of our discussion this type of faith has nothing to do with the justification by faith of the Reformers and of classical Protestantism.

It is certainly true that any sincere conviction can help you do things that would otherwise be impossible, from winning a war to sleeping on a bed of nails. We have no right to underestimate the power of faith as a psychological source of strength. The "faith" of the Nazis helped them sweep all over Europe during the early part of World War II. The "faith" of the Communists has helped them to conquer large sections of the world. It would be indeed foolish to deny that these people have faith or that their faith is effective. But at the same time the very success of these faith movements in this century helps to show clearly that the object of faith makes all the difference in the world. Faith in a Hitler can be a demonic force leading millions of men and women to destruction. Faith in a medical quack can lead to needless suffering and death. Faith is by no means always a positive force in human life. This must be said especially in view of the many books written in recent years which exalt faith as a psychological "gimmick." Here you find the tendency to claim that belief is in and of itself valuable. We grant that it is indeed necessary, but from within the context of the Protestant faith we have to say that justification by faith does not mean justification by sincerity or justification by strength of feeling—but rather justification through God's invasion into history in Jesus Christ. According to classical Protestantism, Christ is the object of the faith which justifies, and no other faith but faith in Christ can save man.

The Protestant emphasis on *sola fide*, only through faith, denies the efficacy of other approaches to God, even as respectable an alternative as the way of reason. There are many people who believe that God can somehow be approached by means of almost

rationalization

mathematical demonstration. There are certain proofs of the existence of God which have been popular since the days of Plato and Aristotle. These proofs are supposed to demonstrate to every reasonable person that there is a God, and if one doesn't believe in God after having been subjected to them, one cannot follow a logical argument. This use of reason to prove the existence of God actually roots unbelief in stupidity rather than in revolt against God and has therefore the tendency to make unbelief a less serious offense than the New Testament indicates. Furthermore, such proofs of the existence of God tend to place God in the same class with the objects of mathematical proof and thus reduce him to one object in the same class with others. And finally, they do not seem to prove the existence of God to people however intelligent who do not want to believe in God. Thus, while many Christians have tried to use reason as one way of demonstrating at least the existence of God, Protestants have generally been reluctant to make use of these proofs. This, too, is a result of their emphasis on *sola fide*— by faith alone!

This brings us to a third emphasis which is typical of Protestantism as a whole, the emphasis on Scripture as the rule of faith. One of the common assertions of Protestantism is stated in the Articles of Religion of the Anglican Communion as follows:

> Holy Scripture containeth all things necessary to salvation: so that whatsoever is not read therein, nor may be proved thereby, is not to be required of any man, that it should be believed as an article of Faith, or be thought requisite or necessary to salvation. In the name of the Holy Scripture we do understand those canonical books of the Old and New Testaments, of whose authority was never doubt in the Church.[7]

This statement is also part of the Methodist Discipline,[8] and similar statements can be found governing all Protestants. While this stress on the authority of Scripture identifies all those who are in the stream of classical Protestantism, church history shows that there have also been other sources of authority in Christendom. The most popular alternatives to the Bible as the "only rule and norm according to which all doctrines and teachers alike must be appraised and judged"[9] are the addition or substitution of tradition, the inner light, and the decrees of the institutional church.

It is easy to understand the development of the authority of tradition, for Christianity has a long history. In two thousand years much happens to any living community of human beings. For some Christians the beliefs which have evolved over the years have become of equal value with the teachings of the Scriptures. In any community a custom can become a law and be enforced long after the factors which gave it birth have disappeared. Thus also in the Christian church practices have become hallowed by usage to the point that to change them would be unthinkable. It is only a short step from the development of such customs to their sanctification. Among some Christians there are regular methods by which such hallowed customs can become officially authoritative. Occasionally a church will actually pronounce a belief an official dogma which apparently up to this point was merely a possible opinion, hallowed by custom. The Immaculate Conception of the Virgin Mary, for example, was merely a possible opinion in the Middle Ages. It was not shared by such outstanding theologians as Anselm of Canterbury or Thomas Aquinas. However, when Pope Pius IX proclaimed the Dogma of the Immaculate Conception in 1854, it became binding on all Roman Catholics. Here tradition is obviously considered a valid source of Christian dogma, quite independent of the teachings of the Bible. Protestantism has consistently rejected all teachings which in its opinion could not be found in the Scriptures. There have been some basic disagreements among Protestants about what is in fact found in Scripture, but classical Protestantism has accepted the Scriptures, that is, the universally accepted books of the Old and New Testaments, as the standard by which Christian teaching is to be judged.

Other Christians, again, have emphasized the direct communication of God with the Christian believer through mystical raptures and inspirations. In Luther's time a number of people whom he called *Schwaermer*, or enthusiasts, claimed to have what one could call in twentieth-century terms a "direct wire to God." Men like Thomas Münzer were convinced that God was guiding them through special dreams and visions. They felt in no way bound by the teachings of Scripture. In the light of their special revelation they were willing to contradict the Bible. Martin Luther, Huldreich Zwingli, and John Calvin wanted nothing to do with these people. Luther, whose language was nothing if not colorful, referred to them as people who sounded "as if they had swallowed the Holy Spirit, feathers and all." And he completely rejected the authority of such direct revelations. This has been the position of the over-whelming majority of Protestants.

In spite of the insistence of classical Protestantism that the Holy Scriptures are the only standard according to which all doctrines and teachers alike must be judged, the temptation has been great to add other statements to guarantee the correct reading or to serve as key to the Scriptures, even to claim that certain translations of the Bible have special standing as over against all others.

To add or subtract (e.g., deny the authority of the Old Testa-ment or of certain books of the New Testament) from the Scrip-tures is, however, counter to the basic assertion of the unique authority of the Holy Scriptures. Even the various confessions of Protestant churches, illustrated by the examples in the appendix of this book, are not considered to have authority equal to the Holy Scriptures. They describe the teaching of the particular Protestant church at a certain time in history, but depend for their authority entirely upon their conformity to the Scriptures. The statements of Protestant leaders like Luther, Calvin, or Wesley are considered authoritative only insofar as they are in accord with the teachings of the Holy Scriptures. For classical Protestantism Scripture is the only source of authority for the teaching of the church.

The fourth emphasis which is part of the common Protestant heritage is the understanding of the church as the fellowship of saints and the priesthood of all believers. In the Apostles' Creed, most Christians confess that they believe in the "holy universal church, the communion of saints." This phrase, "communion of saints," though obscure in its original meaning, is for Protestants an explanation of the holy universal church. The Christian church is the Christian people brought together by the Word of God and the sacraments. We shall discuss these concepts in greater detail later. But this understanding of the church as primarily a fellowship rather than an institution or organization is a significant accent that almost all Protestants have in common. This involves also the universal priesthood of all believers. A priest is generally conceived to be a person who has direct access to God. In many non-Christian religions and in some branches of Christendom the priest is a mediator between God and man. Through the priest the individual believer can address himself to God, and through the priest God speaks to the individual believer. But, guided by the First Epistle of Peter in the New Testament, Protestants in general assert that all Christians are priests through their new birth in Baptism: through the work of Christ all alike are God's people called to serve him and to proclaim his Word to each other. In Christ they have direct access to God without the help of another man.

In the Old Testament priests were not elected but were born to their office. A man was a priest by virtue of the fact that he was a descendant of Levi. In the same manner, say the Protestants, Christians are priests through the new birth in Baptism. In the words of the New Testament:

> But you are a chosen race, a royal priesthood, a holy nation, God's own people, that you may declare the wonderful deeds of him who called you out of darkness into his marvelous light. (1 Pet. 2:9)

And as the Apostle Paul writes in his letter to the Galatians:

> For as many of you as were baptized into Christ have put on Christ. There is neither Jew nor Greek, there is neither slave nor free, there is neither male nor female; for you are all one in Christ Jesus. (Gal. 3:27–28)

This, of course, does not mean that Protestants do not have ministers or pastors or that they might not even call their ministers or pastors priests. But this ministry, which is maintained by the overwhelming majority of Protestants, is a functional office. Ministers are people called by God through the church to serve the fellowship of believers by preaching, teaching, and administering the sacraments. For the Protestant the pastor is not a mediator between him and God. He is a leader and servant of the fellowship

25

and a priest by virtue of the fact that he is a Christian like all other Christians.

This may at first sound rather theological and complicated. However, it has immensely practical results. The relatively decentralized character of Protestantism is a direct result of these beliefs. The church is not so much a human organization as a divine organism, held together not by human laws and decrees but by the divine will. It is therefore not entirely surprising to see Protestantism organizationally divided; the very emphasis on the church as the communion of saints would preclude an emphasis upon hierarchy and organization. Protestants generally do not claim that it is necessary for salvation to belong to any particular Christian organization, although most of them would assert that it is indeed necessary to belong to the Christian organism, to the body whose head is Christ.

It is customary for Protestants to accept other Christians even though they might belong to other forms of organized Christianity. Although they may quarrel about organizational structure, they do not believe that the organizational structure has any particular saving significance.

This attitude is partly the result of their conviction that even in the New Testament an organizational development took place. There is a difference between the structure of the church as described for example in 1 Cor. 12:28 and that described in Eph. 4:11–16. 1 Cor. 12:28 states: "God has appointed in the Church first apostles, second prophets, third teachers, then healers, helpers, administrators, speakers in various kinds of tongues." Eph. 4:11 asserts: "And his gifts were that some should be apostles, some prophets, some evangelists, some pastors and teachers." It appears that the church has developed organizationally between the time of 1 Corinthians and Ephesians. The entire group of somewhat less structured, more enthusiastic activities, like miracle workers, healers, helpers, speakers in various kinds of tongues, was seen in 1 Corinthians as being on a continuous scale with apostles, prophets, and teachers. In Ephesians this entire group of ecstatic enthusiastic offices is not mentioned at all. Neither are the bishops and elders which play a decisive part in the later church.

26

Organization in the New Testament is in flux, it is constantly changing, and Protestants see in this a clue to the functional character of all organizational structures. Organization is never an end in itself, but an important and useful means to the proclamation of the Christian message. Protestants realize that the church was always organized. The twelve Apostles were a rudimentary form of organization. The question is not whether to organize or not organize, but rather, is there a model organization for the church which is binding for all times? The rapid change in structures in the New Testament suggests to Protestants that all organizational models must be evaluated from the point of view of their usefulness to the Christian faith and life. Thus Protestants, as we shall see later, have adopted all kinds of organizational patterns, for example, episcopacy, presbyterianism, and congregationalism, without claiming that the validity of their faith and life depends on the particular kind of ecclesiastical organization. They tend to define the church with the Augsburg Confession of 1530:

> It is also taught among us that one holy Christian church will be and remain forever. This is the assembly of all believers among whom the Gospel is preached in its purity and the holy sacraments are administered according to the Gospel. For it is sufficient for the true unity of the Christian church that the Gospel be preached in conformity with a pure understanding of it and that the sacraments be administered in accordance with the divine Word. It is not necessary for the true unity of the Christian church that ceremonies, instituted by men, should be observed uniformly in all places. . . .[10]

The fifth and final emphasis that characterizes classical Protestantism is upon the fallibility of man and of all human institutions. For the Protestant even the empirical church is an all too human institution. It is a common Protestant belief that human institutions are always in need of reformation, that human pride and sin pervert even our best efforts, and that the perversion of the best is the very worst. For that reason men must operate with a large margin for error. No man, even the finest Christian leader, is infallible, and no human institution is perfect. Methods must be built into the

27

organizational structure of the Christian community that will tend to correct errors that are certain to arise in every generation.

In other words, Protestants are well aware of the fact that the Reformation is not merely something that was necessary in the sixteenth century, but they realize and insist that the Reformation is a principle that must cleanse the church again and again.

In the Old Testament we read how prophets such as Amos would come down from the hills and try to reform the corrupted church of the Old Testament. The Reformers are considered as following in these prophetic footsteps. Protestants generally believe the Reformation must continue. Thus the Reformation is not merely a historical date but a vital principle in the present life of the church. Whenever the church becomes self-satisfied and fat, relying on its own words rather than God's, the Reformation principle must stir it up.

Historically, this has been the function of Methodists and Pietists, of Oxford Movement and Social Gospel, of Neo-Orthodoxy and Christian Existentialism, of the Jesus Movement and the Charismatics. This process has by no means ended, for the Reformation must continue. If Protestantism is to be true to its genius, it can never rest on its laurels. It must always interpret the eternal message of the gospel of Christ in a manner that makes it meaningful to every new age.

This does not mean that Protestants doubt the eternal truth of the gospel which they proclaim. It means, rather, that this truth is so great that it again and again bursts the institutional and systematic chains in which it is bound. It is therefore dangerous to place too much emphasis on these temporal forms.

Perhaps a few illustrations will help. For some people the Christian faith is so closely related to the local congregation where they first heard the Christian message that they are unable to transfer their faith when they leave their home community. There are innumerable people who were active Christians in one town and are completely estranged from the church in a town five hundred miles away. The church for them was a particular brick building on the courthouse square, with a particular picture in front, or with a particular minister; they had entombed the gospel in this local institution. Others entomb the Christian faith in a particular type of architecture, taking the attitude that unless the building is imitation Gothic it is not a church, regardless of what is being preached. There are people who have the gospel chained to certain types of hymns; if they do not hear these hymns, and particularly these melodies, they do not feel that they can find the church.

All these are chains which the Reformation principle must break. There is no type of architecture, no style of music, no systematic theology that is the absolute expression of the Christian gospel for the Protestant. In fact, the Christian gospel must find new expressions in every age in order to speak understandably to contemporary people.

Protestants insist the language of the church ought to be the language the people can understand. Just as Jesus spoke Aramaic to the people in Palestine whose mother tongue was Aramaic, so Paul spoke Greek to the Greeks. Protestants assume that they must have the gospel in a language that they can understand, but they often forget that this means more than mere translation.

Anybody who has translated anything from one language to another knows that it involves more than finding the same words in the other language. If you go to Germany and get hungry on the train, you might want a hot dog. If you should translate the words directly and say that you would like to have *"einen heissen Hund,"* people would think that you lost your mind; what you want is a *"Wiener Wuerstchen."* Even in such a simple transaction, translation involves reinterpretation.

This is far more profoundly true of the message of the church; it has to be reinterpreted to every generation. The Protestant principle of Reformation emphasizes that one can never rest on one's laurels, that the task of proclaiming the Christian message in a non-Christian world is never done. There is no final solution.

In summary, there is such a movement as classical Protestantism. Furthermore, this movement has certain outstanding marks. They are (1) grace and the sovereignty of God, (2) faith, (3) Scripture as the rule of faith, (4) the church as the fellowship of saints and the priesthood of all believers, (5) the fallibility of man and all human institutions.

29

It is now of the utmost importance to remember that among the historical Protestant denominations there are great differences in emphasis. One group might emphasize one point almost exclusively. There are genuine Protestant traditions that are somewhat atypical; none is wholly typical. But the marks listed above have by and large characterized Protestantism, just as they were also marks of the New Testament church. Protestants did not adopt these emphases because they considered them congenial, but because they considered them biblical. The beliefs of Protestantism are not, as some people seem to believe today, merely a matter of personal taste. On the contrary, they are circumscribed by the testimony of Holy Scripture. This emphasis is the particular genius of the Protestant faith.

NOTES

1. "Luther at the Diet of Worms, 1521," in *Luther's Works*, ed. George W. Forell, vol. 32 (Philadelphia: Fortress Press, 1958), p. 115.

2. Karl Brandi, *Deutsche Geschichte im Zeitalter der Reformation und Gegenreformation* (3d ed.; Leipzig: Koehler & Amelang, 1941), p. 183.

3. *Luther's Works*, vol. 32, 112–113.

4. These computations are based upon the *Encylopaedia Britannica* (1974).

5. Harry Emerson Fosdick, *Great Voices of the Reformation* (New York: Random House, Inc., 1952), p. 515.

6. See Appendix.

7. See Appendix.

8. *Doctrines and Discipline of the Methodist Church* (Nashville, Tenn.: Methodist Publishing House, 1952), p. 26.

9. "Formula of Concord," *The Book of Concord*, ed. Theodore G. Tappert (Philadelphia: Fortress Press, 1959), p. 464.

10. See Appendix, Article VII.

Chapter 2

GOD'S REVELATION

It is impossible to speak about Christianity in general and the Protestant faith in particular without using certain technical terms. We have, of course, used a number of them already, such as "grace" and "faith" and "salvation" and "church." Some of these terms we have tried to explain, others we hope to explain in the future. Some, we hope, will become clear as we use them in these pages. "Revelation" is a term that will have to be explained with particular care because of the many misunderstandings that have accumulated about it. We cannot discuss Christianity without discussing revelation because it is a key word for the understanding of the Christian faith.

Most people have highly inaccurate notions about it. Professor Spurrier in a splendid little book called *Guide to the Christian Faith*[1] lists three prevalent misunderstandings of revelation. First of all, revelation as we use it in the study of the Christian religion is not some hallucination that an individual has as a result of great personal stress or some alleged special inspiration. Protestants by and large have been very suspicious of people who hear voices which nobody else can hear and which tell them to do extraordinary things. To be sure, visions are an important aspect of the psychology of religion. In many religions such visions establish one's claim to spiritual authority, and some will encourage the use of certain drugs to produce the desired hallucinations. Since the discovery and inexpensive manufacture of hallucinogens like lysergic acid diethylamide (LSD) some people have advocated "better religious experience through chemistry." But this kind of experience is not what is meant by revelation in classical Protestantism.

31

One could say that classical Protestantism has been almost stodgy, or at least extremely conservative, in its attitude toward claims of "revelations." Hallucinations or visions, however obtained, are not what Protestants call revelation.

Furthermore, creedal statements and theological systems are not revelation. Most Christians accept certain creeds. Some Protestants say that they have no creeds, but that is a very debatable claim. In any case, Protestants do not claim that these creeds or the systems of theology based upon these creeds are revelation. For example, the Apostles' Creed and the Nicene Creed are not revelation, and the writings of Luther, of Calvin, and of Wesley are not considered revelation by Lutherans, Calvinists, or Methodists. Even the most brilliant theological statements are not revelation. They may talk about revelation, but they are not themselves revelation.

Thirdly, in areas of human knowledge where we are still in need of a great deal of information, revelation is not the easy way to information. Protestants do not claim that revelation is a short cut to the kind of knowledge that can be attained by careful research in the natural sciences or the social sciences or even the humanities. You cannot be slipshod, inaccurate, or lazy in the laboratory and then hope that revelation will supply the missing information. There are tremendous unsolved problems in all areas of human knowledge, but revelation is not a short cut to their solution.

Finally, Protestants in general do not use the word *revelation* in connection with the kind of hunches that we sometimes have in making decisions. It is, of course, true that we all have to make many decisions in the course of a day, that people who are believing Christians will pray for guidance in these decisions, and that they will often feel that they have received such guidance. But this guidance is not what we call revelation. Revelation does not tell you what kind of job to take or what kind of woman to marry or who might make a fine husband for you. It is indubitably true that we need help in all these decisions, but the term *revelation* is reserved for an entirely different experience.

Revelation, as this term is used by Protestant Christians, refers to the fact that God reveals himself to human beings, makes himself known. Christians believe that the God who is the "Father

Almighty, Maker of Heaven and earth, and of all things visible and invisible" is vastly beyond the comprehension of all human minds. We could not know him had he not chosen to reveal himself, had he not chosen to remove the veil which hides divine power from human powerlessness, divine wisdom from human ignorance, and divine love from human selfishness.

The basic assertion of all Christians is that the unfathomable God has revealed himself to human beings in Jesus Christ. We shall discuss shortly the meaning of this special revelation, as the theologians call it. But first we should note that Christians distinguish between this special revelation in Jesus Christ and what they call general revelation.

General Revelation

For classical Protestantism general revelation is revelation which hides. What does this mean? In the Acts of the Apostles in the New Testament we have the report of a sermon which the Apostle Paul preached before the curious philosophers in Athens. In this sermon Paul asserts that in God we all—Christians and non-Christians alike—"live and move and have our being" (Acts 17:28). This means that human beings are at all times and everywhere confronted by God. We could not breathe for an instant, we could not do anything we are doing, we could not even deny God, say the Christians, were it not for the fact that *God is*. He is the source of our being and of all being. He created us and all that exists and preserves us and all that exists. God is the most overwhelming reality and thus he confronts us everywhere and at all times.

There are some people who will ask you, "Have you found God?" This is a very odd question, viewed from within the context of the Christian faith, for it seems to imply that God is lost, that it takes effort on our part to find him or to discover him in some out-of-the-way place. On the contrary, Christians assert that it takes a tremendous effort for human beings to ignore God, to deny him. An angry small child may make the effort to ignore his mother, but it is a tremendous effort, because everything he does and sees reminds him of his mother. Everything he has comes through the efforts of his mother; he is fed, washed, entertained, and put to bed by his mother—the most real fact in his life is his mother. He still might try to ignore her but it is a fairly hopeless cause. In a far more profound way all human beings, the Christians say, are at all times and everywhere confronted by God. In him all men, good and evil, and all things, important and unimportant, big and small, live and move and have their being. This is the basic fact of general revelation: *God is!*

In the preaching of the early Christians we find frequent references to this conviction that God has revealed himself and ought to be known by all human beings. Let us look at a few of these instances. In his letter to the Romans the Apostle Paul writes:

> For the wrath of God is revealed from heaven against all ungodliness and wickedness of men who by their wickedness suppress the truth. For what can be known about God is plain to them, because God has shown it to them. . . . Ever since the creation of the world his invisible nature, namely, his eternal power and deity, has been clearly perceived in the things that have been made.

And then St. Paul continues:

> So they are without excuse; for although they knew God they did not honor him as God or give thanks to him, but they became futile in their thinking and their senseless minds were darkened. (Rom. 1:18–21)

The claim of the Apostle Paul is that human beings could indeed know God, since he has revealed himself in his creation, but in fact they chose to ignore this revelation.

In other words, this revelation of God is very real but the human race has chosen to act as if it had not occurred. People try to ignore the God who everywhere surrounds them. There are other examples in Scripture of this idea of general revelation. A very strange thing happened to Paul and Barnabas in Lystra on their journey through Asia Minor. The Apostle Paul had healed a cripple and the people who had seen it were sure that this meant that some of their gods had come down to earth. They believed that

Paul was Hermes, the messenger and spokesman for the gods, and that his fellow missionary, Barnabas, was Zeus, the king of the gods. Since the people of Lystra had in their excitement stopped speaking Greek, the language of trade and international communication, and reverted to their native dialect, Paul and Barnabas had no idea what was going on until a priest of Zeus came with oxen and garlands to begin his sacrifices to the presumptive deities. It was then that Paul spoke to them. He said:

> Men, why are you doing this? We also are men, of like nature with you, and bring you good news, that you should turn from these vain things to a living God who made the heaven and the earth and the sea and all that is in them. In past generations he allowed all the nations to walk in their own ways; yet he did not leave himself without witness, for he did good and gave you from heaven rains and fruitful seasons, satisfying your hearts with food and gladness. (Acts 14:15–17)

This conviction permeates Christian thinking; although God has indeed revealed himself to human beings, they have chosen to ignore and misinterpret the revelation. Although they could have known God they do not know him, and they worship idols rather than the Creator. The Christian claim that the human race is guilty before God, that people are sinners, is based upon the assumption that they could have known what is right and wrong and that it is their fault that they do not do what is right but rather choose to do what is wrong.

It is the Christian position that this general revelation is the root of all religion. Human beings are religious. Everywhere they are trying to find answers to such questions as: Where do I come from? Why am I here? Where am I going? As far as we know we are the only beings on this earth that ask these questions. It is doubtful whether any person can live to be an adult without sometime asking one or all of these questions.

Because these questions are part of their nature, because they cannot help asking them, human beings are religious. Christians assert that they are inescapably religious because they are in fact confronted by God all the time. And it is this confrontation which

35

forces them to try to find answers. Religion is the human answer to the fact of God as he reveals himself to them in general revelation. It is a thoroughly human undertaking and full of the weakness of human beings. Religion is an effort to give answers, but it is an ambiguous effort because the human race cannot find these answers by itself. Christians do not say people in India and China cannot find these answers. Rather, they insist that nobody can find these answers unaided, neither Americans nor Europeans nor Asians nor Africans. While every human being must ask these questions, no human being can find the answers. If an answer is available, it must be an answer which God himself chooses to give us. General revelation is the incomprehensible fact of God all about us, and the human response to this revelation is religion. For Christians this response is ambiguous, misleading, and the cause of all idolatry, the human tendency to worship as God persons and things which are not God; but however deceptive, it is a response nevertheless.

Revelation of Law. A second fact about general revelation is that it is the revelation of law. The way God confronts the human race in the universe is through the words "thou shalt!" and "thou shalt not!" The Apostle Paul claims that human beings know intuitively that they must obey certain rules. He asserts in Rom. 2:15 that those who do not have a written law have a law in their hearts. He claims that, although all people know that there is right and wrong, they do that which is wrong and leave undone that which is right. For our purposes here let us just attempt to understand this one assertion: All human beings know that there is law.

This is indeed a startling assertion, since so many of us are convinced that there really is no absolute law, that we make up laws as we go along, and that these laws are completely arbitrary.

Christians affirm that the human race, living in this world created and maintained by God, is confronted by a definite ready-made structure. People do not make up this world; they have to take it as it is. The rules they do make up are by and large the human reaction to the structure as it confronts them. They are the codified good sense of the race.

For example, people do not make up the fact that fire burns. This is an experience they had on the basis of the way things are. When a mother warns her little boy that he will be burned if he touches the hot stove, she is stating a rule which is not arbitrary but a description of the way things are. If the little boy does not heed his mother's warning—and he probably will not—he will of course be burned. He will probably cry bitterly, but he will stay away from the stove in the future. The mother's rule does not make the stove hot; rather, the fact that hot objects burn you is the structure, and the rule, "Don't touch the stove," is a human adaptation to the way things are.

Or we could say that a heavy object running over a small live object will kill the small live object. This is the way things are. We don't make up this situation. But we make up rules which take this situation into consideration. For example, parents make rules for their small children such as "Don't run into the street without looking." But this rule is based upon the way things are and the mother is merely transmitting her information about the way things are to her little boy by means of this rule. In this instance, unfortunately, if the child does not obey the rule his mother lays down for him and he experiences these facts which have caused people to formulate the rule, it will be too late for him to change his mind and to admit that his mother was right. He will be run over by a car—killed—because he did not obey the rule his mother told him. The rule did not kill him, of course; the situation for which the rule was made did.

It is obvious that wherever there are people there are rules. These rules which we shall call law are the result of the experience of mankind that this world has a structure which is given, which we cannot change, and to which we must conform.

To put it quite simply—there are no noble savages who run around without clothing and without laws. Wherever there are human beings there is law. Every tribe has rules governing its conduct, rules which are the result of the experience of these people living in a world whose structure they have experienced as given. They try to adjust to this structure with the help of rules. These rules are not identical. There are bizarre variations—but rules can be found everywhere. In the interesting book by Professors Ford and Beach called

Patterns of Sexual Behavior[2] the most significant fact is that these researchers have not been able to find any tribe where sexual behavior is not subject to rules. The authors seem to approach the subject with considerable prejudice. Somehow they would like to show that human beings are merely very highly developed cousins of the higher apes. But what they do demonstrate is something entirely different—that, while sexual behavior among the apes is governed by instinct, sexual behavior among human beings is governed by law. To the everlasting disappointment of the admirers of the "noble savage" the laws restraining the sex impulse are frequently far more restrictive among the so-called primitive people than among the so-called higher cultures.

Nowhere is a human being merely nature. He reacts to nature with the help of law. According to the Christians this law is part of general revelation. St. Paul says it is written in the hearts of men. People everywhere know that there is a difference between right and wrong, between good and bad. The character of this law in most cultures may be summarized as the "golden rule." The golden rule was stated by Jesus in the Sermon on the Mount in the following words: "So whatever you wish that men would do to you, do so to them; for this is the law and the prophets" (Matt. 7:12). This is the summary of the law, as Jesus points out. But this law is nothing particularly Christian. There is something like the golden rule in most so-called higher religions. Hindus, Confucians, and Buddhists all have some statements very similar to the golden rule. As the Apostle Paul pointed out, those people who do not have the Old Testament law have the law written in their hearts. It may seem that some have rather poor copies. The law written in the hearts of Ruth Benedict's notorious Dobus is not very impressive. It seems to be an almost illegible version.[3] As Benedict says, "The Dobuan lives out without repression man's worst nightmares of the ill-will of the universe." But, by and large, rules govern the behavior of human beings everywhere.

If the law is essentially universal, then what is the special contribution of Christianity? Why do Christians send missionaries if everybody has the law anyhow? And what becomes of Rudyard Kipling's famous phrase about "the lesser breeds without the law"?

These questions can be answered at this point only in a preliminary manner. Classical Protestantism asserts that the good news proclaimed by the Christian church, the distinctively new message, is not the law at all but the gospel, the good news of what God has done. In other words, most Christians, perhaps one could say all Christians, are Christians not because of the uniqueness of the Sermon on the Mount or the golden rule but because of the good news God has given to the human race in Jesus Christ's birth, life, death, and resurrection. Not the golden rule but Christ is unique. What this actually means will be discussed in greater detail later.

When we observe the fact of law and structure as part of God's general revelation, we notice that this law confronts us essentially in six areas: (1) relation to God, (2) relation to the family, (3) relation to one's neighbor's life, (4) relation to sex, (5) relation to truth and integrity, and (6) relation to property. These are also the areas covered by the Ten Commandments.

Apparently these relations are nowhere instinctively established among human beings; they come into the world strangely unfinished in comparison to other higher mammals. They are humanized by their environment; they are ordered and guided by rules and regulations; they are governed by law. Many people who are not Protestants would agree with that. During the entire recorded history of mankind we find few people who deny the existence of law or that man is bound by this law. The existence of a law that is binding for all human beings is one of the most universal human notions and undergirds institutions, as, for example, the United Nations.

However, Protestants go one step further. They not only assert that such a law exists and that it is valid for all human beings, they assert that the human race is unable to obey this law out of its own resources. In other words, the law condemns mankind. It is universal, it is obligatory—and because human beings always disobey it, it always accuses them. This realization is most clearly expressed by St. Paul in his letter to the Romans. "For no human being will be justified in his sight by works of the law since through the law comes knowledge of sin" (Rom. 3:20).

According to the Protestant faith the law is a wonderful gift. It is like a road map of the United States. If you want to drive from Chicago to New York a road map will be useful in finding your way. But the mere possession of a road map does not guarantee your arrival in New York. You must follow its direction. If the map indicates that your destination is in the east, you must go east. The road map is a most useful tool—but only if you follow it. Similarly, the law is good and useful. This is true of the law of the Old Testament and of the law written in the hearts of all humans, including the laws of Confucius, Mohammed, Buddha, and Zoroaster insofar as they agree with the underlying structure which God has given. But it is the assertion of the Apostle Paul and of classical Protestantism that human beings do not, in fact, obey the law. The road map says to go east and they go west. This is not the fault of the map but of the people who think they know better than the map how to get to New York.

The Apostle Paul says:

> For I know that nothing good dwells within me, that is, in my flesh. I can will what is right, but I cannot do it. For I do not do the good I want, but the evil I do not want is what I do. (Rom. 7:18, 19)

Note that here a great leader and apostle of Christendom is speaking. This is not the description of the predicament of a few bank robbers and murderers but, at least according to classical Protestantism, the condition of the human race.

Most of us have a number of preconceived ideas abut Protestantism which are completely at odds with the claim which has just been made. Most of us associate Protestantism with the conventional wisdom of nice middle-class white Americans. In short, we identify Protestantism with the opinions of people belonging to a particular sociological stratum, who quite generally go to Protestant churches. It is indubitably true that all these good people tend to believe that a good Christian is a person who does not get into trouble with the law—except perhaps when it comes to parking or income tax matters. A Protestant is a pillar of society.

Prevalent as this notion may be, and you must judge that for yourself, it is the unanimous witness of classical Protestantism that all human beings are lawbreakers, that the law accuses and condemns them. If God were only a judge who judges righteously according to the law, all human beings without exception would be found guilty. People may have a glimmering of what is right because of God's general revelation, but they do what is wrong. They disobey the law.

Here classical Protestantism makes a shockingly negative judgment about one of man's highest acomplishments, namely, religion. For the great Reformers religion is deeply enmeshed in this pervasive disobedience; it is the human attempt to ignore the situation created by general revelation. People know that there is a structure, that they are in a world which runs according to rules they have not made. And now, in fear and trembling, they are trying to devise their own methods to get away from this awe-inspiring, marvelous, and terrifying universe.

For Protestants *human religion* is an effort to domesticate Almighty God. In religion people give God the scraps and remnants of their life. They whistle in the dark in order to drive away their justified fears. Here we must look again at the most prevalent forms of religiosity.

There is legalism. The legalist says, "I won't do this, and I won't do that, and I'll give you so much time and money every week, God, but the rest of the time and the rest of the money are my own. I can do with them as I please." Against this attempt to bargain with God Protestantism says that everything that a person has is God's, that he himself belongs to God, and that it is blasphemy to act as if any part of a human life does not belong to God.

The well-intentioned, middle-class attitude states, "I am a good Christian; I go to church once in a while, I contribute to my church occasionally, and I have never been in jail. I live a good life!" This attitude may be perfectly satisfactory to make a person conform to the social customs of twentieth-century American society, but it has precious little to do with the Protestant faith.

A second kind of religiosity is mysticism. The mystic may have raptures, he may see visions, he may hear voices and speak in tongues—but these experiences, be they ever so powerful, impressive, and inspiring, do not make him into a Christian. These experiences may, indeed, blind people to their responsibilities for each other and make religion into the "opiate of the people." Giving symptomatic relief to the pain of life, it may prevent people from diagnosing the disease and looking for a cure.

Similarly, there is religious rationalism. A person may know all the arguments for the existence of God and be able to reason anybody into the acceptance of his theological position. But even the most reasonable philosophical system about God does not make a person a Christian.

This is, of course, the Protestant criticism of the non-Christian religions. The Reformers never denied the sincere religious zeal of other believers. Luther, for example, never tired of pointing out to his fellow Germans how much greater the religious zeal of the Moslem Turks was. He admired their zeal and devotion. But at the same time he asserted that nothing that man can do out of his own power can change the fact that before God's law all men are guilty— Germans and Turks, Americans and Chinese.

But this criticism of religion was not only directed against the non-Christian religions. The Reformers asserted that Christianity can become a mere religion, an escape from God, an effort to limit God's influence on our life by turning over to him some of the least important matters and keeping the rest for ourselves.

Let us return to our illustration which pictures the human race as a person driving his car from Chicago to New York. His trouble is that he is going west. Human religion is his vain effort to correct this trouble by inflating the tires of the car, having the motor tuned up, and having the oil changed. These are good and useful measures, but they do not help a person reach New York if he is driving west from Chicago. In fact, they may help him to go faster in the wrong direction. They may give him a false feeling of security. With the beautifully running motor he may be less tempted to ask, "Am I going in the right direction?" General revelation turns out to be of little use in the solution of mankind's ultimate problem. Indeed through general revelation we know of law and we know of God, but what we know only confuses us and may give us a false sense of security, according to the Protestant faith. General revelation is indeed the revelation which hides!

42

Revelation Rooted in Human Experience. But even though it hides God from us, general revelation has its roots in very real experiences of people. As a living being, a person encounters God. And the experiences which make all human beings so inescapably religious are awe-inspiring and overwhelming.

The first of these experiences is that described by the phrase, *I am impressed by the fact that there is something and not nothing!* It is, of course, quite possible never to have thought of this fact in exactly these words. But, as we begin to reflect on our environment, we sooner or later are tempted to follow in the footsteps of the great French philosopher René Descartes, and doubt all things. It is easy to doubt the reality of the world around us and even our reality. But eventually, when we philosophize in this manner, we are struck by the fact that nothing would have to be—although everything is contingent—there is this vast universe! There is something and not nothing! There are human beings—and what odd creatures they are! Blaise Pascal in his *Pensées* describes beautifully the human reaction to such reflection:

> What shall man do in this state? Shall he doubt everything? Shall he doubt whether he is awake, whether he is being pinched, or whether he is being burned? Shall he doubt whether he doubts? Shall he doubt whether he exists? We cannot go so far as that; and I lay it down as a fact that there never has been a real complete skeptic. Nature sustains our feeble reason, and prevents it raving to this extent. Shall he then say, on the contrary, that he certainly possesses truth—he who, when pressed ever so little, can show no title to it, and is forced to let go his hold? What a chimera then is man! What a novelty! What a monster, what a chaos, what a contradiction, what a prodigy! Judge of all things, imbecile worm of the earth; depository of truth, a sink of uncertainty and error; the pride and refuse of the universe! Who will unravel this tangle? Nature confutes the skeptics and reason confutes the dogmatists. What then will you become, O men! who try to find out by your natural reason what is your true condition? You cannot avoid one of these sects, nor adhere to one of them. Know then, proud man, what a paradox you are to yourself. Humble yourself, weak reason; be silent, foolish nature; learn that man infinitely transcends man, and learn from your Master your true condition, of which you are ignorant. HEAR GOD![4]

43

This is the true meaning of the ontological argument for the existence of God, that is, that the idea of God implies his existence. It is not a mathematical proof but an experience which no one can escape. There is something and not nothing!

The second of these universal experiences which give us a sense of the reality of something far greater than we are is the *reality of law*—the standards of law that we have discussed above. We all know that there is truth and there is falsehood, that there is justice and that there is injustice. And we all are frustrated by the fact that we would like to know more—and will always know so very little.

Some time ago an article appeared in a national magazine by a man who had just come to the realization that he would never become an ice skater. Watching the graceful figures at Rockefeller Plaza, he had suddenly admitted to himself that it was too late, that he would never have the time to learn to ice skate. This brought recognition of a long chain of other things that he would never do. In philosophical terms this man had come face to face with existential finitude, the very limitations involved in being human. You may have had this experience already, the realization that for many things it is already too late—you will never become a great pianist or a great baseball player. This experience is related to the thoughtful person's experience in a library: all these books—most of them of some interest, many of them fascinating—and the great majority he can never read. Each would help him a little bit toward the truth, but he will never attain this goal.

This is in a sense a universal human experience. We all know that there is truth, and we know at the same time that we are very far away from it. What we know is partial and limited.

The same is true of justice. We all believe that there is right and wrong; even if we deny its existence with our mouth, we believe it with our total being. Some of the people who are most insistent that there is no right or wrong, who accuse the Christian of being a spokesman for medieval notions, and who shout loudly that right is only what everybody says is right are actually very sensitive to right and wrong. The very same people who have just denied the existence of justice become very emotional when racism shows its ugly face somewhere in the United States. They know very well that this is wrong. They know that somehow the structure of the universe as people know it has been violated. There are standards of justice that we perceive with our very being. Antigone knew that she had to bury her brother! Electra knew that her father had to be avenged! Go through the myths of the ancients and the preliterate people of the present, and everywhere you will discover that human beings know themselves to be confronted by structures that are greater and more important than they are themselves.

People are willing to die for truth because they believe that this truth is more important than their lives. People are dying for the truth today. Perhaps it is a partial truth, a very confused truth, but the mere fact that these people are willing to die for it indicates that human beings know that there are standards that are more important than life itself. Truth and justice simply are, even if we cannot demonstrate them to everybody's satisfaction. We know that they exist and we try haltingly to live by them.

This is the validity of the so-called ethical or moral proof of the existence of God; that our moral nature, our sense of right and wrong, demonstrates the reality of God. It is not a proof in the sense that it is conclusive to the person who does not want to believe, but it is an argument which describes the situation as it confronts us in life.

Thirdly, there is the *reality of beauty and art.* Some of the earliest human beings of whom we have any records scratched pictures of the animals of their environment into the walls of the caves in which they lived. We are not merely mammals who eat and sleep and reproduce. We want beauty and despise ugliness; we want to create beautiful things and are frustrated by our failures. Have you ever watched a child trying to put on paper what he sees in his mind's eye and being disappointed because he cannot create the beauty he would like to create? What is true of children is more true of adults. One of the most sensitive authors of our century was Franz Kafka. He left all his novels unfinished because they never were what he wanted them to be. It was his last will and testament that all his novels, such as *The Castle* and *The Trial*, were to be destroyed. They were published posthumously by a friend who felt that they expressed this insight into man's confrontation with a beauty that he cannot attain better than most other works which are proudly completed by less sensitive men than Kafka.

Human beings have always been artists. They have used art to come to terms with a universe they could not understand. In Greek tragedy and in William Shakespeare, in Johann Sebastian Bach and in Pablo Picasso, we see the results of general revelation. The human race coming to terms with the universe makes some people become artists and gives all of us a sense of beauty and artistic appreciation.

Fourthly, there is the *reality of love*. The Christian Bible is full of allusions to the reality of love as it confronts us everywhere. And this love gives us some inkling of a structure which includes love. Parental love, the love of parents for children, is one of the most basic facts of our life. Nobody can quite understand it unless he or she has experienced it, and no amount of cynicism touches the reality of the experience.

Further, we observe and experience the overwhelming reality of marital love. The Old and the New Testaments describe the relationship of God to man through the image of marital love as well as parental love. God is our heavenly Father, we are his children. The church is the bride of Christ. For the Prophet Hosea the relationship between himself and his unfaithful wife became a symbol of the relationship between God and his people.

Love is a fact of general revelation. Obviously, not only Christians but all human beings are capable of love. Just as people often talk about love but never perform the works of love, so many people also ridicule love and then show love, to their own surprise and to the surprise of everybody else. Love is a reality. Human beings are capable of showing love. It is often clearly selfish and always at least affected by selfishness and pride, but it is nevertheless real. The experience of love becomes a basic experience for a person's realization that he does not stand alone.

A fifth area in which general revelation confronts us is *history*. This does not mean that in history the good people always come out on top and the evil people are always defeated. This is not at all the witness of biblical Christianity. But there are certain facts in

46

history which point us toward the realization that this is an orderly universe and not chaotic.

This insight is in no way particularly Christian. In fact, it was Plato who pointed out that a minimum of order and honesty is necessary to have any kind of society. Even robbers cannot rob effectively unless there is some "honor among thieves." A gang of robbers who desire to hold up a bank must trust each other to a certain extent in order to achieve their goal. If they do not trust each other at all, they will fail in their attempt. The lookout must look out, the driver of the getaway car must stay in the car, and the man who is getting the money must bring it out to the others. This minimal amount of mutual trust is necessary even for a band of robbers. A society cannot be built on chaos; it needs order and mutual trust.

Furthermore, individuals in a community must have some sense of vocation in order to build a successful society. If everybody is concerned only with his own interests, the society will not flourish. There has to be a service motive besides the profit motive for great cultural achievement. To use Arnold Toynbee's phrase, human beings must answer the challenge of their historical situation with an adequate response. If they fail to do so, the culture fails.

Another aspect of this confrontation by God in history is the peculiar way in which we experience time. As usual, the Greeks had a word for it; in fact, they had two words for it. In the Greek language, the language in which the New Testament is written, we find two different words that we translate as "time," namely, *chronos* and *kairos.*

Chronos time is the time that we can measure with the help of a watch or a calendar. It is the time that can be divided into seconds and minutes or days and years and centuries. Chronological time is measurable time, divisible into parts which are all somewhat alike.

But when the Greeks use the word *kairos* they mean another kind of time altogether. The New Testament translations usually render the word *kairos* by "the accepted time" or "when the time was fulfilled." This means that time, besides being this divisible, measurable, even stream on which we are carried along, has another quality which is quite disturbing. It becomes *kairos*, the accepted time, the time for decision.

This can be illustrated with some examples from everyday life. A young man and a young woman are going steady. They have been good friends for a long time and now they have decided to give up all other girlfriends and boyfriends and go steady. All this takes place in *chronos*. But there comes a moment when this *chronos* becomes *kairos*, when this time becomes the accepted time. The crucial moment arrives in which this particular boy asks this particular girl to marry him—and if he delays too long the relationship will surely deteriorate until it finally breaks, and she will marry somebody else. There will still be lots of *chronos*, but when she is married to somebody else and has half a dozen children the *kairos* is gone. There is still time, but the accepted time is past.

Or a student is taking a course at the university. He gets up early every morning to make it to class, where the instructor drones along for fifty minutes. All this is *chronos*. Then one day, after all this *chronos*, the instructor announces a test for the following Thursday. Suddenly *chronos* has become *kairos*; time has become the accepted time. In this Thursday's fifty minutes the fate of the student is decided as far as this course is concerned. He either knows the answers to the questions he is asked *at this particular time* or he fails in this course. This particular time block has also minutes and seconds but somehow these minutes and seconds are different. They are *kairos*, not merely *chronos*. If the student knows the answers at this time, he passes; otherwise, he fails. It does not help for him to go to the instructor afterward and say, "I knew all this material backward and forward; I just couldn't remember it during the test." This is a heartbreaking story and it may even be true, but it won't do him any good. It is what you do when *chronos* becomes *kairos* that really counts.

Or two people work on a flying trapeze, a man and his wife. The woman flies through the air from one side and the man, holding on with his feet, flies through the air from the other side. Then for a split second *chronos* becomes *kairos*, time becomes the accepted time: the man catches his wife and she is safe or he fails and she will fall. It is not enough for this man to say, "My muscles are generally in wonderful shape," or "My coordination is usually extraordinary." That's all very interesting, but what counts is the split second when *chronos* becomes *kairos* and he can grab his wife.

What has been illustrated here is a general aspect of time as it involves human beings. For all of us, as individuals and as members of groups, time has this double aspect. There comes a time for decision. Indeed, without knowing the technical terminology, without knowing a word of Greek, people know about the significance of decision. They know about this double aspect of time. They know that they must act and that they are held responsible for their actions. Their actions have ultimate significance, for time is not reversible. This reaction to time is the result of man's confrontation with God. It is part of general revelation. It does not prove the existence of God to the unbeliever. It is not "scientific evidence," but it is a very real experience shared by all men.

And this brings us to still another aspect of this confrontation with God in history. The German poet and historian Friedrich Schiller said, *"Die Weltgeschichte ist das Weltgericht,"* "World history is the judgment over the world." Schiller was an idealist, and, as it stands, this statement is far too optimistic. But looked at from the negative side it describes a human experience which results from the human confrontation with God. "Lo, how the mighty are fallen!" All human power is powerlessness in the long run. Think of the founders of the so-called thousand-year Reich, the Nazi leaders in Germany whose empire collapsed after only twelve of the thousand years. "O where are kings and empires now, of old that went and came?" This is a universal human experience. It is pathetic when people attempt to fight this reality by trying to build a structure that will last forever, trying somehow to perpetuate themselves through buildings or institutions and fail miserably. Confronted by this fact of judgment, we try to have at least a vault in which our bones will rest unharmed forever. We are comforted by the double-your-money-back, unconditional guarantee that the vault will last forever. But all these frantic efforts only point up the reality of the judgment, which is one of the most basic experiences of the human race. This is the reality that Greek tragedy and American tragedy speak about.

Finally, human beings also experience general revelation, the confrontation with God, when they realize that this universe is an orderly universe, a *cosmos* and not a *chaos*. When the biologist relates the development of greater and greater complexity in nature, and when the physicist describes the orderly way in which the universe runs down according to the second law of thermodynamics, they are both portraying the order of the universe. Almost intuitively we discover pattern and design everywhere, and in the pattern and design we feel ourselves confronted by God. The purposefulness of the universe is the basis for the teleological proof of the existence of God. Here most people, even if they are not convinced by the proofs as logical proofs, admit that they stand in awe before "nature and nature's God," as our deistic predecessors liked to say.

And so, again, human beings experience in many ways this confrontation with God as the wholly other. They experience it through (1) the realization of their own contingency and the contingency of all that exists, the fact that there is something and not nothing, (2) the existence of standards that confront us from the outside and that we cannot change, (3) the reality of beauty and of art, (4) the reality of love, (5) history, and (6) nature.

But here classical Protestantism takes what may seem to be an odd position. General revelation, it says, is real, and all these things that we have described are real experiences of human beings, but general revelation fails to reveal God. Instead of giving us a way to God, it is, on the contrary, at the root of our unwillingness to listen to God, and causes us to devise our own methods of reaching him. Because human beings are in revolt against God, general revelation gives them just enough knowledge to befuddle them, confuse them, and lead them astray. This is not God's fault, for he wants to reveal himself. It is our fault, says Protestantism. We use even the very revelation of God to deny him. Again we can see how the Apostle Paul expresses this human experience:

> Although they knew God they did not honor him as God or
> give thanks to him, but they became futile in their thinking and
> their senseless minds were darkened. Claiming to be wise, they
> became fools, and exchanged the glory of the immortal God for

images resembling mortal man or birds or animals or reptiles.
(Rom. 1:21–23)

This is the experience of the human race, according to the Christian faith; even God's general revelation is perverted by human beings to hide God. God reveals life and humanity sees only death; God reveals law and humanity sees only punishment; God reveals love and humanity sees wrath; God reveals beauty and humanity sees ugliness. Nature shows not the true God but the *Deus absconditus*, the hidden God. The perverse perception of general revelation creates the situation which makes necessary the special revelation of God in Jesus Christ.

According to classical Protestantism there is no continuity between the religion of human beings and the revelation of God. Religiosity is in a sense human effort to escape God. It is the religious person who is particularly stubborn in his refusal to admit his need for revelation. In the New Testament we read a good deal about Pharisees and publicans. It appears that the Pharisees were very religious people—but their very religiosity was at the root of their trouble. As the New Testament describes it, these Pharisees knew so much about religion that they were unwilling to listen to God when he confronted them in the person of Jesus Christ. The publicans, in spite of their religious ignorance and their moral imperfection, were better off than the Pharisees because they at least admitted their shortcomings. Humanity with its religion, and because of its religion, is in need of the special revelation in Jesus Christ.

Revelation in Jesus Christ

The Reality of Revelation. The Christian church confesses on the basis of the apostolic witness as recorded in Scripture that God has revealed himself to people—who are guilty before the law and driven to despair by general revelation—as Lord and Savior. Protestantism insists that this is God's act. Revelation is not something that people have; it is something that God does. It is an act of his sovereign grace. In other words, we have no right to revelation, we have no claim upon God. It is not something to which we are entitled. But, like creation, it is an act of God's sovereign grace. If you ask why God reveals himself you cannot find the answer in human beings. It is not because people are so good or so valuable, but because God is what he is that he reveals himself in Jesus Christ.

Holy Scripture is the record of this revelation. It tells us what God has done in history through Jesus Christ. Through the witness of the church based on Scripture each generation can hear this message.

General revelation hides the true being of God and, because of their attitude of disobedience, tends to confuse people and fails to save them. Special revelation is entirely different. In Jesus Christ God confronts humanity as Savior (2 Tim. 1:10). In him God speaks to us. This is expressed in the Epistle to the Hebrews in the following words: "In many and various ways God spoke of old to our fathers by the prophets; but in these last days he has spoken to us by a Son . . ." (Heb. 1:1, 2). In Christ the eternal Word (*Logos*) has become flesh (John 1:1 ff.). God as God, apart from his revelation in Christ, would be eternally hidden from us. Christians stand in awe before God. They realize that they have no claim on him. He does not owe them anything. What he says to Job is said to all of them:

> Where were you when I laid the foundation of the earth? Tell me, if you have understanding. Who determined its measurements—surely you know! Or who stretched the line upon it? On what were its bases sunk, or who laid its cornerstone, when the morning stars sang together, and all the sons of God shouted for joy? (Job 38:4–7)

In those religions in which magic is used, the gods can be dominated, they can be controlled. It is possible to punish them by punishing the fetish that contains divine power. There are certain attitudes in contemporary religiosity which would indicate a sub-Christian approach to God, as illustrated by the revival of magic and witchcraft. This is the result of the sentimental misunderstanding of God as an indulgent parent. The God of the Old and New

Testaments is not "the Man upstairs." It is hard to imagine any of the great theologians who have been the spokesmen of classical Protestantism addressing God in the patronizing manner which is part and parcel of so much contemporary religiosity.

Classical Protestantism knows God as the sovereign Lord. Statements which emphasize the absolute sovereignty of God abound in the works of Luther and Calvin. John Wesley said about God, the Creator:

> He has acted in all things according to his own sovereign will. Justice has not, cannot have any place here; for nothing is due to what has no being! Here, therefore, he may, in the most absolute sense, do what he will with his own. Accordingly, he created the heavens and the earth, and all things that are therein, in every conceivable respect, "according to his own good pleasure."[5]

This is hardly the God of contemporary juke-box piety. This is the God of the electrons and the spiral nebulae and he is hidden from human eyes.

Because God is so utterly different from us, because of his sovereign majesty, we can never reach him out of our power. According to classical Protestantism, human beings simply cannot attain God. Every effort to do so is doomed from the start and must lead to despair.

But while humanity cannot reach God, God can reach the human race. The gulf between God and man can be bridged only by God. Special revelation is the assertion of the church that God has in fact bridged the gulf in Jesus Christ.

Perhaps the simplest illustration of what Protestant Christians believe here is one taken from the realm of language. If a person visits a foreign country and wants to make himself understood he will learn the language of that country. It is then possible for him to translate his sentiments and ideas into the language of the people he has gone to visit. In a far more profound sense, asserts Protestant Christianity, God has translated himself into human language in Jesus Christ. He speaks to us in language that we can understand, and he lives with us in a human life, the kind of life that is meaningful to us. In 1 John we read:

> That which was from the beginning, which we have heard,
> which we have seen with our eyes, which we have looked upon
> and touched with our hands, concerning the word of life—the
> life was made manifest, and we saw it, and testify to it, and
> proclaim to you the eternal life which was with the Father and
> was made manifest to us. (1 John 1:1, 2)

The eternal life entered into time, the Christians say. God be-
came a human being. The Immortal took upon himself mortality.
The infinite entered into space, in order that people might know
God.

This is the assertion which Christianity makes and upon which
all other assertions depend. In other words, the key to the Christian
faith in general and the Protestant faith in particular is the statement which was quoted in the beginning: "God was in Christ reconciling the world unto himself." People who believe this are called
Christians. But this is certainly *not* something which is obvious or
self-evident. The possibility of this assertion depends upon the reality of the revelation.

The first assertion which the Protestant faith makes concerning
special revelation, the revelation in Jesus Christ, is that it is real.
The second assertion deals with the form of revelation. Here the
Protestant faith asserts that the revelation in Christ is historical
revelation. It took place in time and history. It is not the revelation
of abstract truths that are accepted but revelation through events.

Here Christianity is quite different from most of the other great
religions. What Confucianism or Buddhism or Hinduism insist
upon is the truth of their ideas or the saving and enlightening
power of the way of life they teach. The historical events connected
with these traditions are of little significance. They have only symbolic meaning. If there had never been a man like Confucius, and if
historical scholarship should establish that such a man never lived,
it would make little difference to Confucianism. The message of
Confucianism is based upon the truth of the ideas which Confucius
expressed. These ideas are valid quite apart from any events in
Confucius' life. The events in Confucius' life are accidental and
have at best a symbolic significance.

We could say almost the same thing about Buddha; the teachings of Buddha rather than the events in Buddha's life are the clue to Buddhism. Hinduism offers perhaps the clearest contrast in this regard, since Hinduism also speaks about God coming to humanity in incarnations. But note that there are many incarnations of which no one is of absolute significance. These incarnations, to continue through all eternity, are opportunities for God to teach the human race the truth, the proper ideas and the proper way of life. For the Hindus incarnations are a pedagogical device which the supreme God uses to communicate ideas. What matters are these true ideas. The events in the life of the various incarnations have merely symbolic significance. Neither history nor time has any significance in Hindu thought. Everything is myth and symbol. To go back to the idea which we mentioned before—there is no *kairos* in Hinduism. There is no accepted time, a time for decision, when a person's destiny hangs in the balance. The Hindu doctrine of the transmigration of souls offers human beings infinite time and infinite opportunities to achieve the goal of identification with God.

It is therefore of considerable significance to note the insistence upon time and history in Christian revelation. Each individual is a historical being; only that which occurs in time is real to him. This does not mean that time is real for God, but it does mean that time is real for human beings and that events must take place in time in order to be real and meaningful to them. Here the Christian church asserts that God entered into time and history in order to save people. This is why Pontius Pilate is in the Apostles' Creed. The Apostles' Creed is a very short statement of the Christian faith. There is not a word about Jesus' ministry on earth or about Peter or John—yet Pontius Pilate is in the Creed. It states that "he suffered under Pontius Pilate." This unimportant Roman politician is mentioned and remembered by Christians as an expression of this typically Christian emphasis upon the historical character of revelation. The incarnation, the translation of God into human terms, is for them not a general principle, not a symbol, but an event! Something that actually happened! As St. John puts it: "And the Word became flesh and dwelt among us . . ." (John 1:14).

Time matters. Christians do not believe that they have infinite incarnations in which to attain God. The challenge of Christianity, the challenge of the Christian gospel is that now is the accepted time—the *kairos*—now is the day of salvation. History is not an eternal circle, a wheel that keeps turning for ever and ever. No! History is a line, with its beginning in God. This is the doctrine of creation. It has a center, the incarnation of God in Jesus Christ. And it has an end. But the significant insight is that history is a line rather than a circle. What we do on this little segment of the line which is ours has ultimate meaning for us.

When we say that the revelation in Christ is historical revelation, we say that Christ entered into this line—intersected this line, if you please. The revelation in Jesus Christ from the time when Quirinius was governor of Syria, recounted in the Christmas story, to the time when Pilate was Rome's representative in Jerusalem, as we read in the Passion story, is revelation in time. It is not repeatable, it is not a parable, it happened once and for all, it is event!

And if the first thing that we can say about the form of revelation according to the Protestant faith is that it is revelation in time and history, then we must say simultaneously that the Protestant faith insists that the historical once-and-for-all character of God's revelation in Jesus Christ is history, but it is not *mere* history. We become Christians when revelation is no longer "mere history" to us and when Christ becomes our own eternal contemporary.

This means that it is certainly not enough to believe in Christ as you may believe in Julius Caesar. You may believe that there was a man like Caesar who crossed the Rubicon and was eventually assassinated in Rome. You may accept these occurrences as events in history. There are some people who believe that there was a certain Jesus Christ in the same manner. They believe that there was a certain Jesus Christ who was the son of a virgin and who lived a life of preaching and healing. They believe that he did all the miracles which the Bible reports, and then he was killed, and on the third day he was raised from the dead. There are people who believe that in the same manner in which they believe that Caesar crossed the Rubicon or that Socrates was a sculptor and the son of a midwife and was executed by the Athenians because he asked too many embarrassing questions.

The Protestant faith asserts that it isn't enough to believe facts about Christ. Jesus Christ isn't another Caesar or another Socrates. You have to believe *in* him; it is not enough to believe things *about* him. One must in a sense become a disciple, just as Peter and John became disciples. There were many people in Jesus' time who saw all the things Jesus did and who did not believe in him. A few people believed and became his disciples. Revelation is revelation *for you* only if it makes you into a disciple. Here we are again dealing with the subject of faith which was discussed at the beginning. Faith is complete and utter trust. It isn't mere information about things that happened or didn't happen.

Revelation is not revelation for us until we accept it in faith. And here we must mention a word which will come up repeatedly in the course of our discussion. The all-important emphasis upon the historical character of revelation and the emphasis upon experiencing personal fellowship with Christ, the eternal contemporary, are *complementary* to each other. This means that in the Protestant faith there are a number of basic convictions which cannot be expressed by saying one thing only. We have to make two assertions simultaneously. Often two such statements will appear contradictory on the surface. But only if both are made do we express the Protestant faith adequately at this point. We borrow this concept of complementarity from physics. There it means that various pictures used to describe atomic systems are adequate to certain experiments, yet mutually exclusive. For example, an atom can be described as a planetary system or as a nucleus surrounded by waves, whose frequency is decisive. These different pictures are complementary to each other. While they seem to contradict each other, they are both correct if used properly. Similarly, in theology we often get at the truth by saying two things simultaneously that seem on the surface to be contradictory. We will notice this again and again in our discussion of the Protestant faith. It is in the letters of the Apostle Paul *and* the letter of the Apostle James that we receive the total message. It is through the Gospel of Mark *and* the Gospel of John that the living Christ is presented to us. The emphasis may seem different, but this very difference helps us to get a deeper insight into the Christian message.

This necessity of using seeming contradictions to describe our experience of God's revelation has been very admirably expressed in Professor D. M. Baillie's book, *God Was in Christ*. He says:

> The attempt to put our experience of God into theological statements is something like the attempt to draw a map of the world on a flat surface, the page of an atlas. It is impossible to do this without a certain degree of falsification, because the surface of the earth is a spherical surface whose pattern cannot be produced accurately upon a plane. And yet the map must be drawn for convenience's sake. Therefore an atlas meets the problem by giving us two different maps of the world which can be compared with each other. The one is contained in two circles representing two hemispheres. The other is contained in an oblong (Mercator's projection). Each is a map of the whole world, and they contradict each other to some extent at every point. Yet they are both needed, and taken together they correct each other. They would be either misleading or mystifying to anyone who did not know that they represent the surface of a sphere. But they can serve their useful purpose for anyone who understands that they are intended simply to represent in handy portable form the pattern covering the surface of this round earth which he knows in actual experience. So it is with the paradoxes of faith. They are inevitable, not because the divine reality is self-contradictory, but because when we "objectify" it all our judgments are in some measure falsified, and the higher truth which reconciles them cannot be fully expressed in words, though it is experienced and lived in the I-Thou relationship of faith towards God.[6]

This is true of the tension between the eventful-historical character of revelation and the subjective personal acceptance of these events as governing and transforming the Christian life. For it is not merely history that revelation deals with but the meaning of these events to men and women today.

Of course, this raises quite a number of very significant problems which we can only touch upon in this context. For example, how are we to depict these events artistically in painting and sculpture? At times people have insisted on the imitation of the historical situation in the artistic reproductions which are supposed to illustrate the life of Christ. This means that the artist has tried to depict Jesus and his disciples as Palestinian natives of two thousand years ago. He has tried to be as faithful as possible to the archeological and historical data that tell us about the dress and customs of the people of Palestine in the first century A.D. The result of this approach has often been that Jesus and the disciples have become people from a faraway land, wearing odd costumes. They have become museum pieces, archeological exhibits, as interesting to our life as the dinosaur or the Neanderthal man. Much of the Sunday school art that is distributed to the children in Protestant churches all over the country has this tendency to attempt historical accuracy in a very superficial sense and to remove Christ from our experience as the eternal contemporary. In an effort to be faithful to history, it becomes unfaithful to the core of the gospel message.

Often the greatest artistic masterpieces dealing with the preaching of the Christian church have been efforts to depict Christ and the events of his life as if they had occurred in the time of the artist. If one looks at the art of the Middle Ages, one finds that the great medieval painters depicted Christ as a contemporary, as a medieval man, a man of their time. No effort was made to be historically accurate or to depict Jesus as a man from a faraway world. Rather, the effort was to make him and his life understandable to the contemporary world. While in a sense historically inaccurate, these great artists were able to communicate the message of the New Testament and of the Old Testament amazingly well. This is not only true of the great painters. It is equally true of the great anonymous sculptors who contributed their artistic masterpieces to the medieval cathedrals. Here, too, we find an effort to make these statues speak to people of the day of the great deeds that God has done in history.

The great music of the Christian church is not an effort to go back to the Palestinian music of Jesus' day but to sing of the wonderful deeds of God in such a manner that contemporary people can feel their deep significance. Here lies the importance of men like Palestrina and Bach. Listening to the *Passion According to St. Matthew* by Johann Sebastian Bach, one discovers that the great musician uses his inspired genius to proclaim the eternal message concerning God's deeds by means of the baroque music of the eighteenth century. Some endeavors to tell the gospel with the help

59

of jazz, rock music, or the folk-song idiom are in line with these classical efforts. If they frequently fail it is not because of their contemporaneity but rather because of the limited talent or commercial preoccupation of author and composer.

Interestingly enough, there are contemporary Chinese Christian artists who depict Christ as a Chinese. Their paintings show an Oriental Virgin Mary and Christ child in Chinese surroundings against the background of a Chinese landscape. Again we see the artistic effort to make the historical relevant and meaningful to contemporary men and women.

Yet this tendency can also go too far. The very effort to make Christ speak to our age can also lead to a denial of the Christ the work is supposed to proclaim. Much of contemporary religious art prettifies Jesus to the extent that we forget what the Scripture teaches concerning him. Looking at some of the popular pictures found in Christian churches today, we wonder: Is this the Man of Sorrows? Is this the Suffering Servant? Is this the crucified Christ, or some American movie star with long hair? The pretty Christ is hardly the Christ of the New Testament. Here an effort to be relevant, to make Jesus appeal to the teen-age set, may have gone so far that the message is utterly obscured by the very effort to make it meaningful.

Perhaps one of the most striking examples is a famous book—written by Bruce Barton and published in many editions—about Jesus that was popular in the first half of this century, *The Man Nobody Knows*. The author tried to depict Jesus as a big-business executive. The motto of the book, "Wist ye not that I must be about my Father's *business!*" was printed on the dedication page with the word *business* in italics! The Table of Contents read as follows: I. The Executive; II. The Outdoor Man; III. The Sociable Man; IV. His Methods; V. His Advertisements; VI. The Founder of Modern Business; VII. The Master. Efforts to make Jesus into a revolutionary hero and the disciples into a liberation army seem equally ill advised.

It is important to maintain the tension between history and contemporaneity. Revelation is never merely history, never merely something that occurred in the distant past. Yet at the same time it is never merely the proclamation of ideas which happen to be popular today. Its contemporary importance is based upon the historical event. Revelation is all-important today *because* it took place in history; it is significant for the world of present ideas *because* it is based upon the fact that God entered time. Whenever Protestantism lets go of one or the other assertion it falsifies the form of revelation.

We must admit that both have happened all too often. Some Protestants have at times become so concerned with the events of the past as to forget their meaning for today, while others have become so concerned with meanings for today that these meanings become dissociated from the events of the past. But classical Protestantism has tried to maintain both assertions at the same time and avoid the pitfalls of theological antiquarianism as well as the futile pursuit of modernity which characterizes the mod-theology of our time.

Now we are ready to turn to the next question: What is the content of revelation? As we have indicated a number of times in passing, for the Protestant faith the content of revelation is Jesus Christ. For Protestants Jesus Christ is not primarily the teacher of a revelation. It is not his message which is the object of our faith but rather his person. Classical Protestantism does not call you to faith in Christ's teachings as much as to faith in Christ as God's revelation. Here we should remember again that the ecumenical creeds of Christendom, the Apostles' Creed and the Nicene Creed, as well as most other creedal statements deal with the person of Christ and not with his teachings. This does not mean that his teachings are insignificant or unimportant, but it does mean that his person validates his teachings and not vice versa. Protestants will try to follow the teachings of Christ because they believe Christ to be revelation; they do not say that they know him to be revelation because of his teachings. Thus the content of revelation is Jesus Christ. But what is it that is revealed through this revelation in Jesus Christ?

In Jesus Christ we learn that God is Creator and Lord. General revelation gives us a vague sense of God the Creator, but special revelation in Christ purifies, clarifies, explains, and focuses these vague notions.

All major religions have some notion of creation and a creator. In much religious thought the creator of the earth is evil. Creation, although always an act of power, is not always an act of goodness. For the Buddhist, for example, this world is a prison to be escaped. To be a living creature is to be imprisoned in a body and estranged from the divine soul. Even the great Greek philosopher Plato held the body to be the prison of the soul. Our attitude toward the world is bound to be quite different if we take seriously the revelation in Jesus Christ that the Father of our Lord is the Creator. Christians know that this is God's world and God is good.

Secondly, in Jesus Christ we learn that God is absolute love. The Greek language used by the writers of the New Testament has a number of words for love. *Eros* is love as desire. It is not absolute since it is motivated by the attractiveness and value of the object or person loved. We can only love people or things we find desirable with *eros*-love. *Philia* is love as friendship. It is not absolute since it is made possible by the common interests of the persons who love each other as friends. But when the New Testament speaks of God as love it uses the term *agape*. This is the absolute love which God shows and which does not depend on the attractiveness or loveliness of the persons whom God loves. This is a love that is able to overcome hate and revolt and bridge continually the abyss of separation which we have established and continue to maintain by our revolt against God. In Jesus Christ the very character of God as *agape*-love is revealed.

Christians are prepared to admit that the evidence presented in nature about God's love is in some ways inconclusive. God's power may be seen more clearly than his wisdom and justice. The study of nature will not tell us anything of God's love, for cruelty and hate are at least as obvious in nature as mercy and love. A fair case could be made, indeed, that they are more obvious. As we read the literature of the ages we find that, while many wise and sensitive men have been overwhelmed by the existence of radical evil in the world, few have caught a glimpse of love as undergirding creation.

A look at some of our contemporary literature shows that the love of God is not obvious on the basis of the data which this world supplies. If this literature does not deny God's existence it questions his love. This is hardly surprising, for we cannot know God as love unless he reveals himself to us as love. To the Christian it is not nature or history or the human personality but Jesus Christ who shows the ultimate character and purpose of God. The Protestant faith asserts that only through Christ can we know that God is absolute, self-giving love—love that is not dependent on our goodness and our worth but love that has its sources entirely in his own goodness and worth.

These statements may appear to some to be the most obvious platitude that could possibly be proclaimed. Everybody knows that God is love. But while we are indeed very familiar with the phrase, this does not mean that we are at all familiar with the reality. There is nothing obvious and self-evident about the assertion that God *is* love. It is far from being a universal assertion. Other people besides the Christians have said that God loves, but that he loves his friends and hates his enemies. Others again have said that God loves the good. Their logic leads them to say that since he himself is the best he will love only himself with a perfect love and that he loves man only insofar as he is perfect.

Against all these very reasonable and intelligible views the Protestant faith asserts that God is love because he has revealed himself as love in Jesus Christ. It is not through an analysis of nature—the observation of flowers or trees or butterflies—that we learn that God is love. Nor is it through an analysis of the human race. The analysis of human beings reveals libido, will to power, interesting drives and responses of many sorts, but no God of love. The Protestant assertion that God is love is based exclusively upon the revelation of love in Jesus Christ.

Holy Scripture as the Bearer of Revelation

This raises the next question: How do we know about Jesus Christ? Protestantism's answer is that we know about him through

God's Word. The peculiar authority which Holy Scripture holds among Protestants is based upon the fact that it is considered the bearer of revelation. Here we come to a subject which has been quite controversial among Protestants for a long time, the question of the authority of Scripture.

The Protestant faith considers Holy Scripture, that is, the canonical books of the Old and New Testaments, the record of the original witness concerning the revelation of God in history. This means that for Protestants in general it is not the Bible which saves people, but the deeds of God which are described and interpreted in the Bible. This may seem obvious, but there are, especially among Protestants, some magical concepts concerning the Bible which have nothing to do with classical Protestantism. There are people who believe that carrying a Bible or a New Testament on your body keeps you from having accidents and prospers you in your business affairs. This is a magical concept. It is not the Bible in your coat pocket but the Christ on the Cross who saves people, according to the Protestant faith.

Protestants do not claim that the Bible fell from heaven. Rather they hold that it is a library of books written over a long period of time and by many different people. For most Protestants, what makes the Bible unique is not its grammar, its spelling, or the scientific world view expressed in it. Its uniqueness rests in the fact that God inspired the writers of these many books in such a manner that what these books say about human beings in their relationship to God, God in his relationship to human beings, and human beings in their relationship to each other, under God, is true. Protestants claim that God speaks to them authoritatively in the Bible. The Bible tells the story of God's dealings with the human race; it contains holy history, or the history of salvation.

This means of course that each passage of Scripture must be understood in the light of all other passages and that it is a very dangerous practice indeed to take passages out of context. Most Protestants reject an approach to the Bible which advocates opening it at random, putting a finger on some passage, and then claiming that this is God's word for you. Although there have always been people who have used the Bible in this manner, this is not the way in which the great spokesmen of the Reformation used the Bible as authority.

For Protestants, Holy Scripture is the means through which the contemporary Word of God reaches each generation in the preaching of the church. The Bible is history, in some cases very ancient history. It is poetry, in some cases very beautiful poetry. But for the Protestant faith these ancient writings are vehicles through which God speaks to people today. It is the task of the preaching of the Protestant churches to proclaim the message for today on the basis of the holy history recorded in the Scriptures.

An illustration of such a relevant use of Scripture can be found in an editorial which appeared in *Life* magazine some years ago. A black youth had been lynched. The murderers were not found. *Life* commented as follows:

In Mississippi the murder of 14-year-old Emmett Till still goes unpunished. It will be punished, nevertheless, for there is a higher law than Mississippi's. Emmett Till was a child. One of the South's traditions is the religion of Jesus, who said: "But whoso shall offend one of these little ones which believe in me, it were better for him that a millstone were hanged about his neck, and that he were drowned in the depth of the sea." Men can be forgiven for prejudice, as a sign of ignorance or an imperfect understanding of their religion; no righteous man can condone a brutal murder. Those in Sumner, and elsewhere, who do condone it, are in far worse danger than Emmett Till ever was. He had only his life to lose, and many others have done that, including his soldier-father who was killed in France fighting for the American proposition that all men are equal. Those who condone a deed so foul as this are in danger of losing their souls. The soul of Emmett Till was known to but a few but it was a thing of value. It was fashioned on July 25, 1941, by the Lord God Almighty who placed on it this distinctive seal: This is my son, akin to all others, but unlike any one of them. Like each of my children he is unique, irreplaceable, immortal. I hereby send him among other men, who are his brothers. He went and was slain. In the dark night of this deed his childish cries for mercy fell on deaf ears. But they were heard, nonetheless, and the Hearer made an entry, that night, beneath certain names, writing once more: "It must needs be that offense come, but woe to that man by whom the offense

65

cometh." Sleep well, Emmett Till; you will be avenged. You will also be remembered, as long as men have tongues to cry against evil. It is true now as it was when Christ said it almost 2000 years ago: "For there is nothing covered that shall not be revealed; neither hid that shall not be known. . . . Whatsoever ye have spoken in darkness shall be heard in the light. . . . Be not afraid of them that kill the body. . . . Fear him, which after he hath killed hath power to cast into hell. . . . Are not five sparrows sold for two farthings, and not one of them is forgotten before God? . . . Fear not, therefore, ye are of more value than many sparrows."[7]

This is good preaching. Its frequent references to Scripture do not make its message irrelevant. On the contrary, Scripture used as authority is the very source of its relevance. Here we become aware of the tension between history and contemporaneity. The Bible is history, an account of events in the past, but at the same time it is God's Word for today. Protestants assert that God speaks to all people by means of this holy history.

The authority of Scripture, then, derives from the fact that it confronts us with the living God through the library of books and through the holy history which they record. For most Protestants its infallibility is the infallibility of Christ, whose "cradle" it is. Luther put it thus:

> . . . think of the Scriptures as the loftiest and noblest of holy things, as the richest of mines which can never be sufficiently explored, in order that you may find that divine wisdom which God here lays before you in such simple guise as to quench all pride. Here you will find the swaddling cloths and the manger in which Christ lies, and to which the angel points the shepherds (Luke 2:12). Simple and lowly are these swaddling cloths, but dear is the treasure, Christ, who lies in them.[8]

The book itself is not the object of Protestant worship, but the Christ who meets us in the Bible. The Bible teaches us that God confronts human beings as a person. He does not reveal himself to us as a logical proposition or an unconscious power—but person to person.

According to classical Protestantism, all Scripture must be understood in the light of the revelation of Christ, and Christ must be seen in the light of all Scripture. You may have had the experience of joining a circle of people engaged in a spirited conversation which makes absolutely no sense to you as a latecomer until someone mentions a key word. This key word suddenly makes the subject of the conversation clear, and the remarks which seemed contradictory and nonsensical fall into a sensible pattern. Similarly, Christ is the key to all of Scripture.

The story of the deciphering of the hieroglyphics also illustrates the significance of Christ for the understanding of Scripture. These hieroglyphics made sense for many centuries—but not to us. We could not make any sense out of them until the Rosetta stone was discovered, which contained an inscription in both Greek and hieroglyphics. What had been utterly incomprehensible suddenly became clear with the help of this key.

This is the sense in which Christ is the key to the Scripture. Without him this holy history and the literature which reports it are merely history and poetry. With him this same history gives sense to all life and all history.

At the same time, Christ must be seen in the light of all Scripture. Just as a conversation becomes clearer to the listener when he knows what subject is being discussed, so the subject becomes clearer as the conversation throws light upon it. Similarly, the other hieroglyphic inscriptions that have been solved through the Rosetta stone, in turn, throw light upon the particular inscription which became the key to solving the mystery of the hieroglyphics. In the same way, while all Scripture must be understood in the light of the revelation in Christ, so must Christ be seen at the same time in the light of all Scripture. Preserving this double relationship is one of the ongoing concerns of the Protestant faith.

One problem in regard to Scripture which separates Protestants from some other Christians is the canon of Scriptures. Canon is a Greek word meaning literally "rule" or "measuring rod." Which books constitute the Holy Scriptures? Protestants assert with the Articles of Religion of the Anglican Communion, "In the name of Holy Scripture we do understand those canonical books of the Old and New Testament, *of whose authority was never any doubt in the Church.*" These are the twenty-seven books of the New

Testament, on which all Christians agree, and the thirty-nine books of the Old Testament, which are also accepted as the Bible of the Jewish religion. The Roman Catholic Church accepts in addition certain other Hebrew writings as "canonical" although they are not so accepted by the Jews nor were they accepted as canonical by the ancient church. For Protestants these books are not acceptable because by definition canonical books are those "of whose authority was never any doubt in the Church." These Hebrew writings were not included in the Jewish canon, and they are not quoted in the New Testament. In the famous passage where Jesus refers to the witness of the Old Testament, these noncanonical books are conspicuous by their absence:

> Then he said to them, "These are my words which I spoke to you, while I was still with you, that everything written about me in the law of Moses and the prophets and the psalms must be fulfilled." (Luke 24:44)

The early church apparently did not accept these noncanonical books. One of the greatest scholars of this period, Jerome, who was the author of the Vulgate, a translation of the Bible into Latin, writes of the apocryphal books of the Old Testament:

> As, then, the Church reads Judith, Tobit, and the books of Maccabees, but does not admit them among the canonical Scriptures, so let it read these two volumes [Wisdom of Solomon and Ecclesiasticus] for the edification of the people, not to give authority to the doctrines of the Church.[9]

This canon of Scripture, that is, these sixty-six books, is normative for the proclamation of the Protestant faith. All Protestant teaching and preaching are supposed to be in conformity with the witness of these books. The famous *Westminster Confession of Faith of 1647* puts it thus:

> The authority of the Holy Scripture . . . dependeth not on the testimony of any man or Church; but wholly upon God (who is truth itself) the author thereof. . . . Our full persuasion and assurance of the infallible truth and divine authority thereof is from the inward work of the Holy Spirit, bearing witness, by and from the Word, in our hearts. . . . Nothing is at any time to

be added—whether by new revelation of the Spirit or traditions of men. . . . The Church is finally to appeal to them. . . . The infallible rule of interpretation of Scripture is Scripture itself.[10]

Although this is a Presbyterian statement, it expresses the consensus of classical Protestantism concerning the normative character of the canonical writings of the Old and New Testaments. The reason for this authority of Holy Scripture is that these books contain the record of the original witness to the Christ event. They tell what God did to reveal himself to human beings. They are the record of revelation.

At this point these questions arise: Was there any disagreement about the canon in the early church? Did Christianity know immediately which books were definitive and which were not? If they, in fact, eliminated some books as unfit for Scripture, were not, then, these church authorities who decided on the canon superior to Scripture? To these questions Protestantism, with common consent, answers *no!*

A study of the discussion of the canon will show that the leaders of the church never claimed to have the power to declare something Scripture. All they tried to do was to select the apostolic writings. The early church very clearly placed itself beneath the authority of the teaching of the Apostles. The books which they rejected were rejected because they were clearly not apostolic. The early church recognized the standard of the apostolic witness; that which was apostolic witness was retained, and that which was not apostolic witness was rejected. They used no personal or subjective criteria. Such arbitrary selection was the procedure of heretics such as Marcion who selected certain books he liked and dropped from his Bible others he did not like. This procedure forced the Christian church to define the canon. Marcion, a gifted amateur theologian, did exactly what the early church did not do; he acted as if his church had the right to pick and choose from Scripture and to accept certain books and reject others. The Gnostic heretics were willing to produce spurious gospels and epistles to spread their particular religious convictions. The early church rejected these "pseudepigrapha" not because the Gnostics liked them but rather because they were sure that these documents were in fact not written by the apostles to whom they had been attributed. There were other parts of the New Testament which notorious heretics like Marcion liked very much—but the church retained them because they were considered clearly apostolic.

For the early church and for the Protestant faith the testimony of Scriptures was authoritative and decisive. The teaching of the church had to be substantiated from the witness of the Apostles to the Christ event. Other doctrines might seem attractive and useful but if they were not scriptural they were rejected. This is the authority of Scripture for classical Protestantism and for those Protestants today who remain in the stream of classical Protestantism.

The Old and New Testaments. As we have indicated, the Bible is divided into two parts, the Old Testament and the New Testament. A question arises as to the relationship of the two parts: Can both be called "the Bible" in the same sense, or is the New Testament more truly the Bible than the Old?

For classical Protestantism, the Old and the New Testaments have equal status; both are God's Word to Christians, and both bear witness to Christ. They are part of the same holy history, both telling of the events through which God has entered history in order to save the human race. The difference is that the Old Testament testifies to a Messiah who is to come, while the New Testament tells of the Jesus Christ who came. For the Christian church and for classical Protestantism they are equally Christian books. Of course, it is quite possible and legitimate to read the Old Testament as Jewish history or as Near Eastern literature—and if one does this it is not likely that one will come to the conclusion that it is a Christian book. But this is not the way the people of the New Testament read the Bible or the way in which the Christian church, in all its branches, has read the Bible through the last two thousand years. For Christians in general and for Protestants in particular, the Old Testament is a book which points to Jesus Christ. It is read because it testifies of Christ and it explains the life and work of Christ.

An illustration may help to show what this means. If a young man receives a letter from his girlfriend telling him that she is very much in love with him and agrees to marry him, this is a document which will change his life, because he is the person about whom it speaks. Now, it is quite possible that an English professor might find this document and discover many grammatical errors, poor spelling, and ambiguous expressions. This is a perfectly valid way to look at the letter, for it is a document in the English language besides being the document that will change the young man's life. But everybody will forgive him if he tells the good professor that he cares little about the spelling—the letter tells him that she loves him and that is all he is interested in. Or if this letter is written from Europe during a political crisis, it may contain interesting political and historical information which makes it a worthwhile subject for the study of a historian. But, again, this is not the way the young man is going to read the letter.

Protestants will readily admit that the Bible is Hebrew and Greek literature and that it contains important historical and political data. They have no objection to people who study it from this or that point of view. But it is the Bible for them because God speaks to them person-to-person about those things that matter ultimately. It tells them the source, the purpose, and the goal of human existence. It is God's Word for them. And this is true of both the Old and the New Testaments. When the New Testament and Jesus speak of the Bible they always refer to the Old Testament, which is the Bible of apostolic times. The Reformers quoted and interpreted the Old Testament as often as the New. Luther, for example, considered Genesis, the first book in the Old Testament, and the book of Psalms among his personal favorites in the entire Bible. For classical Protestantism the Old Testament and the New Testament are equally the Word of God. They both tell the holy history, the story of God's intervention in history for the salvation of mankind.

A second question concerning the relationship of the Old and the New Testaments deals with the specific content of these two main parts of the Bible. If part of the message of God to man is what humans should do (often called the law) and another part is what God has done for them (often called the gospel), some might think that the Old Testament contains only law and the New Testament only gospel. As far as classical Protestantism is concerned, both the Old and New Testaments contain law *and* gospel. Not only the Old Testament tells us what God wants from human beings. The New Testament too reveals God's demands. The Ten Commandments in the Old Testament find their counterpart in the catalogs of vices to be avoided which we find in the epistles of the Apostle Paul. Both Old and New Testaments proclaim God's law.

Similarly not only the New Testament tells us the gospel. Nowhere in the entire Bible is what God has done for human beings stated more beautifully than in the passage concerning the Suffering Servant in the fifty-third chapter of the Prophet Isaiah. And the twenty-third Psalm describes movingly what God has done, is doing, and will do for people.

Thus, as far as classical Protestantism is concerned, the Old Testament is not merely the history of some ancient Near Eastern tribe. It is not merely beautiful and primitive poetry. It is the revelation of God's will for the human race, telling people what they should do—and at the same time what God has done and is willing to do for them.

The contemporary neglect of the Old Testament in the preaching and the worship of so many Protestants only illustrates how far much of twentieth-century Protestantism has deviated from the classical Protestant faith. If modern Protestants say that they cannot do anything with the Old Testament, that it does not mean anything to them, it only shows that they are really no longer within the mainstream of Protestantism. It cannot be overemphasized that, for classical Protestantism, *Old and New* Testaments are God's Word.

Thirdly, the center of the Old as well as of the New Testament is the Cross of Christ. For a Christian to understand anything in the Old Testament or in the New Testament, they must be seen in relationship to the Cross of Christ. A certain balance exists between the message of the Old and the New Testaments. In the phrase of St. Augustine: "In the Old Testament the New lies hid; in the New Testament the meaning of the Old becomes clear." The method used to connect the two "testaments" is commonly called "typology." It has been defined "as the establishment of historical connections between certain events, persons or things in the Old Testament and similar events, persons or things in the New Testament."[11]

The story of the Tower of Babel may serve as an illustration (Gen. 11:1–9). The parallel to this story in the New Testament is the story of Pentecost (Acts 2:1–13). For the Protestant faith, these two stories complement and interpret each other and the Cross is the center of both. The story of the Tower of Babel tells how human disobedience and alienation from God ended in the disruption of human society and the inability of people to understand each other. If human beings are separated from God, in revolt against God, they are also separated from their neighbors and at odds with their neighbors. Peace and understanding among people depend upon their relationship to God. But while the Old Testament tells this story negatively, describing the misunderstanding and disruption caused by disobedience and revolt against God, the New Testament tells of the other side of the same problem. In the story of Pentecost we learn that people who came from different nationalities, people whose languages differed so that they could not understand each other, learned to understand each other through the power of the Holy Spirit. Once they were united with God, the disruption of the Tower of Babel was reversed. Languages no longer separated the crowd that was present at Pentecost. They could all understand the Apostle's preaching. They each felt themselves addressed in their own tongues, in their own languages.

The eternal message which Protestants gain from the Old and New Testaments states that human understanding and peace among people depend upon peace with God. It states that people in revolt against God will also be at war with each other. It asserts that the tension and the strife that embitter the life of people on this earth, the misunderstanding and the hatred that disrupt all human community, are the result of human estrangement from God. Old Testament and New Testament looked at from the Cross proclaim that at the root of every human difficulty lies the fact that people are at odds with God. All other difficulties are the result of this main and basic difficulty.

Similar illustrations could be multiplied. One of the most profound investigations of the nature of faith was written by the Danish philosopher Søren Kierkegaard. The story he uses to interpret the meaning of the Christian faith is the Old Testament story of Abraham and Isaac. He retells the tale of the father who has one son upon whom all his hope for the future rests. And he tells about the decision that this father makes to kill the son, to sacrifice him upon the commandment of God. Kierkegaard does not gloss over this part of the story; he does not try to destroy its seriousness by jumping immediately to the happy end. Rather, he takes the Old Testament absolutely seriously. In doing so he tells us more about the meaning of the Christian faith than most other writers in the last hundred years.[12]

What every Christian interpretation of the relationship of the Old and the New Testaments has in common is the effort to understand both through their center and key, the Cross of Christ. To the Protestant faith, Christ is the clue to the Bible. As Luther puts it in his preface to the epistles of St. James and St. Jude:

> And that is the true test by which to judge all books, when we see whether or not they inculcate Christ. For all the Scriptures show us Christ . . . and St. Paul will know nothing but Christ . . . . Whatever does not teach Christ is not yet apostolic, even though St. Peter or St. Paul does the teaching. Again, whatever preaches Christ would be apostolic, even if Judas, Annas, Pilate, and Herod were doing it.[13]

The Old and the New Testaments cannot be understood apart from each other as far as the Christian faith is concerned; they are complementary to each other. Disregarding either will falsify both. Protestants would say that much of the misrepresentation of Christianity in our time and in times past is the result of the neglect of some part of the biblical message. Wherever the church has ignored social justice and acted as if the plight of the downtrodden were none of its business, the Old Testament prophets have reminded Christians that zeal for justice is part of the Christian life. The Old and New Testaments have helped to subject to close investigation every religious fad and every theological movement—Rationalism and Puritanism, Pietism and Orthodoxy. The message of the Old and New Testaments has upheld the Protestant faith through the ages, in spite of the deviations and conflicts which are freedom's price.

We are now ready to look a little more closely at the content of the Christian faith as proclaimed by Protestantism. The first subject which comes up for discussion is the reality of God.

NOTES

1. William A. Spurrier, *Guide to the Christian Faith* (New York: Charles Scribner's Sons, 1953), pp. 38 ff.
2. Clellan S. Ford and Frank A. Beach, *Patterns of Sexual Behavior* (New York: Harper & Brothers, 1951).
3. Cf. Ruth Benedict, *Patterns of Culture* (New York: New American Library of World Literature, Inc., 1946), pp. 120 ff. and p. 159.
4. Blaise Pascal, *Pensées* (New York: E. P. Dutton & Co., Inc., Dutton Everyman Paperback, 1948), pp. 120 ff. Part of Fragment No. 434.
5. Harry Emerson Fosdick, *Great Voices of the Reformation* (New York: Random House, Inc., 1952), p. 518.
6. D. M. Baillie, *God Was in Christ* (New York: Charles Scribner's Sons, 1948), pp. 109–110.
7. *Life,* October 10, 1955. Copyright, Time, Inc.
8. Martin Luther, "Preface to the Old Testament, 1545," in E. Theodore Bachmann, ed., *Luther's Works* (Philadelphia: Fortress Press, 1960), vol. 35, 236.
9. *Nicene and Post-Nicene Fathers,* ed. Philip Schaff and others, Second Series (Grand Rapids, Mich.: William B. Eerdmans Publishing Co., 1954), VI, 492.
10. Henry S. Bettenson, *Documents of the Christian Church* (New York: Oxford University Press, 1954), p. 347.
11. G. W. H. Lampe and W. J. Woolcombe, *Essays on Typology* (Naperville, Ill.: Alec. R. Allenson, Inc., 1957), p. 39.
12. Søren Kierkegaard, *Fear and Trembling,* trans. Walter Lowrie (Princeton, N. J.: Princeton University Press, 1954).
13. Martin Luther, "Preface to the Epistles of Saint James and Saint Jude, 1545." *Luther's Works,* vol. 35, 396.

Chapter 3

THE REALITY OF GOD

As has been shown previously, the reality of God is not a proposition deduced by our reason, but rather an experience which confronts us everywhere. We experience ourselves as creatures in a universe which we share with other creatures and which is not of our making. We have a beginning—we all know and can even give the exact date of our birth—and we will have an end at a certain day in a certain year. But neither the beginning nor the end is in our power. Our whole life is not in our power at all; it is created and it is dependent. We are dependent upon many factors, from a very small temperature range to the makeup of the atmosphere. If the earth were only a hundred degrees hotter, no human life could exist. Take away the oxygen in our air and our fate is sealed. There are innumerable factors over which we have no control but upon which we depend. And the generations before us who knew little about these factors knew nevertheless that they depended upon the sun and the rain, upon the seasons following each other and upon innumerable other "facts" completely outside their sphere of influence. Human beings are limited in many ways. We are limited in space, for we can be only in one place at one time; we are limited in time, and the older we get, the more obvious this fact becomes. But all these limitations only accentuate the assertion of the Christian faith that *God is power.*

God's Nature

The theologians of the Christian church have frequently discussed this assertion in very technical ways. They have discussed the power of God abstractly, apart from his revelation. This seems

76

to be fruitless and can only lead to all sorts of self-contradictions. One of the great arguments of the Middle Ages revolved around the nature of this divine power—is it in any way limited, even by his goodness? If it is limited by his goodness, is it still absolute? In other words, if God cannot do that which is evil, is he still absolute power? Sometimes these discussions degenerated into pure speculation. How far is God dependent upon the laws of logic? Can he make a four-cornered triangle? Can he make a rock so heavy that he cannot lift it?

All this abstract speculation about the power of God is meaningless and irrelevant to the Protestant faith, for God is not abstract power, nor theoretical power, but power in relation to our weakness, infinity in relation to our limitations, freedom in relation to our bondage. God is holy and personal power as he confronts us in his creation.

This means that in classical Protestantism there is no room for the assertion of a limited God as he is sometimes posited by modern philosophers, a god who is limited by evil or matter or whatever else it might be. The Protestant faith asserts: "With God all things are possible" (Matt. 19:26); and "What is impossible with men is possible with God" (Luke 18:27). The God who confronts the Christian in revelation is a God of power.

Furthermore, the reality of God confronts us in all our intellectual efforts. We are confronted by truth and meaning. Often we make desperate attempts to be coherent, to be meaningful, and to be truthful. We want to convey what we believe, and the more profoundly we believe it, the more difficult it becomes to convey it. With a simple statement it is fairly easy to convey the fact that a dog has four legs. This kind of statement is easily understood. But when we talk about justice and beauty, about the things that really matter to us and to all people, and when we talk about peace and democracy, it becomes very difficult to convey meaning. This is the lesson which political orators teach us in their drab routines. This is also the lesson which our own efforts to search for truth teach us; truth is elusive, and just when we think we have it captured, it has escaped us. It is in this very experience of the limitations of our own spirituality that we are confronted by the *God who is spirit.*

As the Bible teaches in many places: "No one has ever seen God
. . ." (John 1:18); "the blessed and only Sovereign . . . dwells in
unapproachable lights, whom no man hath seen or can see" (1
Tim. 6:15–16). God is spirit, and all efforts on the part of human
beings to reach ultimate truth shatter before this fact. This is the
end of all religious rationalism which believes that God can be
contained in some clever theological formula. The God who is
spirit cannot become a specimen in our collection of solved problems. His very spirituality sheds light upon our lack of it. The
assertion of the Protestant faith that God is spirit should guard
Protestants against vain efforts to identify their own puny accomplishments with ultimate and absolute truth.

The reality of God confronts us further in our experience of
structure in our environment to which we must conform and which
we cannot escape. Our will is never entirely free; we are confronted
and surrounded by another will. This shows the reality of *God who
is will*. To many non-Christian philosophers absolute power and
will appeared self-contradictory. Christians believe that God has a
purpose which he is carrying out. What happens is not the result of
some immutable law but rather of the personal will of God. Again,
one can easily become involved in extended and sophistic argumen-
tation about this divine will in the abstract. But the Protestant faith
asserts that we do not confront God's will in the abstract, but
rather as the will to create, the will to preserve, and the will to
redeem human persons.

This will is holy. This is the only attribute which does it justice.
The holiness of God is more than moral perfection; it describes the
fact that God is God and human beings are human beings. People
can be more or less clever, and they can be more or less good, they
can be more or less religious—but only God is holy. When the
Protestant faith speaks of God as power and God as spirit and God
as will, we must always keep in mind that all these assertions are
made against the background of the holiness of God. As Gustaf
Aulén has put it:

> Holiness stands as a sentinel against all eudaimonistic and an-
> thropocentric interpretations of religion. Holiness meets us as

unconditional majesty. . . . To meet God as the Holy One is to be placed under a supreme compulsion, and to be confronted by a power advancing in sovereign majesty. If God is the Holy One, he is also the One on whom we are absolutely dependent. We are in his power, not He in ours.[1]

How can humanity be related to this holy God? Does God's holiness remove him completely from the reach of our experience? Or do we have access to this holy God when we contemplate quietly the very source of our being? Theologians have stated this problem by asking whether God is transcendent or immanent. The dictionary defines transcendent in this way: "Of God, being prior to and exalted above the universe, and having being apart from it." The Protestant faith asserts that the God who confronts us as reality is indeed *transcendent*. The attributes with which he is described are expressions of this transcendence. When he is called *omnipotent*, or almighty, this is an expression for his transcendent power. He can do everything he wants to do. He is called *omnipresent*, or present everywhere at once, because there is no place where God is not present; there is no escape from him in space. He is called *eternal*, or everlasting. There was no time when God was not and there will never be a time when God will not be. And he is called *omniscient*, or infinitely wise, knowing all things. All these are, of course, mere human attempts to describe, however inadequately, the vastness of God. These words must not be thought of as adjectives which describe God as an "object." They are the language of worship and adoration, rather than the detailed attributes of somebody we can understand and comprehend. As Calvin has put it:

> The majesty of God in itself goes beyond the capacity of human understanding and cannot be comprehended by it, *we must adore its loftiness rather than investigate it*, so that we do not remain overwhelmed by so great a splendor.[2]

The Protestant faith is wary of all efforts to reduce God to the major premise in a syllogism. The Reformers' criticism of the grandiose theological systems that were taught by the church in the Middle Ages was based upon their suspicion that in these systems

God has been reduced to a mere object in the theological enterprise. Protestant Christians do not deny the validity of these theological descriptions which scrutinize the "attributes" of God. They do feel that this approach is presumptuous. They prefer to approach the description of God in the context of worship and adoration. Protestant hymnody is the best expression of this approach. For classical Protestantism the following hymn speaks more adequately of God's almighty power than any logical analysis:

> Praise to the Lord, the Almighty, the King of creation!
> O my soul, praise him, for he is thy health and salvation!
> All ye who hear, Now to his temple draw near;
> Praise him in glad adoration.
> Praise to the Lord! Who o'er all things so wondrously reigneth,
> Shelters thee under his wings, yea, so gently sustaineth;
> Hast thou not seen How thy desires e'er have been
> Granted in what he ordaineth?
> Praise to the Lord! O let all that is in me adore him!
> All that hath life and breath, come now with praises before
> him!
> Let the Amen sound from his people again;
> Gladly for aye we adore him. (Joachim Neander, 1650–1680)

This difference is further illustrated if we examine the brilliant analysis of God's power in Thomas Aquinas' *Summa Theologica* in the discussion "Whether God can make the past not to have been?" He proceeds by stating the reasons for holding this view. Then he states his own view as follows:

> I answer that, as was said above, nothing that implies a contradiction falls under the scope of God's omnipotence. Now that the past should not have been implies a contradiction. For just as it implies a contradiction to say that Socrates is sitting and not sitting, so does it to say that he sat and did not sit. But to say that he did sit is to say that.it happened in the past. To say that he did not sit is to say that it did not happen. Whence, that the past should not have been, does not come under the scope of divine power. This is what Augustine means when he says: Whosoever says if God is almighty, let him make what is done as if it were not done, does not see that this is to say: If God is almighty let him effect that what is true, by the very fact that it

THE REALITY OF GOD

is true, be false. And the Philosopher says: Of this one thing alone is God deprived—namely, to make undone the things that have been done.[3]

This is certainly a very logical argument. Indeed, it is committed to the absolute validity of the logical law of Aristotle: Whatever is, is; nothing can both be and not be; and everything must either be or not be. These laws are known respectively as the Law of Identity, the Law of Contradiction, and the Law of the Excluded Middle. In scholastic theology's approach to God these laws play a most important part.

Now let us look at a typical Protestant reaction to this entire philosophical approach to God. Luther says:

> ... we have to argue in one way about God or the will of God as preached, revealed, offered, and worshiped, and in another way about God as he is not preached, not revealed, not offered, not worshiped. To the extent, therefore, that God hides himself and wills to be unknown to us, it is no business of ours. For here the saying truly applies, "Things above us are no business of ours." And lest anyone should think this is a distinction of my own, I am following Paul, who writes to the Thessalonians concerning Antichrist that he will exalt himself above every God that is preached and worshiped (II Thess. 2:4). This plainly shows that someone can be exalted above God as he is preached and worshiped, that is, above the word and rite through which God is known to us and has dealings with us; but above God as he is not worshiped and not preached, but as he is in his own nature and majesty, nothing can be exalted, but all things are under his mighty hand.
>
> God must therefore be left to himself in his own majesty, for in this regard we have nothing to do with him, nor has he willed that we should have anything to do with him. But we have something to do with him insofar as he is clothed and set forth in his Word, through which he offers himself to us and which is the beauty and glory with which the psalmist celebrates him as being clothed.[4]

These two quotations, the one abounding in philosophical reflection and references to the logic of Aristotle, the other stressing the sovereign grace with which God has revealed himself in his Word, illustrate the peculiar emphasis of the Protestant faith on the

81

mystery of God's power. Philosophers may try to understand and explain God; Christians will try to worship and obey him. If we want to comprehend the transcendence of God as this notion occurs in the Protestant faith, it will be well for us to see it as an expression of adoration and prayer rather than logical analysis or objective description. As the great Calvinist hymn writer Gerhard Tersteegen said, "A God comprehended is no God." But the Protestant faith does assert that God is transcendent, that is, prior to and exalted above the universe!

However—and here again the complementary character of all human assertions about God must be stressed—the God who confronts us as transcendent reality is at the same time *immanent*. The omnipotence of God is not merely an experiment in abstract thought. Rather, the God who is our Father in Jesus Christ is the Almighty. Protestant Christians do not only assert that there is an Almighty God—as one might assert that there is a Pacific Ocean—they assert that they have an Almighty Savior. The Almighty, Omnipresent, Eternal, Omniscient God is closer to the Christian than the Christian is to himself. Perhaps Luther's explanation of the First Article of the Apostles' Creed will help to illustrate the Protestant concept of God's immanence, the fact that he is closer to us than we are to ourselves.

The Creed says: "I believe in God the Father Almighty, Maker of heaven and earth." Luther explains this statement in the following words:

> I believe that God has created me and all that exists; that he has given me and still sustains my body and soul and all my limbs and senses, my reason and all the faculties of my mind, together with food and clothing, house and home, family and property; that he provides me daily and abundantly with all the necessities of life, protects me from all danger, and preserves me from all evil. All this he does out of his pure, fatherly, and divine goodness and mercy, without any merit or worthiness on my part. For all this I am bound to thank, praise, serve, and obey him. This is most certainly true.[5]

Here we see how a statement which could be understood as a fairly abstract statement about God becomes a profoundly personal expression of God's deeds for *me*, not only for humanity in the abstract but for the specific person who is making this confession. For the Protestant faith even those terms which express God's majesty and power in the most overwhelming manner are related person to person. It is this overwhelming God who is always close to me. It is this Almighty God without whose knowledge not one hair falls from my head.

This simultaneous emphasis upon God's transcendence and immanence makes it unnecessary for the Protestant faith to interpose mediators between God and people. There is no need for the Protestant to implore the intercession of other human beings living or dead in order to approach God. He believes that each believer can personally and at all times approach God directly. He will say, "The Almighty God is closer to me than I am to my best friend, my mother, or my father. He is closer to me than I am to myself."

This brings us immediately to another significant assertion of the Protestant faith, namely, that God is person. In the theological discussion of the last one hundred years a great deal has been said about this "personality" of God. The term is dangerous, if we assume that it means that God's personality is the same as any human personality. The great nineteenth-century theologian Friedrich Schleiermacher objected to the use of the term *person* because it seemed to him that it idolized and deified human self-consciousness. If, nevertheless, Protestants by and large retain the definition of God as person, the reason is that it explains many things which otherwise would be beyond comprehension. Although the word *person* as applied to God does not occur in the New Testament, many personal terms are applied to him. In the Old Testament he is always addressed as Lord; the New Testament speaks of him as Father. When we think of the Twenty-third Psalm, we realize immediately that the word *person* is the most adequate expression of the fact that God is an "I" who has become a "thou" for us, that he is a "thou" to our "I," in other words, that our relationship is an "interpersonal" relationship.

The assertion that God is a person guards us against a pantheistic understanding of God. A pantheist believes that God is the universal substance, that he is everything that is. This position means that the human race as well as the universe is only one of God's expressions, one of God's appearances. The Protestant faith rejects this mystical pantheism by the assertion that God is person who confronts us as a person.

At the same time this view guards us against all polytheistic notions that there are many gods. There is not one god in charge of the ocean, another in charge of fire, and other gods and goddesses who fill the heavens. The assertion that God is person excludes all forms of polytheism, which denies that there is a Supreme Being.

God is person, he is thou, he addresses us with his Word. We encounter him person to person.

However, this does not mean that the word *person* is adequate to define the "form" of God. It does tell how he meets us, but it does not describe his appearance nor does it enable us to analyze his consciousness. We must guard against any attempt to use the term *person* to confine God in some anthropomorphic shell. There is no room in a mature Protestant faith for a god who looks and acts like a super-Santa Claus. The picture of God as a bearded sage sitting on a golden throne only confuses our understanding of the meaning of the assertion that God is the Absolute Person who meets us personally.

Here again we must pause to remind ourselves that the truth about God as the Protestant faith sees it is expressed in complementary statements. The Protestant faith asserts that God is the absolute ground of all being. Everything that is has its source in God. Yet at the same time he is the Lord of history, the personal spirit who is executing his plan.

This means that the Protestant faith attempts to avoid a one-sided emphasis upon the omnipotence of God, which takes away the meaning of history and human decision and ends in fatalism. This possibility confronts us in the moment when we concentrate exclusively on God's power. History then becomes merely a performance that is played with prearranged parts. We are not even actors but puppets, who are pulled by invisible strings and whose lines are spoken by a director, who is the master ventriloquist and puts the words he wants us to say into our mouths.

The neglect of the complementarity of our speech about God

may lead to an undue stress upon the omnipotence of God and thus to a complete neglect of the significance of human decision. This would deny the meaning of time as the accepted time and as the time for decision. Such fatalism is not entirely uncommon in our age. It has received theological support from those writers who see God's hand clearly and unambiguously in the events of history. Every current human fad is hailed immediately as God's will, and theologians are busily producing religious vindications for the cultural trends of the day. There are many people today who feel that whatever must happen will happen and who fatalistically and passively suffer their life rather than live it, "making the most of the time" (Col. 4:5). We are reminded of the two soldiers who were discussing their chances of survival in the coming battle. The one said quite fatalistically, "Well, I don't worry except for that one bullet that has my name on it." His friend replied, "I don't worry about the bullet with my name on it, but I do worry about the bullet that says: 'To whom it may concern.'" Christians aware of God's omnipotence nevertheless cultivate the attitude of the second soldier.

At the same time it is equally important to avoid one-sided emphasis upon the importance of historical decisions to the exclusion of the absoluteness of God. There are many Christians who have reduced God to a spectator or at best a referee in the game of life. In modern Protestantism the importance of human action has been so exclusively emphasized that the ultimate future of mankind —indeed, the future of the universe—is conceived to be in the hands of human beings. What we do today, our historical decisions, are alleged to determine the outcome of God's plan. This idea has frequently been expressed in terms of "bringing in the kingdom of God," or "saving the human race from extinction," as if man had it in his power to bring in God's kingdom or to prevent the arrival of God's realm. For such people God is at best the coach on the "good" side in the game of life and history. He can send in some plays, but their execution is up to the human players. The coach will lose the game unless we play better.

This position assumes a very limited God, a God who is no longer the Lord of lords and the King of kings. Forgotten is the

New Testament assertion that God can raise up children to Abraham out of stones (Matt. 3:9). He can accomplish his ends with us or against us, but his ends will be accomplished.

It is highly questionable that such sentiments as "God has no other hands but mine," or words to that effect, are in tune with the complete trust in the power of God which has characterized the classical Protestant faith. It may be a good way to raise money for churches and other worthy causes to claim tearfully that God is lost unless we step in to act as his hands. However, it is dubious Protestant theology. According to the Protestant faith *we* may very well be lost unless we step in and serve God and the neighbor—but God is not lost without us. The Protestant faith asserts that while the human race is lost without God, God is not lost without the human race. His eternal counsels will ultimately prevail, with us or without us.

Here again it is of the utmost importance to maintain both sides of the dialectic. The Protestant faith rejects at the same time a fatalism which reduces people to puppets and a concept of a limited God which reduces God to a spectator.

Law and Gospel

The God whose reality we have attempted to describe within the frame of reference of the Protestant faith confronts people through two basic means—the law and the gospel. A clear distinction between them is essential for an understanding of the Protestant faith. Yet there are few Protestants who can actually tell the difference between these two terms. What do these words mean?

The law is God's "thou shalt!" or "thou shalt not!" It represents God's justified demands upon the human race. The Ten Commandments are law. We are confronted by law when we read:

> I am the Lord your God, who brought you out of the land of Egypt, out of the house of bondage.
> You shall have no other gods before me.
> You shall not make for yourself a graven image, or any likeness of anything that is in heaven above, or that is on the earth

beneath, or that is in the water under the earth; you shall not bow down to them or serve them; for I the Lord your God am a jealous God, visiting the iniquity of the fathers upon the children to the third and fourth generation of those who hate me, but showing steadfast love to thousands of those who love me and keep my commandments.

You shall not take the name of the Lord your God in vain: for the Lord will not hold him guiltless who takes his name in vain.

Observe the sabbath day, to keep it holy, as the Lord your God commanded you. Six days you shall labor, and do all your work; but the seventh day is a sabbath to the Lord your God; in it you shall not do any work, you, or your son, or your daughter, or your manservant, or your maidservant, or your ox, or your ass, or any of your cattle, or the sojourner who is within your gates, that your manservant and your maidservant may rest as well as you. You shall remember that you were a servant in the land of Egypt, and the Lord your God brought you out thence with a mighty hand and an outstretched arm; therefore the Lord your God commanded you to keep the sabbath day.

Honor your father and your mother, as the Lord your God commanded you; that your days may be prolonged, and that it may go well with you, in the land which the Lord your God gives you.

You shall not kill.

Neither shall you commit adultery.

Neither shall you steal.

Neither shall you bear false witness against your neighbor.

Neither shall you covet your neighbor's wife; and you shall not desire your neighbor's house, his field, or his manservant, or his maidservant, his ox, or his ass, or anything that is your neighbor's.

These words the Lord spoke to all your assembly at the mountain out of the midst of the fire, the cloud, and the deep gloom, with a loud voice; and he added no more. (Deut. 5:6–22)

Most people would agree that this is law. Now let us look at another quotation from the Bible; is this also law?

You have heard that it was said to the men of old, "You shall not kill; and whoever kills shall be liable to judgment." But I say to you that every one who is angry with his brother shall be

liable to judgment; whoever insults his brother shall be liable to
the council, and whoever says, "You fool!" shall be liable to the
hell of fire. So if you are offering your gift at the altar, and
there remember that your brother has something against you,
leave your gift there before the altar and go; first be reconciled
to your brother, and then come and offer your gift. Make
friends quickly with your accuser, while you are going with him
to court, lest your accuser hand you over to the judge, and the
judge to the guard, and you be put in prison; truly, I say to
you, you will never get out till you have paid the last penny.
You have heard that it was said, "You shall not commit adultery." But I say to you that every one who looks at a woman
lustfully has already committed adultery with her in his heart.
(Matt. 5:21–28)

These verses are part of the famous Sermon on the Mount. They
are clearly law, for they too tell us of God's demands upon us.

The Old Testament and the New Testament abound in such
passages of law. According to the Protestant faith these passages tell
people what the righteous demands of God are. But the same God
who confronts human beings in the law confronts them also in the
gospel. The word *gospel* is a literal translation of the Greek word
euaggelion which means "good news." The nature of this good news
is probably best summarized in the famous passage which most
Protestant children memorize in Sunday School: "For God so loved
the world, that he gave his only Son, that whoever believes in him
should not perish but have eternal life" (John 3:16). The gospel is
the good news of what God has done for people and is willing to do
for every individual. This gospel is found already in the Old Testament. For classical Protestantism, Isaiah 53, for example, describes
what God will do for all people in Jesus Christ:

Who has believed what we have heard? And to whom has the
arm of the Lord been revealed? For he grew up before him like
a young plant, and like a root out of dry ground; he had no
form or comeliness that we should look at him, and no beauty
that we should desire him. He was despised and rejected by
men; a man of sorrows, and acquainted with grief; and as one
from whom men hide their faces he was despised, and we
esteemed him not. Surely he has borne our griefs and carried

our sorrows; yet we esteemed him stricken, smitten by God, and afflicted. But he was wounded for our transgressions, he was bruised for our iniquities; upon him was the chastisement that made us whole, and with his stripes we are healed. All we like sheep have gone astray; we have turned every one to his own way; and the Lord has laid on him the iniquity of us all. He was oppressed, and he was afflicted, yet he opened not his mouth; like a lamb that is led to the slaughter, and like a sheep that before its shearers is dumb, so he opened not his mouth. By oppression and judgment he was taken away; and as for his generation, who considered that he was cut off out of the land of the living, stricken for the transgression of my people? (Isa. 53:1–8)

Whatever this passage may mean to others, to classical Protestantism it represents the gospel, that is, the good news of what God has done for people in Jesus Christ, in its absolute purity—even though it is found in the Old Testament.

But granted that God confronts human beings in law and gospel, what is the specific purpose of the law? Essentially the law has two functions which theologians have sometimes called the political use of the law and the theological use of the law.

The *political use of the law* describes that function of the law which contributes to civil righteousness. Because there is law and order people act a great deal better than they would otherwise act. This is the same sort of reasoning that we find in many political philosophers, for example, in Thomas Hobbes. He asserted that without authority and law there would be a universal war of all against all. Hobbes described this situation very colorfully in the following words:

In such condition there is no place for Industry; because the fruit thereof is uncertain: and consequently no Culture of the Earth, no Navigation, nor use of the commodities that may be imported by Sea; no commodious Building; no Instruments of moving, and removing such things as require much force; no Knowledge of the face of the Earth; no account of Time; no Arts; no Letters; no Society; and which is worst of all, continual fear, and danger of violent death; and the life of man, solitary, poor, nasty, brutish, and short.[6]

Although the Protestant faith does not claim that there ever was a time like this, but rather asserts that mankind has always been confronted by the law, this law in its political use prevents the collapse of society and culture. The relative justice which obtains in this world, fragmentary and imperfect as it may be, is the result of the political use of the law.

The law in this political use affects all people. One does not have to be a Christian in order to use or benefit from the law in its political use. All human beings are subject to it, all people do in fact benefit by it, and all human beings are to some degree aware of it. It may be regrettable, but it is unfortunately true that for many persons the only reason for socially acceptable behavior is the fear of punishment. This does not mean necessarily that they are afraid to go to jail—but they are afraid to lose face. The law in its political use is designed to prevent the complete collapse of justice and equity among people by subjecting them to quite obvious pressures in the direction of order.

In this form the law is extremely useful not only in order to maintain some sort of national civilization, it is of the greatest importance also for all international understanding. Because there is law among all people the terms *good* and *bad* make sense across national and religious boundaries. Organizations such as the United Nations depend for their success very largely on what Protestant theologians would call the political use of the law.

It is also interesting and noteworthy that people who are estranged from Christianity or have never even heard of it may be expert in the political use of the law. Luther, for example, never tired of pointing out the political superiority of the Turkish Empire, which was, of course, a Moslem empire. In many ways, he asserted, the Turkish Empire was governed far better than the German Empire. He also cited with approval the civil righteousness of Roman statesmen who had lived in pre-Christian times and who were pagans but nevertheless men of justice.

It is not too difficult to see this political use of the law in operation, for example, on the campus of a great modern university. All kinds of religious and irreligious, philosophical and antiphilosophical ideas may be current. The subjects on which universal agreement could be achieved in such a community would be fairly small. But because of the law and its political use it would be easier to achieve some sort of common consent on propositions like "honesty is desirable" or "racial justice is good" or "respect for the rights of other people is necessary" than on almost any other propositions that might be offered. Here we see the political use of the law in action. The law suggests and establishes minimal justice and for this reason alone it is good and ought to be proclaimed.

Some of the approval for religious groups in our culture comes from people who have no use for religion personally but who notice that religion in the Judeo-Christian tradition, at least, tends to contribute to civil righteousness. It was for this reason presumably that Voltaire said, "If there were no God he would have to be invented!" It was for this reason that Plutarch asserted: "It is easier to erect a city in the clouds than a state without religion." Much of the pro-religious propaganda of our age is based upon this sentiment. It was because of the religious contribution to civil righteousness that the United States Congress inserted "under God" into the pledge of allegiance to the flag, which school children repeat so often. The same reason probably motivated the legislators to insist that "In God We Trust" be added to coins and postage stamps.

However, from the point of view of the Protestant faith, the contribution to civil righteousness of the law is distinctly secondary in importance to the *theological use of the law*. The theological use of the law is to drive people to Christ. Because of the law and its demands people become aware of their alienation and separation from God. The law reveals to human beings how different they are from what they ought to be. The law shows them that they do not do the good deeds which they should do, and they commit the evil deeds which they should avoid. This is what the Apostle Paul meant when he said, "Through the law comes knowledge of sin" (Rom. 3:20). It is because of the law that people are willing to listen to the gospel. The Christian message that in Christ God bridges the gap which human beings have caused by their revolt against God makes very little sense to people who are not aware that such a gap exists.

91

Through the law most people become aware of the abyss that separates them from God, for the law describes the rightful demands that God can make. This is shown clearly in the New Testament summary recorded in Matthew:

> And one of them, a lawyer, asked him a question, to test him. "Teacher, which is the great commandment in the law?" And he said to him, "You shall love the Lord your God with all your heart, and with all your soul, and with all your mind. This is the great and first commandment. And a second is like it, You shall love your neighbor as yourself. On these two commandments depend all the law and the prophets." (Matt. 22:35–40)

This shows that the Christian faith states the law in all its sharpness. It doesn't weaken the law nor does it change its demands. On the contrary, it accentuates the demands, as in the statement in Matt. 5:48: "You, therefore, must be perfect, as your heavenly Father is perfect." This is the ultimate demand; no higher requirement can even be imagined. Yet the Protestant faith insists that this mandate must be taken absolutely seriously. It does not permit glossing over. Neither must it be explained away. We might be tempted to say, "This doesn't really mean 'perfect'; it merely means try to do the best you can!" But such modification of the Bible goes counter to the very spirit of Protestantism. On this point the theologians of classical Protestantism are in basic agreement. God's demands are serious demands, and they must be taken seriously. Only if we take the law seriously will it fulfill its theological function and drive us to Christ.

When taken seriously the law shows people their true condition. They are supposed to be perfect—as God is perfect. But they are in fact most imperfect. The more seriously the Christian compares himself with the revelation of God in Jesus Christ, the more aware he becomes of his own imperfection. This is the reason why people do not like to measure themselves by the standard of Jesus Christ. They prefer to compare themselves to other people who are just as imperfect as they are. Indeed, there is no one who cannot find somebody whom he considers even worse than himself. Even in a prison there are caste distinctions; a burglar or a murderer, for ex-

ample, feels himself vastly superior to a political criminal, a traitor
to his country. It is fairly easy for a person of normal intelligence
to use the process we call "rationalizing" in order to make a fairly
good case for his own superiority over most of his neighbors. The
Protestant faith points out that the law does not say, "Be perfect as
the Jones family or the Smith family is perfect"; it says clearly, "as
your heavenly Father is perfect"!

This closes all exits through which a person could flee and
makes such an escape utterly impossible. The Protestant faith asserts that under the judgment of the law nobody can say, "I'll stand
on my record"; for in comparison with the demand for God-like
perfection every human record looks shabby indeed. Thus, in the
light of the law all must realize that they are utterly dependent
upon the mercy of God as revealed in Jesus Christ.

However, only when the law is taken absolutely seriously does it
have the effect indicated. What is commonly called "legalism"
tends to obscure man's understanding of the seriousness of the law.
If the law is understood as little moral rules of legalism, rather than
the demand to be as perfect as God, it becomes possible, even easy,
to obey the law. For example, if "do not smoke" becomes the law,
a person may become a paragon of virtue merely because he
doesn't like to smoke. Or if "do not dance" becomes the law, a
person who cannot dance because he gets dizzy when he turns
around more than once achieves a moral distinction which has its
roots in his inadequate sense of balance rather than in his superior
sense of God. The great classical Protestant thinkers took the law
seriously—and in doing so they asserted that no one can be justified by his own goodness, by his own moral accomplishments, by
his own moral perfection. The law accuses people and drives them
to Christ.

Furthermore, only if the law is taken seriously is the gospel what
the word implies, "good-spell," the "good news." The Protestant
faith asserts that the "divine love cannot be contained within the
framework of the law or a legal system."[7] The "good news" is
simply that God has decided out of his sovereign power to deal
with us according to his love. To the people who are condemned by
the law the Apostle Paul says:

> While we were yet helpless, at the right time Christ died for the ungodly. Why, one will hardly die for a righteous man—though perhaps for a good man one will dare even to die. But God shows his love for us in that while we were yet sinners Christ died for us. . . . For if while we were enemies we were reconciled to God by the death of his Son, much more, now that we are reconciled, shall we be saved by his life. (Rom. 5:6–10)

The gospel announces that God is willing to base his relationship to people not on justice but on his spontaneous and unmerited love. What this means has been stated in far less theological terms in the stories of the lost sheep, the lost coin, and the prodigal son (Luke 15). In all these stories it is the housewife, the shepherd, the father, the symbols for God, who find what is lost and who forgive the prodigal. It is not the coin that finds itself. It is not the sheep that returns to the shepherd. The prodigal son has wasted his entire inheritance. He comes to the father penniless. He deserves only punishment—and this is what he would receive were it not for the fact that the Father is love.

In Jesus Christ this love has been revealed. In Jesus Christ God has identified himself completely with the human being in the lostness and the meaninglessness of his life and death. Christ is the reality of God overcoming for us the undeniable reality of God in the law. Indeed, says the Protestant faith, the law is of God—but so is Christ. In Christ God fulfills the law and cancels it. Here we must state again what we pointed out as the clue to any understanding of the Protestant faith: "God was in Christ, reconciling the world unto himself!"

Lest we misunderstand this distinction between the law and the gospel as implying the existence of two gods, let us remind ourselves again that, as far as the Protestant faith is concerned, the law *and* the gospel are valid expressions of God's will. Protestants do not believe in two gods, a god of law and a god of love. This was the heresy of the Gnostics and of Marcion and it is rejected by all Protestant theologians. The gospel is God's expression of love overcoming the barrier of God's law which would eternally separate human beings from God. The gospel is God's miracle of love that makes it possible for people to live with and in spite of God's law.

94

God as law is not a lower form of God than the God of the gospel. The same God meets people in law and gospel. For the Protestant Christian law and gospel are not contradictory but complementary. This is the only way in which human beings can speak about God. If God speaking to us in law is neglected—as he has been at various periods in the history of the Christian church— Christianity degenerates into sentimentality. God becomes a super-Santa Claus or an overindulgent grandfather. The result is the understanding of the Christian faith as symbolized by Heinrich Heine. On his deathbed he is alleged to have said: "God will forgive me—it is his business." The neglect of the proclamation of the law makes the gospel a meaningless platitude. Unless people see that their separation and alienation from God are a serious matter, the healing of this breach seems irrelevant and immaterial. To the extent to which the proclamation of the law has disappeared from Protestant preaching the Protestant proclamation of the gospel has lost its meaning. If the message of Protestantism consists of stale jokes and superficial travelogues, it is not surprising that many people prefer the sharper jokes of the professional comedians and the more penetrating political analyses of the professional news analysts. The Christian message is betrayed if the law is not proclaimed as an essential element of the Christian witness.

The Protestant faith holds that the proclamation of the law is so important because it explains the situation in which all human beings find themselves even before they ever heard its commandments. Paul Tillich has described it as the state of anxiety.[8] The word *anxiety* is the translation of the Greek word *thlipsis*, which is usually rendered in the English translations of the New Testament as tribulation or affliction. Literally it means pressure and describes the plight of all people. The word is used in John 16:33, where Jesus says to his disciples: "In the world you have *thlipsis* [anxiety, pressure, tribulation]; but be of good cheer, I have overcome the world."

Tillich analyzed this word and suggested that human beings experience three forms of such anxiety. One he calls ontic anxiety, the pressure that comes from the fact that we have no control over the most important features of our lives, that we are subject to genetic and environmental forces completely out of our power. This gradually developing universal awareness of our dependence on such forces results in the anxiety of fate and death. This is the law accusing us.

But we are also under pressure because we are not what we want to be. In more technical terms there is a profound difference between our assumed potentiality, what we think we could be, and our actuality, what we really are. Even if what we think we could be is not realistic, it does not affect the profound sense of anxiety which our failure to live up to our own expectations produces. Tillich calls this moral anxiety, the anxiety of guilt and condemnation. This is again the law accusing us.

Finally, we are also under pressure because we would like our life to have a purpose and goal. We would like to feel that life makes sense. But most people are aware that such meaning and significance escapes them and that their life is routine and shallow. The acquisition of material goods thinly veils a profound emptiness. Tillich calls this existential anxiety, the anxiety of emptiness and meaninglessness. Here once more the law accuses us.

Thus the law is not introduced artificially into a human life which would otherwise be happy and serene, but rather serves to explain the anxiety which is an inescapable part of human existence.

But once this has been stated it must be added that without the proclamation of the gospel, the proclamation of the law soon degenerates into mere scolding. Again we can say that the history of Protestantism shows many periods in which the Protestant faith has been obscured because of a one-sided emphasis upon the proclamation of the law, to the exclusion of the proclamation of the gospel.

Many Protestants associate their own religious experiences with constant tongue-lashing about the fact that they are all miserable sinners. The admonition may be well deserved, but it is not particularly helpful unless it is delivered in the context of the gospel—the good news of what God has done, is doing, and will do with people who so clearly deserve his condemnation.

It is significant that most people, if asked concerning the meaning of religion, define it almost exclusively in terms of law. Religion is for them the obedience to certain rules, most quite marginal to life, which are supposed to relieve the pressure and quiet the conscience. They are often rules that have been inherited from the past and that make little or no sense in the present. Few would define religion as being a proclamation of God's deeds for us. Yet even as stern a Protestant as John Calvin knew perfectly well that the law without the gospel is not Christian proclamation. He says:

> The testimony of the law, which convinces us of iniquity and transgression is not made in order that we should fall into despair, and having lost courage, stumble into ruin. Certainly the apostle (Rom. 3:19, 20) testifies that by the judgment of the law we are condemned, in order that every mouth be closed and the entire world be found guilty before God. Yet that very apostle elsewhere (Rom. 11:32) teaches that God has enclosed all under unbelief, not in order to ruin them or let them perish, but on the contrary, in order that he may exercise mercy on all. The Lord therefore, after reminding us (by means of the law) of our weakness and impurity, comforts us with the assurance of his power and his mercy. And it is in Christ his son that God shows himself to us benevolent and propitious. For, in the law he appeared only as remunerator of perfect righteousness (of which we are completely destitute) and, on the other hand, as upright and severe judge of sins. But in Christ his face shines full of grace and kindliness even toward miserable and unworthy sinners; for, he gave this admirable example of his infinite love, when he exposed his own son for us, and in him opened to us all the treasure of his clemency and goodness.[9]

Again it was Tillich who found a most helpful expression to describe this gospel for our age. He said, "We must accept our acceptance in spite of the fact that we are unacceptable." This is the gospel of the absolute love of God which, as Calvin stated above, does not depend on human merit but only on divine mercy.

We repeat: For the Christian, law and gospel are not contradictory but complementary. Protestant Christians experience God as the source of law and the source of the gospel. If either aspect of God's revelation is neglected, the Christian message is falsified and obscured.

Righteousness and Love

The Protestant faith asserts that God is *both* righteousness and love. When the Protestant faith speaks of God's righteousness, it speaks about it not as an abstraction, logically deduced from the nature of God, but as the righteousness of the God who is revealed in his dealings with his people recorded in Scripture and experienced in the life of his church and of every individual Christian.

It is impossible to read the Bible with any degree of attentiveness and still hold to the Santa Claus or "man upstairs" notion of God. The fact that strikes the reader is that God is a righteous God. This is stated repeatedly in the Old Testament. The Psalmist sings: "For the Lord is righteous, he loves righteous deeds" (Ps. 11:7). And Jesus prays in the famous high priestly prayer of the Gospel according to St. John: "O righteous Father, the world has not known thee, but I have known thee; . . ." (John 17:25).

Because of God's righteousness his own chosen people must suffer for their disobedience and betrayal. Because of God's righteousness the church and the Christian are punished for unrighteousness. The righteous God reveals his law, and punishes evildoers. But this is not all the Protestant faith has to say at this point. Although his righteousness is revealed in his wrath—and this word *wrath* as applied to God occurs innumerable times in the Old and the New Testaments—this is again not all that can be said about the righteousness of God. According to the Protestant faith God reveals his righteousness also by carrying out his plan of salvation. In other words, his grace is also part of his righteousness. Because God is righteous and faithful he keeps his word even to the unrighteous. Even though human beings are not trustworthy, God is! For the Protestant faith "In God We Trust" is not merely a numismatic platitude but a *faithful* assertion based upon the righteousness of God. The Christian can trust God, even though he cannot necessarily trust his best friend, his wife or parents or children—even though he cannot trust himself! He can trust God because God is righteous altogether! Thus, if the righteousness of God is frightening, it is at the same time comforting. For it is this righteous God who has established his covenant with his Old and New Testament people.

Here again the Protestant position is best stated by saying that God's righteousness is part of his holiness. It contains both his wrath and his grace without abolishing either.

At the same time God is love. Again the Protestant faith asserts that this statement rests upon God's self-disclosure in his dealings with his people as recorded in Scripture and demonstrated again and again in the life of the church and the individual believer. "God is love" is for the Protestant faith not an abstract philosophical proposition which is deduced from the nature of God. As Plato, Aristotle, and, later, Spinoza have shown, one can construct philosophically very impressive deities—but any similarity between these philosophical constructs and the God who has revealed himself to his people and in the life of his church is quite coincidental.

God's love is revealed in his relationship with people. God desires to have communion and fellowship with human beings—to meet each person to person. God is therefore far more than goodness; he is love. Goodness gives things, while love gives itself. Of course, God's goodness gives us many things. Religious people have always praised God for all the things they have received. There is a thanksgiving holiday among all people who have some sense of the eternal. Protestants will gladly join in the chorus of praise that sings hymns of gratitude for the gifts of God's goodness. We experience the goodness of God as creatures. And therefore our fellow creatures are just as much objects as we are. As Jesus says in the Sermon on the Mount:

> Look at the birds of the air; they neither sow nor reap nor gather into barns, and yet your heavenly Father feeds them. Are you not of more value than they? . . . And why are you anxious about clothing? Consider the lilies of the field, how they grow; they neither toil nor spin; yet I tell you, even Solomon in all his glory was not arrayed like one of these. (Matt. 6:26–29)

All creatures are beneficiaries of this divine goodness. It is an impressive, in fact, an overwhelming, part of our experience. We are able to make long catalogs of the gifts of God's goodness which we and all other creatures receive.

But the love of God is something different. We experience the love of God not as creatures but as children! The Protestant faith asserts that God's love is personal, involving a personal relationship which makes certain personal demands upon us.

The love of a parent for a child does something to a child. It transforms him. Psychologists tell us that it makes a better person out of the child. Children need the love of their parents, and there is no substitute for this love. Modern child psychology has shown again and again that children who have the best of care, technically speaking—who have all the food they need, all the clothing they need, all the shelter they need—but who are not loved are likely to show in their personalities the results of this lack of love. It seems easier for a child to put up with a deficiency of shelter or food or clothing if he is supplied with an abundance of love. There is no substitute for love. The Protestant faith asserts that God loves us—not in general, as one might love the British or the Irish, the Germans or the Swedes, or some other group of people—but he loves us personally. The Twenty-third Psalm says: "The Lord is my shepherd, I shall not want." For that one sheep that is lost the shepherd in Jesus' parable goes out into the night and leaves the entire flock of sheep. God's love is a personal love, a parental love.

If this is taken seriously it must have certain consequences. Parental love creates fear in me—the fear of hurting my father or my mother. Because my mother loves me I do not want to do anything that will hurt her. I am afraid to hurt her. This is a fear that is the result of love. The theologians have called it "filial fear," in contrast to the slavish fear of a person who is afraid to do something because he thinks he will be caught and punished. The love of God creates this filial fear. Personal love makes me fear to hurt the person who loves me. I do not want to disappoint such love. God's love, according to the Protestant faith, is personal, individual, and fatherly.

There is another strange thing about this divine love. It is, as we said before, *agape*. This means that it has its source in God, the

100

loving subject, rather than in a human being, the object of divine love. God's love is the result of the fact that God is love. It does not depend on the attractiveness of the object but only on the *agape* of God.

The Protestant faith asserts that God's love is something entirely different from all forms of human love. We love because the object we love does something for us. Perhaps we love it for its beauty or for its goodness. It may even be that we love it because of its helplessness, which gives us an opportunity to show our power. Human love is always acquisitive. It always wants something from the object of its love. In most cases this is quite obvious, while in some cases it takes some training in psychology to discover what we want for ourselves in loving something or somebody. *Eros*, mentioned earlier and described so beautifully by the Greek philosophers, deals with the love of the True, the Good, the Beautiful. It purifies a person by directing his attention toward these objects that will make him better. *Eros* is, in fact, the human way to all that is worth while, and ultimately the human way to God. For the Greek philosopher Aristotle, God is the unmoved mover, the goal of the universe to which all creation is moving. It is God's complete perfection which makes him so desirable. Because of his perfection everything loves him. Through his perfection he draws all love toward himself. God himself does not love anything except that which is absolutely perfect. This means that he loves only himself. To love anything but himself would be to love that which is imperfect and thus would detract from God's absolute perfection.

Aristotle's God loves only himself, but he is loved by everybody and everything, and through this love for God everybody and everything is moving toward its goal. It is *eros* that makes the world go around, the love for the absolute perfection of God.

It is important to keep this *eros* concept of love in mind in order to understand the complete reversal of *agape* in the Christian faith in God. The God who has revealed himself in Jesus Christ loves imperfect, sinful, miserable human beings. He loves sinners. Not because they are imperfect and miserable and sinful, but because *he is love*. According to the Protestant faith God is overflowing, self-giving, radiating love. The love is in him, not the result of the object. In fact this divine love does not find but creates its lovable object. God does not love us because we are lovable; we are lovable because God loves us. Nowhere has this been stated more clearly than in the First Epistle of John. Here we read: "In this is love, not that we loved God but that he loved us and sent his Son to be the expiation for our sins." And a little later: "We love, because he first loved us" (1 John 4:10–19).

As Bishop Aulén puts it:

> Every attempt to demonstrate something in man, some incorruptible essence or some quality pleasing to God, which would explain rationally why God meets man in love, is in principle foreign to Christian faith. Such attempts prove only that divine love is again incarcerated within the walls of rationalism and legalism.[10]

According to the Protestant faith the most accurate description of God is that he is love. He is self-giving, self-sacrificing, overflowing love. He is *agape*.

Again, for the Christian the righteousness and the love of God are not contradictory but complementary. God's righteousness ultimately reveals his love, and God's love ultimately reveals his righteousness. This assertion may seem almost completely self-contradictory at this point of our discussion of the Protestant faith. The meaning of such a paradoxical statement becomes clear only in the doctrine of Christ and his atoning death. In him that which is here merely a paradoxical assertion becomes a saving event.

NOTES

1. Gustaf Aulén, *The Faith of the Christian Church* (Philadelphia: Fortress Press, 1948), pp. 123–24.

2. From John Calvin, *Instruction in Faith*, trans. Paul T. Fuhrmann (Philadelphia: Westminster Press, 1949), as quoted in Harry Emerson Fosdick, *Great Voices of the Reformation* (New York: Random House, The Modern Library, 1952), p. 216.

3. From *Basic Writings of Saint Thomas Aquinas*, edited and annotated by Anton C. Pegis (New York: Random House, 1945), Vol I, p. 265.

4. Martin Luther, "The Bondage of the Will," in Philip S. Watson, ed., *Luther's Works* (Philadelphia: Fortress Press, 1972), vol. 33, 139.

5. *Book of Concord*, ed. Theodore G. Tappert (Philadelphia: Fortress Press, 1959), p. 345.

6. Thomas Hobbes, *Leviathan* in *The English Philosophers from Bacon to Mill* (New York: Random House, The Modern Library, 1939), p. 161.

7. Aulén, *The Faith of the Christian Church*, p. 40.

8. Paul Tillich, *The Courage to Be* (New Haven: Yale University Press, 1952), pp. 40 ff.

9. Harry Emerson Fosdick, *Great Voices of the Reformation* (New York: Random House, Inc., 1952), p. 222.

10. Aulén, *The Faith of the Christian Church*, pp. 133 ff.

Chapter 4

GOD'S WORLD

An important part of the Protestant faith is that the world in which we live and of which our little earth is such a very small part is God's world. This is what the doctrine of creation means. This world is not a cosmic accident but rather the expression of the divine will. "I believe that God has created me and all that exists."

Creation

The Christian faith in creation is the result of our confrontation with God in Jesus Christ and his Word. It is the result of revelation. Faith in creation is an axiom of the Christian faith. It is important to emphasize this against the well-intentioned efforts to deduce creation logically from the evidence that surrounds us.

There are, indeed, many theories about the origin of the world. Some, neither more nor less logical than others, arrive at a "god" as the ultimate cause of the universe. These theories may argue from the design observable in the world to the necessity of the existence of a designer. They may argue from the causal chain that everything must have a cause and conclude that God is the first cause. They may in many other interesting ways deduce the existence of a creator and therefore of the universe as creation.

The Protestant faith is not particularly concerned with any of these theories about the origin of the universe or of this earth. The doctrine of creation is an article of faith, describing the human situation in this world. The Christian faith does not furnish a theory about the origin of the world. Such theories are more or less interesting scientific speculations and hypotheses which do not need to clash with the Christian assertion that this is God's world, unless they become articles of faith for the "believer in science."

The Protestant faith believes that "God has created me and all that exists" because the Christian has met the living God in revelation. He knows this universe to be creation because he has encountered the Creator. Genesis tells us: "In the beginning God created the heavens and the earth." Through faith this becomes a personal experience. As the great Quaker George Fox put it:

> One morning, as I was sitting by the fire, a great cloud came over me, and a temptation beset me; but I sate still. And it was said, "All things come by nature"; and the elements and stars came over me, so that I was in a manner quite clouded with it. But inasmuch as I sate still and silent the people of the house perceived nothing. And as I sate still under it, and let it alone, a living hope arose in me, and a true voice, which said, "There is a living God who made all things." And immediately the cloud and temptation vanished away, and life rose over it all; my heart was glad and I praised the living God. After some time, I met with some people who had such a notion that there was no God, but that all things came by nature. I had a great dispute with them and overturned them and made some of them confess that there is a living God. Then I saw that it was good that I had gone through that exercise.[1]

As Bishop Aulén puts it:

> It is, therefore, of fundamental importance to emphasize that faith's affirmations about creation do not imply a theoretical proposition about the origin of the universe, but rather a religious statement about the nature of the relation between God and man.[2]

In this regard we ought to distinguish clearly between the Christian faith in the almighty Creator of heaven and earth and the alternative positions of deism, pantheism, and dualism.

There are many people who believe in creation, but according to the ideas of deism. Deism's belief in the Creator reduces the relationship between God and the world to a causal connection that took place in the distant past. Once upon a time in a faraway age

God created the machinery of the world, set the clock, wound it up and started it, and it has been running ever since. God is the watchmaker, and the universe is the giant clock which he built and set in motion. This reduces God to the distant, dim cause of the world. Instead of creation we have in deism the past event of the construction of the marvelous mechanism. Against these views the Christian faith asserts that God indeed created the world but that he also creates and maintains it continuously. This creative relationship of God to the universe has never stopped. God is still the Creator today. That is why we can sing with the Psalmist, "Create in me a clean heart, O God, and put a new and right spirit within me" (Ps. 51:10). Creation continues! In every moment all the universe is upheld by God's creative power. The deistic view must be categorically rejected by the Protestant faith because it reduces faith in the Creator to a theoretical proposition about something that happened a very, very long time ago. Whenever Christians think of creation merely as a past event they are in danger of the deistic perversion of the doctrine of creation.

But there is an equally dangerous pantheistic perversion. The Protestant faith distinguishes carefully between faith in the Creator who is clearly above his creation and the divine process of creation of pantheism. In pantheism everything that is real *is God*. God and the universe are conceived as being identical; God is the world and the world is God. Every tree, every flower, every rock, every star, every person is part of God. There is nothing that is not God. Sometimes the relationship between the world as we see it and the God who is underneath all this visible world is defined as one of reality (God) and appearance (world), but not in the sense that there is any conflict between the two. They are essentially identical. If we look from the limited point of view of a small part of divine reality, or from your point of view or my point of view, it might appear as if there were a difference between God and the world. However, the pantheists say that *sub specie aeternitatis*, that is, from the point of view of eternity, there is no difference whatsoever. God and the world are identical.

This view makes God into the soul of the world, or the inner-most essence of the world. Any distinction between God and nature becomes meaningless. God is nature and nature is God. The human being is a part of God, his limitations being the result of the fact that he is such a small part. Good and evil disappear also, for an evil action appears evil only because of the limitation of our insight; if we had full knowledge, if we had comprehensive rather than a particular view of reality, all evil would disappear. There is, of course, no creation in the sense that something came into being that was not. There is only eternal being, which may change superficially but which does not change essentially. This eternal being has always been and will always be. There is no creation and there is no end.

Against these views of pantheism the Protestant faith asserts that God created and creates through his sovereign Word. Creation is the result of God's freedom. He created the world—which he did not have to create. Although creation is real, it is not necessary. The world is not the automatic emanation of God's Being but rather the result of a free act. This free act is not merely an event of the past but rather an eternal act. It is a result of God's will that the world continues to exist. Although God is creatively present in the universe he also transcends it. It does not contain him, and he is not identical with it. Whenever Christians speak of nature as divine they are in danger of the pantheistic perversion of the Christian doctrine of creation.

There is a third interpretation of the relation of God to the world which in the light of the revelation in Christ must be rejected by the Protestant faith. This is dualism. Dualism is the view that asserts that the universe must be explained as the result of the conflict of two eternal principles. These two principles are sometimes called light and darkness, good and evil, mind and matter, or soul and body. Whatever terms are used, this view implies two absolute and coequal principles which are engaged in an eternal struggle. The key to the understanding of life is the understanding of the nature of this conflict. In this view one aspect of nature is generally favored over its opposite—usually mind over matter or light over darkness, form over formlessness or soul over body. Here we find the theories which assert that matter and body are the result of the evil principle and that only mind and soul are the creation of the good principle. Actually, dualism operates with gods who are engaged in an eternal struggle in which man is in the middle.

In this world view the body becomes the prison of the soul, and nature as it appears to our senses, the bait of the evil one. God himself is here the fighter against darkness and chaos, and instead of creation we find the eternal struggle of form to overcome formlessness, of light to overcome darkness, of mind to subdue matter, and of the soul to subject the body.

Against this view the Protestant faith asserts that God created the universe *ex nihilo*, out of nothing. All of it is ultimately the product of his creative power. This is true of darkness as well as light and of the body as well as the soul. While Plato could say that the body is the prison of the soul, the Apostle Paul says that the body is the temple of the Holy Spirit. Even those powers which oppose God have their source in God's creative will. They are not eternal or independent from God but are dependent upon God's creative power. Whenever Christians depreciate matter and the body in a false spiritualism, dualism has obtained a hold on them. The Christian doctrine of creation is categorically opposed to the dualistic conflict between good spirit and evil matter, good soul and evil body. The one God is Creator of all that is. We repeat: According to the Protestant faith the world is the product of God's sovereign power and in its totality in every instant completely dependent upon him. However, this is not a reversible dependence. Although the universe is dependent upon God, God himself is not dependent upon the universe.

It is of some importance that the difference between the Protestant faith and deism, pantheism, and dualism be clearly defined because these very ideas have frequently penetrated deeply into Protestant thought. It would not be too difficult to produce numerous people who consider themselves "'good" Protestants who hold a deistic view of the relationship of God to the universe. They do believe that God set the whole process in motion a long time ago. Now the universe runs, so to speak, by itself. God must be busy somewhere else. Such deism is far more prevalent than the doctrinal statements of Protestantism would lead one to believe.

Furthermore, there is a good deal of pantheism among people

who consider themselves Protestants. It usually appears in the form of various kinds of nature worship. The most common form is probably to be found in the worship of the green grass of the golf course on Sunday morning. But there are many Christians who tend to think that God is nature and nature is God.

Like pantheism and deism, dualism is not unknown in Christian garb. In the very earliest time of the history of the Christian church, certain Christian sects claimed that the Creator God and the Savior God were two different Gods, that there was a difference between the Old Testament God who had created matter and the New Testament God who had saved the human race. This view was resolutely rejected by the mainstream of Christian thought. Nevertheless, a certain depreciation of the body and of the world accessible to our senses seems to have been a lasting result of the dualistic approach, which can still be discovered among Protestant Christians. Such dualistic deviations from the mainstream of Christianity are not uncommon in our own time.

It would therefore be wise in our study of the Protestant faith not to ignore these alternatives which we have discussed briefly, namely, deism, pantheism, and dualism. They may throw a great deal of light on some of the contemporary pressures upon Protestantism by new religious and antireligious movements. The Christian faith in God, the Creator of heaven and earth, has always had to be stated in contradiction to very lively views which considered God merely the first cause, or which identified him with the universe, or which had two gods fighting an eternal war for human souls.

For the Christian faith creation means that the universe had a beginning and will have an end. This, of course, does not say anything about space and time. For the Christian, space and time, whatever they are, are in themselves part of God's creation. The Protestant faith does not take sides for a Newtonian or an Einsteinian universe; whatever the universe is, whatever space is, whatever time is, the Christian sees them as God's creation.

Before we leave the subject of creation it may be advisable to describe briefly the attitude with which the Protestant Christian accepts the world as God's creation. This doctrine of creation prevents two attitudes which could easily arise and which have, in fact, arisen in the past as far as the human understanding of the universe is concerned.

On the one hand, creation means that this is God's world, that all of it is God's world. The insistence upon matter as well as spirit as God's creation is in opposition to all those beliefs which tend to depreciate matter. The material world is not inferior and not in itself evil or demonic. The Protestant Christian has every right to enjoy the world of matter, to love the stars and admire the majesty of the universe, to love the flowers and the trees which beautify our world. There is nothing in the Protestant faith which says that the material world is to be ignored or belittled. As God's creation we may love it. The manner in which Jesus preached seems to indicate that he loved it. There is nothing in the Protestant faith that would command us to desire ugliness instead of beauty and to run down the material world. The doctrine of creation is a constant reminder that it is God's material world. Man has the right, even the duty, to love and admire it because of its Creator.

On the other hand, the doctrine of creation means we must make a clear distinction between creation and the Creator. While we may enjoy creation, we must never worship it, says the Protestant faith. This is, of course, not an idle warning. Much pagan religion is, indeed, the worship of the creature and creation instead of the Creator. The stringent prohibitions against the manufacture of graven images, or idols, which we find in the Old Testament are an attempt to safeguard the Jewish people against the worship of creation, which was so common among the neighbors of the Israelites and which was such a serious temptation to the Hebrew people. The worship of creation in all its forms is always idolatry. The Protestant faith insists that you cannot worship beauty, or nature, without being guilty of idolatry. Creation always points beyond itself to the Creator. That is what the Psalmist means when he sings: "The heavens are telling the glory of God; and the firmament proclaims his handiwork" (Ps. 19:1). Here the doctrine of creation protects the Protestant faith against what is commonly called "secularism," which is essentially the deification of all those things which are not God, the deification of God's handiwork. This is as much a temptation in our age as it was a temptation when Israel confronted the Canaanites. There are many people today who worship the creature instead of the Creator. There are those, for example, who worship the family. To have a family is a wonderful thing; to love and cherish a wife or a husband and children is a glorious experience. However, the man who worships his family is idolatrously worshiping the creature instead of the Creator. When Jesus said to one of his disciples who wanted to go and bury his father, "Follow me, and leave the dead to bury their dead" (Matt. 8:22), he insisted on higher loyalties than even the universally respected loyalty toward one's family. The same message is stated in Matt. 10:35-36: "For I have come to set a man against his father and a daughter against her mother, and a daughter-in-law against her mother-in-law; and a man's foes will be those of his own household." This meant the abolition of the family as the object of absolute loyalty.

The worship of the creature instead of the Creator offends against the First Commandment: "I am the Lord your God. . . . You shall have no other gods before me" (Exod. 20:2, 3). Christian rejection of such worship applies also if the object of our worship is not the family but rather our work or money or even our country. There are many people who have made their work into a god and who will sacrifice everything, even their family and their faith, to achieve success in their work. The temptation of Jesus described in Luke 4:9, where the devil suggests that Jesus should demonstrate to everybody his divine mission and thus accomplish his task by throwing himself from the pinnacle of the temple in a spectacular display of divine power, is a paradigm of the idolatrous temptation of salvation through success in one's work. While work, according to the Protestant faith, offers people the opportunity to serve God and all mankind, it is not work which saves. The history of the Protestant movement has been plagued by the tendency to idolize work. Even if the books of Max Weber[3] and R. H. Tawney[4] about the connection between Protestantism and capitalism must be read with considerable reservation,[5] the tendency of some Protestants to believe in salvation through work is an important and peculiarly Protestant idolatry.

The worship of money is also frequently excoriated in the New Testament, where Jesus exclaims: "No one can serve two masters; for either he will hate the one, and love the other, or he will be devoted to the one and despise the other. You cannot serve God and mammon" (Matt. 6:24). The obsession with money is seen as so destructive that Jesus can say: "How hard it is for those who have riches to enter the kingdom of God! For it is easier for a camel to go through the eye of a needle than for a rich man to enter the kingdom of God" (Luke 18:24, 25).

The replacement of loyalty to God by loyalty to country or nation was repudiated by the Prophet Jeremiah in the Old Testament. He proclaimed the will of the Lord saying: "Behold, I set before you the way of life and the way of death. He who stays in this city [Jerusalem] shall die by the sword, by famine, and by pestilence; but he who goes out and surrenders to the Chaldeans who are besieging you shall live and shall have his life as a prize of war" (Jer. 21:8, 9). Yet, in spite of the Prophet's effort to put the love of country into proper perspective, nothing has produced greater terror and destruction in the twentieth century than the idolatry of nationalism. No people seems immune against this plague.

Family, work, money, and country are gifts of God's creation to be used by humanity to honor God, serve the neighbor, and enjoy life. But if made absolute and worshiped these divine favors lead human beings to idolatry and result in error and destruction. The Protestant faith rejects this kind of secularism, the autonomy of creature and creation.

Providence

Faith in God as Creator includes faith in God's providence, which grows out of the faith in God's power and love. This means that everything that happens in the universe happens as the result of God's will and in order to accomplish his purpose. Again it must be stressed that this is not an effort to explain logically the events which in fact occur. The Protestant Christian does not pretend to have an answer for everything. Indeed, he is quite suspicious of those who always have a ready explanation. Perhaps this is best illustrated by the story that was told about Count von Zinzendorf, the famous leader of German Pietism and of the Moravian Brethren. Asked by an inquiring lady to explain such theological conundrums as, "What did God do before he created the world?" and, "If God is Love and Almighty, why is there evil in the world?", he refused to answer, but replied, "Madam, I am trying to be God's servant—not his brain trust!"

This response throws some light upon the Protestant understanding of providence. If the Protestant faith asserts that all events are subject to God's power, this does not mean that Christians claim to have explanations for all events. Faith in providence does not supply pat and glib answers to the perplexing questions confronting the human race. It rather proclaims that all events in nature and in history, however bewildering, are ultimately subject to God's purpose.

In the New Testament we read a story in which Jesus is asked to give the reason why a certain man was born blind. His questioners had a ready explanation. They gave him two alternatives, that the man was born blind either because of his own sin or because of the sin of his ancestors. Jesus rejected both these answers and said: "It was not that this man sinned, or his parents, but that the works of God might be made manifest in him" (John 9:3). This shows that faith in the providence of God is not intended to supply a simple explanation for all that occurs. Christianity does not only fail to provide simple answers to complicated questions, but, as this story shows, it occasionally raises complicated questions where people are satisfied with simple answers. Again, it is impossible to understand the Protestant faith if we remove the assertions of faith from their proper context. Within the context of worship and adoration the Protestant faith asserts that all events in nature and history are ultimately subject to the divine purpose. This is not supposed to be a substitute for scientific explanations. Protestants are prepared to accept these gladly—as far as they go. They only claim that they do not go far enough. The Protestant faith deals with humanity's ultimate questions. To the individual believer, this means what the Apostle Paul states in Romans in the following words: "We know

113

that in everything God works for good with those who love him, who are called according to his purpose" (Rom. 8:28). If we trust God, if we lay hold on him in faith, we will understand all the events in our life in the context of this faith. This is perhaps one of the most exasperating aspects of the Christian faith for those who do not share it. People who do not trust God but trust their bank account, or their health, or their luck are utterly confounded when they meet with Christians who are willing to take whatever comes as an expression of the divine will. And since these Christians know that this will is good, they are firmly convinced that *ultimately* no harm can come to them.

Here we cannot be careful enough to separate this faith in God, which expresses itself in the conviction that ultimately no harm can come to those who trust in God, from its popular counterfeit. There are many people who claim that Christianity will make you rich, or healthy, or lucky. Their slogan goes somewhat like this: "Become a Christian and God will give you wealth." Unfortunately they have innumerable tedious case histories to fortify their position. They'll tell you about some impoverished traveling salesman who hadn't sold a vacuum cleaner in weeks. Wherever he went people would slam the door in his face saying, "We don't want any!" The poor vacuum cleaner salesman trudged through the ice and snow and nobody wanted to buy any vacuum cleaners. And then he met some minister, or perhaps he found his grandfather's Bible in the attic. It doesn't really matter what the "gimmick" is. In any case, we are told he became a Christian. And now everything changed. Customers greeted him with, "I have been waiting for you; would you please sell me your vacuum cleaner?" To make a long story short: After he became a Christian, the man sold thousands of vacuum cleaners; his salesmanship brought him to the attention of the boss, whose beautiful daughter he subsequently married, and now this poor unsuccessful traveling salesman owns the biggest vacuum cleaner concern in the world—all because he became a Christian. This may be a somewhat exaggerated version of this popular manner of establishing the truth of Christianity, but basically this is the form in which the Christian faith is perverted and peddled like a patent medicine which will cure everything from falling hair to athlete's foot. "Become a Christian," they say, "and you will have everything you want. Try Jesus; he satisfies!"

It would be a waste of time to give much attention to this perverted view of what the providence of God means to the Protestant faith were it not for the fact that so many people, especially in our time, are led to believe that this *is* the Protestant faith. For this reason we should point out a few facts: In the Bible we find no such materialistic perversion of the effects of the Christian faith. It is common knowledge that Jesus Christ was not elected president of the Chamber of Commerce of Jerusalem, but rather that he was executed as a common criminal. And so, it appears, was every one of his disciples with the possible exception of St. John. None of them became rich. Paul was a sick man all his life. His Christian faith did not take away his illness, but it made it possible for him to live with it. He tells us: "Three times I besought the Lord about this, that it should leave me; but he said to me 'My grace is sufficient for you, for my power is made perfect in weakness'" (2 Cor. 12:8, 9). And Paul, too, was eventually executed for his Christian faith. Trust in God's providence does not mean that all events are understandable to the Christian. It does not mean that he does not have to suffer, that he will have a trouble-free life. It means that nothing can separate him from God, that he personally knows God, because God has made himself known to him, and that therefore in all events, good, bad, or indifferent, the works of God are made manifest to him.

This has, perhaps, been put most succinctly by the French-Jewish writer Simone Weil. In her book *Gravity and Grace*, she says: "The extreme greatness of Christianity lies in the fact that it does not seek a supernatural remedy for suffering, but a supernatural use for it."[6] The Protestant faith does not deny suffering, anxiety, despair, and death. It asserts rather that God can use all of it for his purpose of love. This he demonstrated most profoundly when he himself suffered and experienced anxiety, despair, and death in Jesus Christ. This is the point of reference, the perspective from which the Protestant faith makes its assertions concerning the providence of God. It is never a theoretical proposition to be debated, but always a personal confession which must be lived.

Here we must add that, as far as the Protestant faith is concerned, there is a vast difference between faith in providence and fatalism. Fatalism is the assertion that man "can't win," that there is a cold, immutable destiny which rules gods and human beings and nature. For the Greeks, for example, gods and human beings are equally caught in the net of this inexorable fate. Whatever a person does, he will finally be strangled by his fate; in fact, the harder he tries to escape it, the more obvious it becomes that nobody can ever escape his fate. This philosophy is best illustrated in Greek tragedy, for example, in the story of King Oedipus. Oedipus has been told that he would kill his father and marry his mother. When he tries to avoid his fate by leaving the people whom he believes to be his father and mother, he immediately fulfills the very fate he is trying to escape. For the Greeks, fate was unchangeable and impersonal, and gods and mortals were equally subject to it.

By contrast the Protestant faith speaks of providence as a personal trust in a personal God, a living faith in a living God who confronts living people. The Christian faith in providence is the absolute opposite of the Greek surrender to fate. There is likewise no place in Protestantism for modern American fatalism which expresses itself in such slogans as, "You can't win, the dice are loaded," and all the other expressions of despair which are part of our everyday life. The Protestant faith guards the Christian simultaneously against the superficial optimism of the men and women who think that trouble will go away if you ignore it and the profound despair of the people who insist that this life is the "tale told by an idiot, full of sound and fury, signifying nothing." Providence is personal trust in a personal God. As Luther sings: "Take they then our life, goods, fame, child and wife, When their worst is done, They yet have nothing won: The Kingdom ours remaineth."

Prayer

In the relationship of prayer to the Protestant faith in the providence of God, what does it mean that Christians pray? Do they actually believe that they know better what should happen than

God in his providence? Are they trying to give unsolicited advice to the Creator and Ruler of the universe?

Again, it is utterly impossible to discuss the Christian meaning of prayer in an abstract, philosophical manner. The right and duty of the Christian to pray to God are not something that we can deduce logically from the nature of God as Creator and Preserver of the universe and of humanity. For the Protestant faith prayer is not like sending an order to a mail-order house or, worse, giving orders to somebody who has to obey. There are religions where prayer is a form of magical incantation which can be used to make God do something that he apparently does not want to do. While prayer is central to most religions, it has often been sacrilegiously distorted by the religious. Even among Christians it has been perverted into routine and magic. Here again Jesus' words are abundantly clear:

> When you pray, you must not be like the hypocrites; for they love to stand and pray in the synagogues and at the street corners, that they may be seen by men. Truly, I say to you, they have their reward. But when you pray, go into your room and shut the door and pray to your Father who is in secret, and your Father who sees in secret will reward you.
> And in praying do not heap up empty phrases as the Gentiles do; for they think that they will be heard for their many words. Do not be like them, for your Father knows what you need before you ask him. Pray like this: ... (Matt. 6:5–9)

And here follows the Lord's Prayer. Note that Jesus says, ". . . your Father knows what you need before you ask him." Yet he wants us to pray. This can only be understood if we remember that, for the Christian, prayer is not informing God about things he might otherwise not know, although admittedly many prayers sound as if they were trying to fill God in on something he might have missed by failing to read the newspaper. The clue to prayer is the fact that here a child is speaking to his father. It is an expression of the father-child relationship, in which the child knows the father and the father knows the child. Thus prayer is an expression of confidence and faith. Once this has been established it becomes clear why there is nothing, absolutely nothing, that cannot be brought to God in prayer, according to the Protestant faith.

The Protestant faith does not say that people must only pray for high and exalted ends, such as world peace and brotherhood. Prayer is personal communication in the context of the divine-human encounter which undergirds it. If world peace and brotherhood personally concern and move you, you may and should pray for it. But if your inability to get along with other people or your inability to make ends meet troubles you, you may pray about these matters just as readily as about world peace.

The essential ingredients in prayer are faith and sincerity. Since human beings are most sincere when their own interests are involved, our most sincere prayers are often those prayed when we are in trouble. There is nothing wrong with such prayers, for they may be, in fact, a real expression of our dependence upon God. In such prayer, we may earnestly feel that we are children and God is our heavenly Father. If this is the case, this is true prayer!

Perhaps an illustration will help. A father who loves his children wants his children to have confidence in him. This confidence may sometimes express itself in very odd ways. If you have a small boy, he may ask you, "Daddy, I want a gun which shoots real bullets." Of course, this is the kind of request that you will not fulfill as long as the child is too young to handle a gun. But you **are** glad he asked you. This is an opportunity for you to explain something about guns and about shooting, and even this unreasonable request is an expression of confidence.

According to the Protestant faith, we can and should speak to God about everything. This does not mean that God will grant all our requests, but he will hear all our prayers. Although he knows what we need, he wants us to ask him. This personal God desires to have personal fellowship with his children. Prayer is the most profound expression of this fellowship.

Prayer as a problem in metaphysics is unsolvable. (The controversy of freedom versus determinism drowns us in philosophical difficulties.) But in the Protestant faith prayer is not presented as a philosophical problem. On the contrary, whenever the Bible speaks about prayer, it speaks about the father-child relationship which

God has established with people. Prayer is the action which gives expression to the reality of this relationship. Thus, there has never been a Christian leader, a prophet, an apostle, or a saint who did not pray! For through prayer the Christian shows that his theological assertions are not merely intellectual games.

The acute problem which confronts contemporary Protestantism is the failure of the movement to teach people how to pray. A remarkable feature of the current scene is that many people raised in Protestant churches have never learned to pray. The interest in Eastern religions, especially among young people, is to some extent attributable to the skill with which their teachers expound the practice of prayer and meditation.

No amount of theoretical approval of prayer is a substitute for the practice. Luther constantly counseled prayer and in a lengthy letter to a friend who happened to be a barber offered very practical guidelines:

> So, a good and attentive barber keeps his thoughts, attention, and eyes on the razor and hair and does not forget how far he has gotten with his shaving or cutting. If he wants to engage in too much conversation or let his mind wander or look somewhere else he is likely to cut his customer's mouth, nose, or even his throat. Thus if anything is to be done well, it requires the full attention of all one's senses and members. . . . How much more does prayer, if it is to be a good prayer, require a heart that is undistracted and completely concentrated on its task.[7]

The Protestant faith must reject firmly the contemporary efforts to reduce prayer to some sort of psychological self-hypnosis. Nothing could be more misleading and dangerous than to say that, although God is in his heaven, running the universe without regard to your prayer, go ahead and pray if it makes you feel better. Either prayer is communication between the child and the father—or it is not Christian prayer. Much can be said for the psychological value of a quiet hour and even of some routine prayers. But in the moment the quiet hour and these words are used as a psychological device to make me feel better, to help me in business, or to soothe my ulcers—I am not praying to God. All these devices may be indeed very helpful. This is a question for a competent psychologist to decide. All that the theologians can say is that self-hypnosis is not prayer. Prayer is the supreme human expression of the father-child relationship.

Miracle

Deeply involved with the creative power of God is the subject of miracle. The word *miracle* has suffered a great deal from the inflationary tendencies of our language. We use it loosely for all sorts of events that we consider astonishing from the catch of a forward pass in football to the description of the effects of some soap by the advertising fraternity. "Joe Doaks made an absolutely miraculous catch," we will say; or we will hear, "Glutch's soap is truly a miracle soap."

The dictionary defines a miracle as "event or effect in the physical world deviating from the known laws of nature, or transcending our knowledge of these laws." However, this definition implies that if no laws of nature were known, then nothing could be considered miraculous, in other words, that the breach of the laws of nature makes the event miraculous.

If we want to look at miracle from the point of view of the Protestant faith, we might as well ignore the event's relationship to the laws of nature. For the believer, any event that opens his eyes to God is a "miracle." God can make any event translucent, so that it leads to faith and thus becomes miracle for the person who meets God in this event. Strangely enough, the same event may not be miracle to the unbeliever; he will have some other explanation, some device which enables him to remain an unbeliever although he has observed the very same event.

An example from the New Testament may help explain what this means. In the Acts of the Apostles, we read the story of Pentecost as follows:

> When the day of Pentecost had come, they were all together in one place. And suddenly a sound came from heaven like the rush of a mighty wind, and it filled all the house where they were sitting. And there appeared to them tongues as of fire, distributed and resting on each one of them. And they were all

filled with the Holy Spirit and began to speak in other tongues, as the Spirit gave them utterance.

Now there were dwelling in Jerusalem Jews, devout men from every nation under heaven. And at this sound the multitude came together, and they were bewildered, because each one heard them speaking in his own language.... And all were amazed and perplexed, saying to one another, "What does this mean?" But others mocking said, "They are filled with new wine." (Acts 2:1–13)

Even the Pentecost miracle was for those who did not want to believe merely the result of alcoholic overindulgence. In other words, for the committed unbeliever, no event, even the most miraculous, is "miracle"; it does not help him to have faith, it does not automatically make him a believer. Judas probably witnessed as many miracles as any of the other disciples, but this did not keep him from betraying Jesus to his enemies. These events did not open Judas' eyes to God. For him they were not miracles. On the other hand, some of the most ordinary events, the most explainable events, can be transfigured into miracles for a person who believes. There was a rather well-known eye specialist to whom the ordinary working of the human eye was the miracle of miracles; if you gave him the opportunity, he would explain to you in great detail how the structure and operation of the human eye had helped him to come to faith in God.

The Protestant faith is not committed to the absoluteness of the causal chain or the absoluteness of any physical law. We assume that what has happened a million times in a certain sequence will happen in the same sequence the one millionth and first time. This seems a most reasonable assumption until something else happens. All the Protestant faith asserts is that nothing in this universe, including the causal chain or the law of gravitation is independent of God. In fact, all events depend upon God; without him the "miraculous" as well as the "nonmiraculous" event could not occur. The unusual event may in a very specific sense become an occasion for faith, but not all unusual events do become occasions for faith. From the point of view of the Protestant faith the significance of an event is dependent upon the power it has to help people meet God.

121

However, faith in the reality of miracle in the Christian past, the Christian present, and the Christian future must not lead us into a very serious misunderstanding. This is the notion that, in general, events run without God, by themselves, so to speak, and only occasionally does God enter into the processes of nature and history and perform a miracle, afterward withdrawing again and letting things run by themselves.

Such a position is deistic, even if defended by a good Protestant. It reduces God to a spectator to the processes of nature and history, a spectator who only occasionally takes any interest in these processes. In contrast to this view, the Protestant faith asserts that God the Creator upholds the universe at all times. Whether events seem to us ordinary or extraordinary, they happen because of the creative and maintaining power of God. Any event, the most routine as well as the most spectacular from our human point of view, can become the occasion for faith if this is God's will.

NOTES

1. *The Journal of George Fox*, revised by Norman Penney (New York: E. P. Dutton & Co., Everyman's Library, 1924), p. 15, entry of 1646.

2. Aulén, *The Faith of the Christian Church* (Philadelphia: Fortress Press, 1948), p. 182.

3. Max Weber, *The Protestant Ethic and the Spirit of Capitalism* (New York: Charles Scribner's Sons, 1958).

4. R. H. Tawney, *Religion and the Rise of Capitalism* (New York: New American Library, Inc., 1947).

5. See George Wolfgang Forell, *Faith Active in Love* (Minneapolis: Augsburg Publishing House, 1954).

6. Simone Weil, *Gravity and Grace* (New York: G. P. Putnam's Sons, 1952).

7. Martin Luther, "A Simple Way to Pray," in Gustav K. Wiencke, ed., *Luther's Works* (Philadelphia: Fortress Press, 1968), vol. 43, 199.

Chapter 5

THE HUMAN CONDITION

There are many different ways in which we can and do look at human beings.[1] We can look at them from the point of view of what is generally called "common sense." From this point of view we recognize that human beings are different from the animals and things that surround them. The human being is *homo faber*, he makes tools, he uses language, he creates culture. Somehow, he knows himself to be different from the rest of creation, yet at the same time he knows also that he is a part of it. All this is a pretty disorganized approach to the human condition. Yet every person has some sort of anthropology, some idea about what it means to be human. It may not be very scientific, it may not be very articulate, but almost anyone can give you some idea of what he thinks human beings are.

But, besides these disorganized, common-sense ideas, there is the scientific approach to the question "what constitutes a human being?" The answer will depend a good deal on what science you choose. Professor Arthur Eddington once said, "If a mathematical physicist were asked for his definition of a human being, he would probably reply: 'a rather complex differential equation.' "[2] This means that a human being is also, among other things, a physical object that can be studied like other physical objects. The biochemist might give us an even better description of the human being than the physicist, while a biologist, concerned with living cells, would have still a different approach. If we asked a psychologist to answer the question "What constitutes a human being?" his answer would depend upon which school of psychology he happened to belong to—behavioristic, psychoanalytic, or Gestalt. In its own way, each of these different schools of psychology is trying to answer this question. If we look further, we will find that the economist offers another answer: People are producers, distributors, consumers of goods. The political scientist says: People acquire, exercise, regulate, and are subjected to political power.

The answers to our question become even more complicated and varied when we turn to philosophy. The dualistic philosophers will tell us that the human being is an interesting and unique combination of body and soul. They have devised many fascinating theories about this body and this soul and how they act upon each other. Other philosophers will say that a human being is merely body, merely matter. "Mind" or "soul," they assert, are merely words, or perhaps the description of some special functions of the body. And then there are the idealists, who deny the reality of matter and body and claim that the human being is "really" mind, and the body merely an illusion.

It is easy to see that it would take us forever to find all the answers that have been given to the question "what constitutes a human being?" In a sense it is the most important question people can ask. The Protestant faith asks this question also, but the answer is very different from all the views which we have listed because the Christian faith sees people primarily in their relationship to God. For the Protestant faith this relationship of a person to God is the key to the understanding of the human condition. Without knowing about this relationship we may have all sorts of interesting ideas about humanity, but we will not have that meaning which brings all other meanings together, the ultimate meaning of human personhood.

Of course, this does not mean that these other views of humanity are without value. As far as their specific insights are concerned, each one of them is of the greatest importance. It is not only proper, but necessary, to study people from all these different points of view. But the answers which economics and political science, medicine and psychology give concerning humanity are only partial answers.

The Protestant faith asserts that if any of these answers is made into the whole story, if people are considered merely "political animals" or a bundle of reflexes, then the true nature of the human being is seriously misinterpreted.

If these partial views are accepted, everything that is said about people and their life is perverted and falsified. One example will suffice. Two human beings are in love and become engaged. This relationship is in a sense economic, for without it jewelers would have a hard time selling diamond rings. This relationship is political; it involves a power structure and the distribution of power. It has important physiological and biological aspects. It can be studied psychologically and philosophically. And yet we all know, at least those who have ever been in love, that it is all of these things and more. We can only smile at the person who is trying to understand this relationship of one human being to another in such narrowly limited ways.

The Human Being as Creature

Christianity asserts that the human being is unique, that he cannot be contained and enclosed in any of these partial descriptions, because he alone of all the creatures of this earth is on speaking terms with God. God speaks to the human being and the human being can respond. This fact about the human race has been described by the theologians with the phrase *imago dei*, the image of God. According to the witness of the Bible, human beings are created in the image of God. "So God created man in his own image, in the image of God he created him; male and female he created them" (Gen. 1:27). The reality of this image is expressed by the fact that human beings know *agape* and God is *agape*, and by the fact that human beings know freedom and God is freedom.

But before we become too proud about this *imago dei*, the image of God, the Protestant faith says also that, although human beings are created in the image of God, this image has been effectively destroyed through sin. It has become a broken image. This means that human knowledge of *agape* does not lead people to love God and their neighbor. Rather, although people know of love, they hate; they do not know how to love. They want to be loved, they want everybody to love them, but this very desire creates hate.

While human beings want everybody to love them, they do not know how to love anybody. And the same tragedy occurs when human beings are trying to use their freedom. Because of sin, because they are in revolt against God, they cannot use freedom except to enslave everybody around them and ultimately themselves as well. The human person who imagines himself to be free is in fact a slave.

To use a very simple example, the small child that is given absolute freedom tyrannizes and terrorizes the entire family—and in the process of doing so becomes terribly unhappy. The child is enslaved by his own so-called freedom.

Because of our alienation from our Creator, classical Protestantism asserts, we turn love into hate and freedom into slavery. Whatever we do works our destruction. Yet the destruction of the image of God in people does not turn them into animals. Even the enslaved human being is still human. Even a person who is full of hate is still a person. People cannot escape their humanity. They can try to escape, but they never succeed.

There are many attempts on record in which people have tried to be merely a part of nature. They have said, "Let us be animals. We are unhappy, miserable human beings; perhaps we can be simple and happy animals. Let's go back to nature!" But whenever people have tried to abandon their humanity, to take it off as one takes off uncomfortable clothes, the effort has failed.

It has failed first of all because humanity has never been merely a part of nature. As we observed earlier, there has never been a time in which human beings were merely animals. We might gain the impression that our prehistorical ancestors were animals if we were to depend on comic strips and magazine cartoons for our information about them. But these characteristics are amusing precisely because they depict human beings as animals, just as we find cartoons which depict animals as human beings entertaining. A human being who acts like an ape is odd (e.g., Tarzan) just as a duck or a mouse who acts like a human being is peculiar (e.g., Donald Duck and Mickey Mouse). It is the uniqueness of the human race that makes these artistic flights of fancy so interesting. The cartoons depicting our prehistoric ancestors tell us something about the way in which the cartoonist views the contemporary situation but nothing about these early human beings.

Such drawings as those found in the caves in Dordogne, France really tell us something about cave dwellers. One of the oldest records we have of our early ancestors, they are beautiful pictures of animals. They reveal that our early ancestors were not brutes but artists. As G. K. Chesterton has put it:

> It is the simple truth that man does differ from the brutes in kind and not in degree; and the proof of it is here; that it sounds like a truism to say that the most primitive man drew a picture of a monkey and that it sounds like a joke to say that the most intelligent monkey drew a picture of a man.[3]

People are always unique. The reason is, according to the Protestant faith, that they stand in a unique relationship to God. The fact that this relationship has been terribly disturbed does not make it any less unique. There is no escape from our humanity into some animal ancestor. The effort to escape our humanity by claiming that some contemporary primitives are not really human, and that humanity is therefore merely an acquired characteristic that we can abandon if we so desire, is equally doomed. As we said before, there is no noble savage; there is no contemporary primitive who is merely animal. The more we learn about the various patterns of culture among human beings today, the more we must realize that, in spite of all the variety, every group of people is human. None of them act like animals, none of them act as if they were merely nature. Like "civilized" people, the contemporary primitives, too, know love and practice hate, know freedom and are enslaved. People are always human; there is no escape from our humanity.

The same rule holds for those forlorn efforts of eighteenth-century Europeans who dressed up as shepherds and shepherdesses in order to "go back to nature." It is equally valid for our contemporaries, whatever they call themselves, who let their hair grow and wear animal skins and sandals. Such efforts do not provide an escape from our humanity—they only illustrate how we are bothered by the fact that we are human beings who are not what human beings are supposed to be. We are human but not humane. The

Protestant faith claims that we are people alienated from our Creator. We are the broken image of God. It is always true that the perversion of the best is the worst. Because of humanity's special destiny the failure of humanity is so uniquely tragic. As we can see all about us, what is wrong with people does not only threaten other people but all creation. Human beings estranged from their Creator lose sight of their responsibility for his creation. The result is the ecological crisis of our time. Because of humanity's unique power, the result of the image of God, we have the ability to poison the air and the water, devastate the land and place all life on earth in jeopardy. Because of the brilliant potentialities of the human race we have become a threat to the world we inhabit.

The Human Being as Sinner

Classical Protestantism asserts that the human being is a sinner. This is his tragedy! This is the source of *all* his problems. Created for free fellowship with God, he uses his freedom to make himself into God and thus revolts against his Creator and Heavenly Father. The desire to be God is the basic sin. Nietzsche once said, "But that I may reveal my heart entirely to you, my friends: *if* there were gods, how could I endure it to be no god! *Therefore* there are no gods."[4] The human being wants to be God—and he wants everything to turn around himself. He wants to be the center and the meaning of the universe. He resents the fact that he is marginal, the experience that he is finite. He knows that there was a time when he was not, and he dreads that there will be a time when he will not be!

What human beings resent most is that they are so dispensable. Life goes on without any of us. It would go on without all of us. Thus we do not want to die—but not because we will leave such a great vacuum that it will never be filled! On the contrary, we fear death because we know that life will go on as if we had never lived. It is our obvious dispensability which terrifies us. We envy God his godhead. People want to be like God and therefore they revolt (Gen. 3:1-5). Sin is the human revolt against God.

128

But how does this revolt specifically express itself? What in particular is sin? If we look at it psychologically, sin is pride. The Greek word for this pride is *hybris,* and the ancient Greeks suspected that *hybris* was the source of human suffering. It was the flaw in the hero of the great tragedies. The Greeks saw in it both the expression of the hero's greatness, that is, his awareness of his affinity to the gods, and the expression of his enmity toward the gods, his defiance of their superiority. In the Greeks' tragic view of life *hybris* causes humanity's downfall and destruction.

For the Christian, *hybris* means that people, who are created to live their lives in grateful dependence upon God, who are supposed "to fear, love, and trust God above all things," believe that they can manage without God. Sin is to fear, love, and trust other things besides God. Classical Protestantism says that we are sinners because we do in fact worship other gods. Turning away from the one true God, human beings choose to worship idols. This means that in a sense all sins are sins against the First Commandment: "I am the Lord your God, . . . You shall have no other gods before me."

In fact, humanity has other gods. One could say that we make up our gods as we go along. We worship ourselves and do everything to please ourselves. We live as if there were no God. This is sin. But it is also sin if we worship other idols, for example, our nation. We then act as if our country or our "race" were the highest good—we hate and even murder to maintain the supremacy of our "race"—and sin. Or money can be the idol. There are many people who will do anything for money, because having money gives them the feeling of being independent, sovereign—like God. They will lie, deceive, betray, and murder for money. This is sin.

According to the Protestant faith people are created to return their lives as a living sacrifice to God; they are supposed to live in God and for God. But when they live in fact apart from God and only for themselves, glorifying their own happiness and their own pleasure, they sin.

Sin may find innumerable expressions. In the New Testament we find the so-called catalogs of vices, which indicate the many forms in which sin appears. Thus St. Paul writes:

> Now the works of the flesh are plain: immorality, impurity, licentiousness, idolatry, sorcery, enmity, strife, jealousy, anger, selfishness, dissension, party spirit, envy, drunkenness, carousing, and the like. (Gal. 5:19)

All these specific sins are the result and the expression of humanity's revolt against God. Since the perversion of the best is the worst, it is in the sins of the spirit that human beings sin most profoundly.

Through the mind people are superior to the animals. Through their imagination they can accomplish the particularly human tasks, yet the imagination enables them to revolt against God in the most sophisticated manner. As far as the Protestant faith is concerned, an action is sinful to the degree that it expresses human revolt against God.

This is most movingly illustrated in Fyodor Dostoyevsky's famous novel *Crime and Punishment.* In this novel we meet a murderer and a prostitute. Dostoyevsky shows that the murderer, Raskolnikov, sins in the most horrible manner. He murders a pawnbroker, because he is convinced that he, a brilliant student, will make a greater contribution to society than this worthless old woman. As Professor Jaroslav Pelikan has put it:

> The murder of the old pawnbroker was a sin, but not merely because it was a breach of conventional morality. This made it a crime, not a sin. Raskolnikov's sin was brought on by his egocentricity, his assumption that his position in the universe was so important that he could suspend the existence of another person to advance his own ends. . . . Sin, therefore, was not the violation of some precept or prohibition, it was the assumption: I am God.[5]

In the same novel we meet Sonia. She is a girl who sells her body into prostitution to secure food for her stepmother and her small brothers and sisters who are starving. She sins; she transgresses the moral law knowingly and deliberately. But while Raskolnikov "acted out of an egocentric belief that he had a claim upon another person's life," Sonia "acted out of the belief that her stepmother and the children had a claim upon her life."[6]

There are vast differences between the kinds of evil deeds human beings do. But the most terrible aspect of sin, according to the Protestant faith, is that it is revolt against God. This is perhaps most shockingly illustrated in another of Dostoyevsky's novels, *The Brothers Karamazov*. Here the Grand Inquisitor of Seville is confronted by Jesus, who has come to this city in Spain during the time of the greatest power of the Inquisition. Christ is put in prison by the church. The church has become an institution for the acquisition of power. As such it has no use for Christ, and so the Grand Inquisitor can tell the very Christ in whose name he has usurped his power:

> I repeat, tomorrow Thou shalt see that obedient flock who at a sign from me will hasten to heap up the hot cinders about the pile on which I shall burn Thee for coming to hinder us. For if any one has ever deserved our fires, it is Thou. Tomorrow I shall burn Thee![7]

Here a man of the church shows sin in its most severe and serious form. It is revolt against God which leads the Grand Inquisitor to burn the Christ, as it once led Caiaphas and Pilate to crucify him. Because the Grand Inquisitor wants to be God, because he refuses to let God be God, he sins most profoundly of all. In the perversion of our highest aspirations we commit our worst sins.

Psychologically speaking, sin is pride. Theologically speaking, it is unbelief. Because people do not believe in God, because they believe in that which is not God, they are sinners. If a human being analyzes his life he discovers again and again that his actions are inspired by trust in other gods besides the Lord God. A person is a sinner because he has other gods before the Lord his God! The Old Testament supplies many illustrations. The Israelites trust the golden calf—and sin! They trust their own kings instead of God—and sin! They trust Egypt—and sin! They trust their wealth and prosperity—and sin!

What the Old Testament says about the Israelites is equally true of contemporary Americans. The Protestant faith asserts that Americans sin when they trust their natural resources, or their economic prosperity, or their military strength, when they put their trust in anything besides God, when they have other gods besides the Lord God. There is a story in the New Testament which helps to show that sin is unbelief, the trust in things instead of God. It is a very simple story taken from the everyday life of a rural society.

> The land of a rich man brought forth plentifully; and he thought to himself, "What shall I do, for I have nowhere to store my crops?" And he said, "I will do this: I will pull down my barns, and build larger ones; and there I will store all my grain and my goods. And I will say to my soul, Soul, you have ample goods laid up for many years; take your ease, eat, drink, be merry." But God said to him, "Fool! This night your soul is required of you; and the things you have prepared, whose will they be?" So is he who lays up treasure for himself, and is not rich toward God. (Luke 12:16–21)

Because a person does not believe in God, because he trusts in all sorts of false gods, in himself, in his family, in his wealth, because of his unbelief, he is a sinner.

The Protestant faith asserts furthermore that sin is a responsible act. There is no doubt that sin has a long history. Our own deeds of injustice are conditioned to a large extent by deeds done long ago. Sin has a way of proliferating, of giving birth to more sin, that is truly frightening. This has led some people to say that there is indeed evil in the world, but humanity is rather to be pitied than censured. It is a victim of circumstances over which it has no control. Sin is never personal sin, these people say; it is always a social disease. Each person as an individual is good; it is society that makes him bad.

This argument has a great deal of attraction because it is so obvious that our life in society aggravates all our shortcomings from the most superficial to the most profound. It also involves our pride and our revolt against God. It seems obvious that people are worse in society than as individuals. A mob will commit crimes that no individual member of the mob would do by himself. Perhaps the family supplies the most striking illustration of the fact that we act worse as members of a group than we would act as individuals. A mother will lie, cheat, and steal if need be in order to protect her children—even though she would never do any of these acts to protect herself. A college student who would never cheat in a test in order to obtain a better grade himself will condone and protect the cheating of his classmates. And there are many other illustrations of this fact that we act less responsibly as members of collectivities than we would act if we were all by ourselves. The excesses of the mass movements of our time have further substantiated this judgment.

This observation has led some to speak of evil as a product of society and its maladjustments. According to these people, there is no sin; there are only poorly designed societies. If we would correct the inadequate design of our society we would immediately eliminate evil.

In some sense this seems to be the assertion of the Marxists, who blame all the shortcomings of humanity upon the deficiencies of the capitalist system and who seem to think that evil will disappear if we redesign society according to a socialist pattern. But the Marxists are not the only voices proclaiming that persons are good individually and they are made evil by society. In America behaviorist psychologists like B. F. Skinner have dismissed the whole debate about good and evil by saying: "An experimental analysis shifts the determination of behavior from autonomous man to the environment—an environment responsible both for the evolution of the species and for the repertoire acquired by each member."[8] He and his followers advocate the abolition of "autonomous man, the inner man," what they call "the man defended by the literature of freedom and dignity," and suggest "his abolition has long been overdue."[9]

Against all these views the Protestant faith asserts that sin is a personal and a responsible act. It is a personal revolt against God, which is aggravated by society and its shortcomings, but which is nevertheless our personal responsibility. In fact, the shortcomings of society are in turn the result of personal failures. And so we are involved in a vicious circle. Personal sin creates a corrupt society, and the corrupt society aggravates and encourages personal sin. But the human being remains responsible. Although he will always try to blame his moral failures on others, ultimately the responsibility is his own. In the story of Paradise Eve blames sin on the serpent, and Adam blames sin on Eve. This is a most human reaction; the pattern has continued ever since. Although we know deep down in our hearts that we are responsible, we will always find somebody to blame. Not only are human beings sinners, but they are sinners who cannot face their sin honestly and always need a scapegoat.

But in addition to emphasizing the reality of personal responsibility, classical Protestantism says simultaneously that human beings are sinners because of original sin. Here we see again the principle of complementarity in operation. Sin is at the same time personal and collective responsibility. For classical Protestantism, original sin describes the fact that the human being is born in revolt. The revolt against God is not something which he must gradually learn but is the pattern of human nature, because humanity collectively since the dawn of history has been in revolt against God. People living on a dirt road in the country will tell visiting drivers in the winter, "Choose your ruts carefully; you will be in them for a long time!" This illustrates the predicament of the human race. It is in a rut, says the Protestant faith. Sin surrounds and embraces humanity. Not only individual human beings but the entire human race is in revolt against God. And this revolt afflicts everything we do. This is what is meant by the total depravity, a Protestant concept that has come in for much criticism. When Calvin wanted to summarize this concept, he turned to the Apostle Paul and his letter to the Romans:[10]

> None is righteous, no, not one; no one understands, no one seeks for God. All have turned aside, together they have gone wrong; no one does good, not even one. Their throat is an open grave, they use their tongues to deceive. The venom of asps is under their lips. Their mouth is full of curses and bitterness. Their feet are swift to shed blood, in their paths are ruin and misery, and the way of peace they do not know. There is no fear of God before their eyes.

This passage is a collation of quotations from the Psalms and the Prophet Isaiah. None of these authors means that we cannot act like ladies and gentlemen. They do not mean that we are beasts, that we are animals. They do mean, however, that nothing we do is unaffected by sin, by our revolt against God. Our social life as well as our personal life is perverted by sin. It affects our relationship with our friends as well as with our enemies. In every area and nook of human life the fact that humanity is in revolt against God is noticeable. In the moment when we think we have escaped it, it becomes most obvious. This is repeatedly illustrated by the Pharisees in the New Testament. These Pharisees were good people, solid citizens; and their very goodness and righteousness resulted in pride and conceit and made them sinners! Ironically, many a modern Protestant has contemplated the story of the Pharisee and the publican and completely missed the point of the story. Where the Pharisee says, "Lord, I thank thee that I am not like this publican," the modern Protestant has said, "Lord, I thank thee that I am not like this Pharisee," and in doing so he has indicated that he is just as much of a sinner as the Pharisee of old, even if his pride is not pride because of righteousness but rather pride because of his lack of pride!

There is nothing that cannot become sinful. Humanity's highest aspirations, even our loyalty to family and country, can become the source of pride and the point of revolt against God. Even religion can become the focus of sin. This was the problem of the Grand Inquisitor. The very zeal of the religious person who burns the unbeliever to the greater glory of God is the expression of sin. Nobody is safe from it, says the Protestant faith, and no aspect of human life is untouched by it. Even my awareness of sin can lead me to become careless about sin, to take it for granted and thus not to take it seriously.

This is a temptation which threatens with greatest subtlety those who take their religion seriously. Dealing with the concept of sin as part of the language of their daily worship, they may become so accustomed to the word as to forget the dangerous reality it describes. People who work with high explosives in their daily routine must be constantly reminded that familiarity dare not breed contempt. If that happens they may carelessly risk their lives. Similarly, those for whom sin is part of their daily religious speech must be on guard lest familiarity with the word breed contempt for the ever-dangerous reality. This is why Holy Scripture warns the Christians constantly against overconfidence.

Thus the Protestant faith asserts that all human beings are sinners and that people express their alienation from God in all they do. The facts thus described must not be taken for granted.

But one comment must here be added. When the Protestant faith speaks of original sin, it does not state or imply that this sin is sexual. The notion seems to be quite prevalent that "original sin" is "sexual sin," and that sex is somehow the result of sin. Whatever its origin, this is not Protestant teaching. Any basic drive in the human species can be perverted and made sinful. This is just as true of the drive toward self-preservation as of the sexual urge. We should not forget that the commandment dealing with adultery is not the first of the ten; it is not the key to the understanding of sin. The tendency in religious circles, probably not uninfluenced by Victorianism, which makes so many people identify sin and sex has quite obscured the pervasiveness and profundity of human depravity.

The Protestant faith asserts that sex is God's invention. He made man male and female. Thus nothing is wrong with the sexual urge as such, for it has been given to the human race by God. Of course it can be perverted, but so can every other basic drive of the human being.

Here the Protestant faith wants to be clearly distinguished from what could be called the modern attitude of positive or negative pansexualism. Positive pansexualism is the effort to explain the human being entirely in sexual terms, making the libido, the sex urge, the center of the human personality. This is certainly a tendency in contemporary life. It has been brilliantly described and explained by various social scientists. David Riesman in his book *The Lonely Crowd* has called sex "The Last Frontier." He claims that, for modern man, the so-called "other-directed person," "it [sex] provides a kind of defense against the threat of total apathy."[11] Whatever the reason for preeminence of sex in the thought of our age, the Protestant faith asserts that sex is simply not that important. It is part of life, an important part of life, but not all of life. It is quite possible to be a sinner, in revolt against

God, without focusing the revolt in the area of the relationship of the sexes. This tendency to think of sin in sexual terms, which has dominated our culture, has had the effect of making us take less seriously all the other ways in which human beings revolt against God. All sorts of people who have revolted against God "intellectually" or in the way in which they have made other people into means to their ends have felt deceptively secure from sin because their particular revolt was not "sexual."

We read in the Gospel of Mark that Jesus, when asked by a scribe, "Which commandment is the first of all?" answered:

> The first is, "Hear, O Israel: The Lord our God, the Lord is one; and you shall love the Lord your God with all your heart, and with all your soul, and with all your mind, and with all your strength." The second is this, "You shall love your neighbor as yourself." (Mark 12:29–31)

A human being is a sinner because he has broken and is breaking these commandments. He has other gods whom he loves, and he does not love his neighbor as he loves himself. All the specific sins which ruin human life are the result of this. People are in revolt against their God—yet without this God they cannot live! Humanity has always been in revolt against God; it is a revolting community, a race in revolt. Each individual is involved in the collective guilt of the human race. This is the meaning of the doctrine of original sin in classical Protestantism. But in the Protestant faith, this revolt is always at the same time personal responsibility and collective guilt. The personal responsibility explains the collective guilt—and the collective guilt throws light upon the personal responsibility.

The clue to the understanding of the predicament of each person in the world, according to the Protestant faith, is the fact of sin. All human troubles stem from this one source. None can be solved ultimately unless the relationship to God, broken through sin, is restored.

Perhaps it is now in order to say a few words about some theoretical questions which always arise when the subject of sin is discussed. How can we explain the origin of sin? Where does evil come from? How can a universe created by a good God have evil in it? These questions are not answered by simply attributing evil to the activities of the devil or other demonic powers, for the question arises immediately—how did the devil become evil? Is he not also the creature of a good God?

To ask for an explanation of evil is actually a fairly "un-Protestant" question. Protestantism begins with the encounter of God and the human person. In this encounter the human being knows himself as evil. He says with Isaiah: "Woe is me! For I am lost; for I am a man of unclean lips, . . . for my eyes have seen the King, the Lord of hosts!" (Isa. 6:5). But while we experience ourselves as sinners, as alienated from God, and while this is an utterly personal experience which needs no explanation of the origin of evil as far as the individual is concerned, some explanations of its origin which have been offered by Christian thinkers could be mentioned.

Perhaps one of the most brilliant efforts is the explanation that the origin of evil does not have to be explained because it is essentially *nothingness*. It is nonbeing. An evil person is not a person plus something, namely, evil. Rather an evil person is not fully human. He is a deficient human being. Evil is nothingness, nonbeing, and the vile person is the person whose deficiencies have perverted him. This is the explanation offered by Plato, which Augustine adopted with minor modifications. For Augustine, evil is not nothingness, but rather the turning of the human being from God to nothingness. Nothingness in itself is not evil. But the movement of the human being who turns from God to nothingness is evil. Here no explanation of evil is needed because pure evil has no being. Human sin is to turn toward nothingness instead of turning toward God.

The other equally ingenious effort to explain evil has been suggested by men like Nicolaus Cusanus at the end of the medieval period and by the German philosopher-shoemaker, Jacob Boehme, in the post-Reformation period. They asserted that evil is a lack of balance. If all things are in perfect balance, there is no evil. These various aspects of being are in themselves good if they are properly balanced against all other aspects of being. However, when a part goes off by itself, leaves the whole and becomes an independent part—then we have evil.

Perhaps this could be best illustrated by the example of the red and the white corpuscles in our blood. Both are in themselves good. Both white and red are necessary for the well-being of the human being. Neither is evil. But if the number of white corpuscles rapidly increases and the number of red corpuscles rapidly decreases, the person is sick. The same happens if the red corpuscles increase and the white corpuscles decrease. Health is not having white corpuscles or having red corpuscles but having both in proper balance. Similarly, nothing in the universe is in itself evil. Evil originates if something that is part of the whole separates itself, makes itself independent from the whole, and thus upsets the divine balance.

Ingenious as these explanations of the origin of evil are, from the point of view of the Protestant faith they serve only to illustrate that it is revolt which is at the root of sin—the revolt that turns people from God to nothingness or that makes them forget the balance and go off by themselves. A human being is a sinner because he is in revolt against his Creator. There is no intellectual answer to the problem of evil—the only Christian answer is repentance and faith.

The Result of Sin

The human revolt makes God's judgment necessary. The holy God appears to the sinner as the God of wrath. The Protestant faith insists that God takes sin seriously. Against all efforts to reduce God to an overindulgent grandfather who overlooks disobedience and ignores it, the Protestant faith asserts that God is holy and righteous altogether. He does not ignore the revolt of a person any more than a good physician would ignore disease in the body. God would not be God if evil and sin were not abhorrent to him. This is the unanimous witness of the Old Testament prophets. Amos sings:

> Seek the Lord and live, lest he break out like fire in the house
> of Joseph, and it devour, with none to quench it for Bethel, O
> you who turn justice to wormwood, and cast down righteous-

ness to the earth! He who made the Pleiades and Orion, and turns deep darkness into the morning, and darkens the day into night, who calls for the waters of the sea, and pours them out upon the surface of the earth, the Lord is his name, who makes destruction flash forth against the strong, so that destruction comes upon the fortress. They hate him who reproves in the gate, and they abhor him who speaks the truth. Therefore because you trample upon the poor and take from him exactions of wheat, you have built houses of hewn stone, but you shall not dwell in them; you have planted pleasant vineyards, but you shall not drink their wine. For I know how many are your transgressions, and how great are your sins. . . . (Amos 5:6–12)

It is because God is holy, because he is the Creator of heaven and earth, because he is all that has been said so far, that the Protestant faith insists that God cannot and will not tolerate the revolt, the pride, and the unbelief of people.

The meaning of God's punishment is the assertion of his authority. He has not abdicated as ruler of the universe and he does not intend to do so. Thus humanity's revolt results in punishment. The fact that God is Lord, which is here expressed, was not hard to understand for the people of biblical times. In our democratic age, this notion is not so obvious. The Protestant faith proclaims it nevertheless. God is not a constitutional monarch. The manner in which some Protestants tend to speak of God in our day would lead one to believe that God is a little like an elected chairman of the board of a great corporation of which the Christians are the stockholders. For this reason Rabbi Liebman's argument in his book *Peace of Mind* has found willing listeners among Protestants. For Dr. Liebman advocated a democratic god, an American god, when he wrote:

The story of the human race, until the age of technological democracy, has really been the story of dependence and helplessness—of men really feeling impotent in the presence of poverty and disease, of tyranny and autocracy, before which they had to bow their heads in resignation. . . . America is different from Europe. In Europe the emphasis was too often upon obedience to and dependence upon some strong power to whose will man had to submit. In America . . . the emphasis has been upon self-reliance, upon every generation doing better than its fathers, on becoming more successful in human attainments. One of the great troubles is that in our religion we have continued to picture our relationship to God in terms of the helpless, poverty-stricken, powerless motifs in European culture. Now, a religion that will emphasize man's nothingness and God's omnipotence; that calls upon us to deny our own powers and to glorify His—that religion may have fitted the needs of many Europeans, but it will not satisfy the growing self-confident character of America. . . . We must be brave enough to declare that every culture must create its own God idea rather than rely on outworn tradition. . . . The religion of the future, for the first time, may become a partnership religion in which men will not only *say* but will *feel*, that they are indispensable to God.[12]

It is hard for modern people to remember that God is independent of us and not a democratic leader subject to reelection. He is absolute Lord with absolute power. This aspect of the Protestant faith, which is so eloquently proclaimed by a man like Calvin, has been frequently forgotten by the descendants of the Reformation, yet it remains an essential aspect of the classical Protestant faith.

God is holy, and human revolt, human sin, brings about punishment. But here it is important to understand the peculiar double character of sin within Protestant theology: because a person is a sinner, he sins; and because he sins, he is a sinner. Sin is both cause and effect. Again, we should remember that the theologians are attempting to describe in words what is in fact part of the experience of the Christian. He knows himself separated from God, and he feels responsible for this separation.

This is clearly indicated through the liturgical service of most Protestant churches. Episcopalians, Lutherans, Presbyterians, and to some degree other Protestants have at the very beginning of their main religious service—if they use any kind of formal service—a section called "confession of sins." In the *Morning Prayer* of the Episcopal Church, it reads as follows:

Almighty and most merciful Father: we have erred and strayed from thy ways like lost sheep. We have followed too much the

141

devices and desires of our own hearts. We have offended against thy holy laws. We have left undone those things which we ought to have done; and we have done those things which we ought not to have done. And there is no health in us.

And here follows a request for forgiveness. The words in *The Service* of the Lutheran Church are very similar:

Almighty God, our Maker and Redeemer, we poor sinners confess unto thee, that we are by nature sinful and unclean, and that we have sinned against thee by thought, word, and deed. Wherefore we flee for refuge to thine infinite mercy, seeking and imploring thy grace for the sake of our Lord Jesus Christ.

It would not be difficult to quote similar confessions of sins from all those Protestant churches which use some sort of formal worship. Even among those Protestants who do not use any kind of formal service, the confession of sins forms an important part of the worship. One of the most universally held beliefs of Protestants is that every human being is indeed a sinner. And this revolt against God, this pride and unbelief, has deserved God's punishment. This is also expressed in most of the popular and ancient hymns of Protestantism. It forms the introduction to all the other proclamations of the Protestant faith. Thus Luther sings:

Out of the depths I cry to thee, O Lord, my sins bewailing!
Bow down thy gracious ear to me, Make thou my prayer availing.
Mark not my misdeeds in thy book, But on my sins in mercy look,
Or who can stand before thee?[13]

The Protestant faith asserts that sin, in which all people are involved, has some very real and observable results. These results are real—even for those people who deny the cause. All mankind, Christians and non-Christians alike, indeed the entire created world in which human beings live, feels the consequences of sin. Briefly summarized, they are strife, meaninglessness, and death.

According to the Protestant faith, conflicts between people in their many forms are the result of sin. This applies equally to the quarrels between individuals and the quarrels between nations. The murder of Abel by Cain is such an individual expression of sin

(Genesis 4). It is the ancestor of all family strife. Sin is at the bottom of the quarrels between husband and wife and between parents and children. Wherever there is real anger and real revolt there is humanity in revolt against God. The Protestant faith insists that it is important to take these quarrels seriously and to reduce their incidence. This is beautifully illustrated with another story from the Sermon on the Mount. Jesus, speaking of a man who wants to worship God, but is angry with his neighbor, said:

> So if you are offering your gift at the altar, and there remember that your brother has something against you, leave your gift there before the altar and go; first be reconciled to your brother, and then come and offer your gift. (Matt. 5:23, 24)

For Jesus, estrangement from our neighbor implies estrangement from God. As long as we are willful in our hate of our fellow human beings we cannot worship God.

Sin leads to estrangement from those closest to us. It is at the root of all our personal difficulties. This is a significant insight of Christianity and clearly part of the Protestant faith.

But this is true not only of individual strife. Collective hatred, the hatred of one family for another, or of one nation for another, or of one race for another, is part of this sinfulness of the human race. This is seen in the Old Testament story of the Tower of Babel. Here, people in revolt against God are cast into confusion and strife (Genesis 11). Because of their revolt the various nations can no longer understand one another. The Bible proclaims that international conflict and interracial conflict are the result of sin. Here again sin is both cause and consequence! Sin is the cause of the hatred between Germans and Frenchmen, Russians and Americans, Israelis and Arabs—and all the other hatreds which embitter our international life. But the resulting hatred is in turn sinful! Because of our estrangement from God, we hate, and because we hate, we are further estranged from God.

The Protestant faith asserts quite simply that all our strife, all our conflict, be it between a husband and his wife or the Soviet Union and the United States, is rooted in man's revolt against God.

This is the ultimate source of all strife and hatred. As long as this revolt lasts, strife and hatred will last. The results of sin might temporarily find other forms of expression—husband and wife may become reconciled and hate the neighbors or the mother-in-law. But it is naive to assume that the "object" of hostility, be it the existence of the mother-in-law or of Russia, is the real source of hatred. Even if people had the power to make these hated "objects" disappear altogether, they would not be able to get rid of their hatred. They would have to find other objects of hatred, because their revolt will always find expression in strife. Furthermore, human beings not only hate God and revolt against him, and hate the neighbor and try to do him harm—as long as their revolt against God persists, they even hate themselves. The result of sin is not only self-love but also self-hatred. We do not want to accept ourselves as children of God; we want either to be God and love ourselves idolatrously, or the devil and hate ourselves with a holy hatred. Sometimes it takes a psychoanalyst to reveal this deep-seated self-hatred, which is as much a result of sin as the idolatrous self-love. This self-hatred will drive people into accidents and suicide; it will make them hypercritical of their own achievements; it will make it impossible for them to accept themselves as children of God with all the personal limitations which are part of their life.

This is the story of Shakespeare's Hamlet, Goethe's Faust, and Ibsen's Peer Gynt. They all tell us that human beings are not able to accept themselves as children of God. They either love themselves with an idolatrous love or hate themselves with demonic hatred. This is the result of sin: each human being is involved in strife—with God, with the neighbor, and with himself!

A further result of sin is that life does not make sense: it is meaningless, it is "the tale told by an idiot full of sound and fury, signifying nothing." The Protestant faith asserts that humanity in revolt against God cannot find any meaning in life. Life for them has no source, no present meaning, and no ultimate purpose. The appearance of the human race on this earth is some ghastly cosmic joke. It is the result of the combination of some infinitely impossible accidents. Here we are—coming from nowhere and going no place.

This is how Bertrand Russell describes the mood:

The endless praises of the choirs of angels had begun to grow wearisome; for, after all, did he not deserve their praise? Had he not given them endless joy? Would it not be more amusing to obtain undeserved praise, to be worshiped by beings whom he tortured? He smiled inwardly, and resolved that the great drama should be performed.

For countless ages the hot nebula whirled aimlessly through space. At length it began to take shape, the central mass threw off planets, the planets cooled, boiling seas and burning mountains heaved and tossed, from black masses of cloud hot sheets of rain deluged the barely solid crust. And now the first germ of life grew in the depths of the ocean, and developed rapidly in the fructifying warmth into vast forest trees, huge ferns springing from the damp mold, sea monsters breeding, fighting, devouring, and passing away. And from the monsters, as the play unfolded itself, Man was born, with the power of thought, the knowledge of good and evil, and the cruel thirst for worship. And Man saw that all is passing in this mad, monstrous world, that all is struggling to snatch, at any cost, a few brief moments of life before Death's inexorable decree. And Man said: "There is a hidden purpose, could we but fathom it, and the purpose is good; for we must reverence something, and in the visible world there is nothing worthy of reverence." And Man stood aside from the struggle, resolving that God intended harmony to come out of chaos by human efforts. And when he followed the instincts which God had transmitted to him from his ancestry of beasts of prey, he called it Sin, and asked God to forgive him. But he doubted whether he could be justly forgiven, until he invented a divine Plan by which God's wrath was to have been appeased. And seeing the present was bad, he made it yet worse, that thereby the future might be better. And he gave God thanks for the strength that enabled him to forgo even the joys that were possible. And God smiled; and when he saw that Man had become perfect in renunciation and worship, he sent another sun through the sky, which crashed into Man's sun; and all returned again to nebula.

"Yes," he murmured, "it was a good play; I will have it performed again." Such, in outline, but even more purposeless, more void of meaning, is the world which Science presents for our belief. Amid such a world, if anywhere, our ideals henceforth must find a home. That Man is the product of causes which had no prevision of the end they were achieving; that his origin, his growth, his hopes and fears, his loves and his beliefs, are but the outcome of accidental collocations of atoms; that no fire, no heroism, no intensity of thought and feeling, can preserve an individual life beyond the grave; that all the labors of the ages, all the devotion, all the inspiration, all the noonday brightness of human genius, are destined to extinction in the vast death of the solar system, and that the whole temple of Man's achievement must inevitably be buried beneath the debris of a universe in ruins—all these things, if not quite beyond dispute, are yet so nearly certain, that no philosophy which rejects them can hope to stand. Only within the scaffolding of these truths, only on the firm foundation of unyielding despair, can the soul's habitation henceforth be safely built.[14]

Here is an honest man speaking. This is what he honestly believes. Since this is apparently a universal reaction of people, the Protestant faith asserts that the result of sin is meaninglessness. Whenever people have contemplated the human predicament in ruthless honesty, they have despaired. The oldest Greek Hedonists who tried to persuade people to live lives dedicated to the pursuit of pleasure finally turned into advocates of suicide (Hegesias) for the same reason that Bertrand Russell has given here—the ultimate meaninglessness of life. Who can read a Greek tragedy and fail to be overwhelmed by the brilliant clarity with which it proclaims the meaninglessness of all human efforts?

The Protestant faith says that this is the result of sin. Because of their revolt against God human beings are separated from the one source of meaning and eventually overwhelmed by meaninglessness. Even if the sage can escape involvement in the strife and the bickering that wastes the time of the fool, he soon realizes that meaninglessness is the alternative to the foolishness of strife and conflict. Therefore the Preacher says,

> Remember also your Creator in the days of your youth, before the evil days come, and the years draw nigh, when you will say, "I have no pleasure in them"; before the sun and the light, and the moon, and the stars are darkened and the clouds return after the rain; in the day when the keepers of the house tremble, and the strong men are bent, and the grinders cease because they are few, and those that look through the windows

are dimmed, and the doors on the street are shut; when the sound of the grinding is low, and one rises up at the voice of a bird, and all the daughters of song are brought low; they are afraid also of what is high, and terrors are in the way; the almond tree blossoms, the grasshopper drags itself along and desire fails; because man goes to his eternal home, and the mourners go about the streets; before the silver cord is snapped, or the golden bowl is broken, or the pitcher is broken at the fountain, or the wheel broken at the cistern, and the dust returns to the earth as it was, and the spirit returns to God who gave it. Vanity of vanities, says the Preacher; all is vanity. (Eccles. 12:1–8)

The other result of sin is death. This is stated briefly and strikingly in the New Testament in the sentence: "The wages of sin is death" (Rom. 6:23). This is all there is to it! The universal revolt of the human race against its Creator results in universal death. Everybody dies; there are no exceptions. To live means to die and there is no escape. The poets and sages of the human race have faithfully proclaimed this fact. Shakespeare declares:

> Tomorrow, and tomorrow, and tomorrow,
> Creeps in this petty pace from day to day,
> To the last syllable of recorded time;
> And all our yesterdays have lighted fools
> The way to dusty death. Out, out, brief candle!
> Life's but a walking shadow, a poor player
> That struts and frets his hour upon the stage
> And then is heard no more. . . .[15]

Yet while death is the destiny of the human race, our entire culture is so designed as to avoid the very mention of the word. Death is simply not referred to in polite society, and we make every effort to remain unaware of it. In his little story *The Loved One* Evelyn Waugh showed how far our civilization is willing to go in order to preserve the illusion that nobody we care about really dies, even to the establishment of mortuaries for household pets. But one does not have to get very old to realize that our own efforts are no more successful than the efforts of the ancient Egyptians who tried to avoid the stark reality of death through embalming.

Our attempts to gloss over the inescapable fact of death by means of sophisticated mortality statistics have proven equally futile. Whatever the health professions may temporarily accomplish the ultimate result is always the same. One thousand years ago one hundred percent of all people died; one hundred years ago one hundred percent of all people died; and today the percentage is the same. In spite of the outrageous increase in medical costs over the last decade, the life expectancy has not lengthened significantly during the same period of time, and the death rate per thousand population went from 9.3 in 1955 to 9.4 in 1972. As in previous ages, so now, the wages of sin is death—and, asserts the Protestant faith, as we are all sinners, we shall all, without exception, die.

There is nothing "subjective" about this result of sin. It is not merely the allegedly morbid imaginations of the religious which cause people to die. Death is real for everybody. It is as objective as anything we experience. In no way does it depend for its reality upon the individual's faith or unbelief. Obviously we do not have to "believe" in strife in order to have our life made miserable by strife and conflict. Strife and conflict are part of the given, part of the world in which we live. Even if we personally should make a heroic effort to avoid all strife, it is possible for others to involve us in their strife against our will. Again, there is nothing merely subjective about Hiroshima, where the first atom bomb killed thousands; this was not a state of mind. Strife is a reality which as a result of sin confronts us everywhere. In a less dramatic sense, the personal bickering and quarreling which may make the home life of an individual miserable is not merely a state of mind; it is often the most real experience a person has in his entire life.

To be sure, meaninglessness is more subjective. It is not so objectively demonstrable as death and strife. But it is real nevertheless. And in some ways it is worse than either strife or death. We can put up with a lot of conflict if we believe that the conflict has some ultimate meaning. It is not impossible to die courageously for country or for friends if we believe that country and friends are worth dying for. If we believe that such a death "makes sense," it is quite possible to face it with equanimity and to say with Nathan Hale, "I only regret that I have but one life to lose for my country." But if the acid of meaningless has destroyed all genuine friendship and all spontaneous loyalty and patriotism—then indeed we have become more miserable than those who have to fight or die. Though perhaps the least objective of the effects of sin, meaninglessness may be the worst of all because it is the most difficult to face and the hardest to bear.

But whatever value judgment we may make, whatever our attitude, the Protestant faith claims that strife, meaninglessness, and death are all three the inevitable results of sin. To some degree all human beings are aware of them.

The Protestant faith asserts that the entire world as we know it is involved in human sin. The world which the human race knows participates in its sin and suffers the consequences. In a sense sin has cosmic significance. It does not merely affect the individual human being; it affects everything with which the human race comes into contact. This again has been described by the Apostle Paul in a very colorful phrase: "We know that the whole creation has been groaning in travail together until now" (Rom. 8:22). As a result of our revolt against God, we have the ability to inject our own failure and strife and meaninglessness into all things we touch.

War, atomic death, genocide are ways in which sin involves the whole world. Human beings do not only destroy each other in war, they destroy nature as well. With ever more powerful bombs they poison the air and the water not only for other human beings but possibly for all life on earth. Through the increased radiation level, which is the result of experimental bombs, the heredity of hundreds of generations yet unborn may be jeopardized. At least this seems to be the view of some of the most competent experts. And all this is the result of sin for the entire world. But while it may be fairly easy to see these universal effects of human revolt against God in case of war and atomic experimentation, the same harmful consequences, even if more subtly, result from human greed. What the human race has done to its rivers and forests, to its soil and air, affects not only humanity but all those creatures who share this earth with the human race.

Because it means easy profit, because it is cheap for the politicians who administer our cities, we poison our rivers and turn them into sewers. The vile polluted smell of some of America's great rivers bears witness to the results of our greed. So does the land turned into a dust bowl, and the desert left behind by strip-mining operations. All the earth is involved in human greed and has to pay the price. There are innumerable ways in which human cruelty, selfishness, greed, in short, human sin, affect all creation.

Even if Albert Schweitzer can hardly be considered an exponent of classical Protestantism, his doctrine of reverence for life, which insists. that humanity has the obligation to respect all life, derives from the witness of Scripture. Schweitzer said: "A man is ethical only when life, as such, is sacred to him, that of plants and animals as that of his fellow men, and when he devotes himself helpfully to all life that is in need of help."[16] This earth does not belong to the human beings who inhabit it temporarily; they are not owners, but merely stewards and administrators of God's possessions. This insight is clearly a part of the Protestant faith. The complete disregard and the sovereign selfishness with which human beings dispose of all those riches which they are supposed to administer are surely the result of sin. *The whole creation has been groaning in travail together until now.*

But what about the relationship of "natural" catastrophes and sin? Is there any special theological meaning to earthquakes and hurricanes, floods and other disturbances? There was a time in which Protestants, and probably all Christians, would have answered this question with an unambiguous *yes!* There wasn't a comet in the sky which was not believed to have religious significance. Every natural catastrophe was immediately explained as a direct act of divine punishment.

Here again, the Protestant faith does not offer an abstract interpretation of meteorological or astronomical phenomena. Whenever this has been done under the cover of Christianity, Christians have forsaken their principal message, that God speaks to human beings personally and they must respond as persons. But if it is understood that the church does not compete with the weather bureau or the observatory, all sorts of events can in fact become occasions for faith. A natural catastrophe may become the incident through which God speaks to me. Or the absence of such an expected catastrophe may become an incident which God uses to address me. But such an interpretation is vastly different from the glib explanations of earthquakes and floods as punishment for other people. The use of "natural catastrophes" to demonstrate the power of God to punish the people we don't like comes from a spirit different from the Spirit who reveals himself in the New Testament. It is significant that Jesus rejects this easy, moralizing interpretation of natural catastrophes when it is suggested to him in the Gospel of Luke:

> There were some present at that very time who told him of the Galileans whose blood Pilate had mingled with their sacrifices. And he answered them, "Do you think that these Galileans were worse sinners than all the other Galileans, because they suffered thus? I tell you, No; but unless you repent you will all likewise perish."

And then he continues, referring to a major accident:

> "Or those eighteen upon whom the tower in Siloam fell and killed them, do you think that they were worse offenders than all the others who dwelt in Jerusalem? I tell you, No; but unless you repent you will all likewise perish." (Luke 13:1–5)

In view of the clear-cut statement of Christ that such catastrophes are not to be used in a moralizing manner—and in the light of the entire book of Job in the Old Testament which indicates that personal misfortune should not be used by the outsider in such a moralizing manner—it is hard to understand why occasionally Christians have insisted on drawing nice comforting lessons from the catastrophes that have befallen other people. This is certainly a sub-Christian way to look at God's dealings with men and women.

Perhaps the most unfortunate example of this moralizing approach has been the complacent and self-righteous manner in which Christians have dealt with the suffering of the Jewish people since the fall of Jerusalem in 70 A.D. Instead of helping their Jewish brothers and sisters in Christian love they sometimes acclaimed their plight as divine punishment for their rejection of Jesus. The appropriate theological position of classical Protestantism in regard to the betrayal and crucifixion of Jesus is best expressed in the hymn by Johann Heermann (1585–1647):

> Who was the guilty? Who brought this upon thee?
> Alas, my treason, Jesus, hath undone thee.
> Twas I, Lord Jesus. I it was denied thee:
> I crucified thee![17]

The Protestant faith rejects simultaneously the idealistic theodicy, which claims that this is the "best of all possible worlds," as well as the "naturalistic" despair, which insists that we are "lost in the stars." Both views have been submitted. Those who have said that this is the best of all possible worlds have claimed that all the evil that we do in fact observe is merely the opportunity for God to show his goodness.

No less a philosopher than the great Gottfried Wilhelm Leibnitz defended the goodness of God against all attacks in this manner in his book *Theodicy*. But the underlying assumption of such an effort is that God needs such a defense. That he must appear before the judgment throne of human reason and morality is completely out of order as far as the Protestant faith is concerned. The Protestant faith confesses with the Apostle Paul: "Let God be true, but every man a liar" (Rom. 3:4) God does not need to be vindicated before the tribunal of the human race. It is rather the human being who needs to be justified before God.

On the other hand, the Protestant faith rejects with equal vigor the despair of those who claim that the life of the universe and the life of people make no sense whatsoever. Such despair itself is for the Christian a result of sin. Indeed it is one of the most dangerous forms in which sin appears. Despair cuts people off from God's mercy more effectively than any other sin. There are those who would say that Judas Iscariot was doomed not for his betrayal of Jesus but because he despaired of God's mercy. Had he gone to the Cross after his betrayal when he repented of what he had done and asked the man hanging on the Cross for forgiveness—it would have been granted to him. What doomed Judas was not his crime but the despair that followed the crime. The Protestant faith rejects this despair just as firmly as it rejects the shallow optimism of the people who assert that this is the best of all possible worlds. Those who speak optimistically of the best of all possible worlds seem to have far too shallow a view of sin and its ravages; those, on the other hand, who claim that despair is the only stance possible for human beings have far too limited a vision of the God who has spoken to them in Jesus Christ.

These false alternatives, an optimism out of touch with the seriousness of the human situation and a pessimism oblivious to the greatness of God's love, indicate that people today have trouble with the basic Christian concepts of "sin" and "salvation."

Indeed, one of the major problems which an interpretation of the Protestant faith confronts is the fact that the word *sin*, which has been used so frequently in these pages, is largely meaningless to us. Although it meant a great deal to Martin Luther and John Calvin, to John Wesley and Jonathan Edwards, it conveys little meaning to the men and women of our time. Is there a reason why this once powerful and lucid word has neither force nor clarity today?

A large number of factors have apparently contributed to this development. Three seem of sufficient importance to deserve some attention here. First, there is the general mood of relativism, which affects every aspect of our life. Many people no longer believe that "right" and "wrong" are words that make much sense. They say that "right" and "wrong" are completely "relative" to the situation and mean that it depends entirely on the prejudices of the group or the individual whether a particular action is considered right or its very opposite. In one society murder may be frowned upon, in another society murder may become a sign of distinction. Among some people the eating of human flesh may be considered terribly evil, while in another society it may be the condition for membership in the most distinguished group. Examples like this have been produced in large numbers, and all have tended to make the notion of sin appear obsolete. Of course, these examples are important to show that it is not easy to discover an "absolute norm." It is true that quite often in the history of the human race people have confused their particular way of doing things with the absolute norm. Observing this, the Greek philosopher Xenophanes commented 2,500 years ago,

Mortals fancy gods are born, and wear clothes, and have voice and form like themselves. Yet if oxen and lions had hands, and could paint with their hands, and fashion images, as men do, they would make the pictures and images of their gods in their own likeness; horses would make them like horses, oxen like oxen.[18]

Relativism has rendered an important service by showing that what was considered the absolute law in one society did not turn out to be very absolute when all societies were taken into consideration.

Even when this significant contribution of relativism to the clarification of human behavior is granted, this idea of the relativity of all concepts of right and wrong can also be carried too far. But it is the popular, unscientific "poor man's relativism" which has subverted all moral standards. The belief that "right" and "wrong" are arbitrary has made it difficult to explain what the Protestant faith means when it speaks of sin. Sin is revolt against God, but if God's will is not known to people or is even unknowable, the concept of sin does not make a great deal of sense.

We have discussed the Protestant faith's answer to this problem previously. The Protestant faith asserts that God's law is known and that there is right and wrong. No amount of statistics can change the facts that lying will make human communication eventually impossible and that homosexual behavior is sterile and, if consistently and exclusively practiced, dooms the human race to extinction. These are the facts of life which give the lie to those people who claim that all moral standards are equally valid or invalid, that they are in fact meaningless. Yet moral relativism has made it difficult for modern people to take sin as seriously as it must be taken according to the Protestant faith.

The same can be said about naturalism. Here we have the assertion that all knowledge, even moral knowledge, is empirical. The key to the understanding of the human being is not his unique relationship to God but rather his relationship to nature. To the "man on the street" it means that human beings are no less and no more a part of nature than any other animal. Whatever he does he does as an animal and it is therefore natural. Just as one would not speak of the sinful behavior of dogs or cats, it would be equally senseless to speak of the sinful actions of human beings. The assumption is that the human being is merely animal. He is merely nature. To quote the eloquent B. F. Skinner again: "[Joseph Wood] Krutch has argued that whereas the traditional view [of the human being] supports Hamlet's exclamation, 'how like a god!' Pavlov, the behavioral scientist, emphasized, 'How like a dog!' But that was a step forward."[19] This, of course, runs counter to the definition of the human being given by the Protestant faith. Here each human being stands in a unique relationship to God. He is not merely animal; he is human. As a human being he is uniquely responsible to God. His relationship to the Creator is different from the relationship of a dog, a cat, or even a chimpanzee. The popular versions of naturalism, however, have obscured the difference, and as long as people believe that the human being is merely a highly developed animal the notion of sin cannot make much sense to them. The idea that the human being is in revolt against God is meaningful only if human beings stand in a unique relationship to God, according to the Protestant faith. The notion of sin has to be understood from this point of view. People today, however, tend to ignore this unique relationship between themselves and God, and thus their sense of sin is affected. If the human being is merely an animal it is no more reasonable to try him for his offenses, to blame him for his sins, than it would be to try a rattlesnake for striking, to blame a cat for chasing mice, a mouse for stealing cheese. The notion of sin has become meaningless for many people in the twentieth century because of the widely held view that we can explain the human being as merely animal apart from his origin and destiny in God.

A third factor which has contributed to the difficulties of communicating the insights of the Protestant faith to modern people is the superficial psychologizing and psychoanalyzing which have become part of our civilization. Sigmund Freud and his associates have made important contributions to human self-understanding. It would be foolish and obscurantist to deny the profound insights into the human mind which depth psychology in all its various forms has provided. But when accepted by modern people as a religion offering salvation, depth psychology can make it difficult for a person to comprehend that sin describes the broken relationship between God and him.

For Freud religion is the result of the Oedipus complex. It is the result of man's guilt, traceable to the dim past, when, according to Freud, human beings traveled in herds, and the young men killed the father and took over the females.[20] This is not the place to debate the validity of these notions concerning the past history of man. Suffice it to say that most anthropologists and psychologists believe that Freud's theology is probably the weakest link in his system. But quite apart from the accuracy of his theories, their effect on the understanding of the Christian faith among those who are influenced by Freud is considerable. Faith is reinterpreted into something quite different from trust; it becomes an expression of fear.

Religion is "neurotic" and prayer is "compulsive." All feelings of guilt and the consciousness of sin are considered dangerous. Especially when this kind of psychology has been popularized by novelists, amateur psychiatrists, and cocktail-party psychologists, sin becomes a "dangerous" notion which a healthy person must by all means throw overboard. These popularizers have tended to say that consciousness of sin is dangerous for a person's mental health. They claim that every effort has to be made to free mankind from all feelings of guilt. It has become fashionable to speak disdainfully of the "repressed" people who worry about sin. In this frequently garbled form depth psychology has become the property of all literate Americans and of a good many illiterate Americans as well. All these developments have made the interpretation of the concept of sin as held by the Protestant faith very difficult. For many modern people it no longer makes any sense.

While the reality of sin has been denied or rationalized away, the consequences of sin have become ever more apparent. The Protestant faith claims that the biblical witness does in fact describe the human situation most accurately. Thus, regardless of our subjective views of the meaning of life, the actual, observable, empirical life of sinful human beings has been blighted. Modern men and women may be able to deny the *existence* of sin. They may be able to discard the very notion as old-fashioned and irrelevant. Yet the Protestant faith insists that the *results* of sin are demonstrable, observable, and painfully apparent to anybody who looks at our age.

However successful modern people may have been in denying the existence of sin, they have been spectacularly unsuccessful in avoiding its consequences. This is not merely pious talk on the part of those who are committed to the Christian point of view. This is the universal witness of all those people who take time to observe our situation and then take the trouble of writing down their observations. It would take us too far afield to quote all the evidence adduced by those outside the Christian faith in support of this view. One example will have to suffice.

Nobody will accuse Jean-Paul Sartre of being a spokesman for Christianity, yet even a cursory reading of his plays and novels shows that he describes a situation identical with the human situation distorted by sin. The picture he shows is an accurate view of the situation of men and women without God according to the Protestant faith. In his play *No Exit* Sartre shows three very modern and emancipated people who are being destroyed by sin. Significantly, the play takes place in hell. The three people are in a drawing room, two women, Estelle and Inez, and one man, Garcin. It is Garcin who finally discovers the secret of Sartre's hell. He says, "So this is hell, I'd never have believed it. You remember all we were told about torture-chambers, the fire and brimstone, the 'burning marl.' Old wives' tales! There is no need for red-hot pokers. Hell is—*other people!*"[21]

Sartre's pessimistic description of the human situation is eloquently supported by American authors. In every serious play, we encounter strife, meaninglessness, and death. This is the story of Willy Loman in Arthur Miller's *Death of a Salesman* and of Blanche in Tennessee Williams's *Streetcar Named Desire*. Everywhere the same message is being proclaimed. Modern people may have trouble understanding the theological concept of sin as used in the Protestant faith, but the consequences of sin are all about them. Whether we like it or not, whether it makes sense to us or not, whether we approve of it or not—the Protestant faith asserts: The wages of sin is death—and all the evidence seems to support this analysis of the human condition.

NOTES

1. To the following, cf. Robert L. Calhoun, *What Is Man* (New York: Association Press, 1939).

2. Ibid., p. 21.

3. G. K. Chesterton, *The Everlasting Man* (New York: Dodd, Mead & Company, 1925).

4. Friedrich Nietzsche, *The Philosophy of Nietzsche* (New York: Random House, The Modern Library, 1927), p. 91.

5. Jaroslav Pelikan, *Fools for Christ* (Phildelphia: Fortress Press, 1955), p. 74.

6. Ibid., p. 76.

7. Fyodor Dostoyevsky, *The Brothers Karamazov* (New York: Random House, The Modern Library, 1929), p. 270.

8. B. F. Skinner, *Beyond Freedom and Dignity* (New York: Bantam Books, Inc., 1972), p. 205.

9. Ibid., p. 191.

10. John Calvin, *Institutes of the Christian Religion* (Philadelphia: Presbyterian Board of Education, 1936), book II, chap. III, sec. 2.

11. David Riesman, *The Lonely Crowd* (New Haven, Conn.: Yale University Press, 1950), p. 154.

12. J. L. Liebman, *Peace of Mind* (New York: Simon & Schuster, Inc., 1946), pp. 172–173.

13. *The Service Book and Hymnal of the Lutheran Church in America*, No. 372.

14. Bertrand Russell, *Selected Papers of Bertrand Russell* (New York: Random House, The Modern Library, 1927), pp. 1–3. Used by permission of original publisher, George Allen & Unwin Ltd.

15. Shakespeare, *Macbeth*, Act V, sc. 5.

16. Albert Schweitzer, *Out of My Life and Thought* (New York: Holt, Rinehart, and Winston, Inc.), p. 232.

17. *Service Book and Hymnal of the Lutheran Church in America*, Hymn 85.

18. C. M. Bakewell, *Source Book in Ancient Philosophy* (New York: Charles Scribner's Sons, 1939), p. 8.

19. Skinner, *Beyond Freedom and Dignity*, p. 192.

20. Cf. "Totem and Taboo," *The Basic Writings of Sigmund Freud*, trans. and ed. Dr. A. A. Brill (New York: Random House, The Modern Library, 1938), pp. 807 ff.

21. Jean-Paul Sartre, *No Exit and Three Other Plays* (New York: Vintage Books, Inc., 1955), p. 47. Reprinted by permission of Alfred A. Knopf, Inc. and Vintage Books, Inc.

Chapter 6

THE DOCTRINE OF CHRIST

Because of their original and actual sin human beings are doomed to despair and eternal death. They experience the wrath of God. This is not only the description of a future state but of a present experience. While the experience is universal, the explanation for it varies greatly. The non-Christian will attribute his feeling of anxiety and despair to circumstances over which he has no control. The Christian, however, sees this situation as the result of his revolt against God. Human life is meaningless because humanity has torn itself away from the source of all being, from the power which alone can give direction and ultimate purpose to life. The Christian knows that his hopeless state is his own responsibility and not God's.

The Reasons for the Incarnation

People have broken the father-child relationship by their revolt against God, and classical Protestantism asserts that they cannot reestablish it out of their own power. While they can break the relationship they cannot restore it. It is as if a man were held by a friend while climbing a high mountain. Beneath him yawns an abyss. In this situation he can push the helping hand of his friend away. He can free himself from this helping interference. But once he has done so, he falls, and now he cannot reestablish the connection which he could dissolve. While he was free to push the friend away, he is not free to get a hold on him again. Through the very act of pushing him away his situation has radically changed. He is now hurtling through space and will surely be smashed on the ground unless something happens. But this is something which he cannot produce or control. It is entirely outside of his power. Søren Kierkegaard, dealing with this problem in his *Philosophical Fragments*, uses a very lucid illustration to make this point. He says:

> Suppose a child had been presented with a little sum of money, and could buy with it either a good book, for example, or a toy, both at the same price. If he buys the toy, can he then buy the book for the same money? Surely not, since the money is already spent. But perhaps he may go to the bookseller and ask him to make an exchange, letting him have the book in return for the toy. Will not the bookseller say: My dear child, your toy is not worth anything; it is true that when you still had the money you could have bought the book instead of the toy, but a toy is a peculiar kind of thing, for once it is bought it loses all value. Would not the child think that this was very strange? And so there was also a time when man could have bought either freedom or bondage at the same price, this being the soul's free choice and commitment in the choice. He chose bondage; but if he now comes forward with a proposal for an exchange, would not God reply: Undoubtedly there was a time when you could have bought whichever you pleased, but bondage is a very strange sort of thing; when it is bought it has absolutely no value, although the price paid for it was originally the same. Would not such an individual think this very strange? Again, suppose two opposing armies drawn up in the field, and that a knight arrives whom both armies invite to fight on their side; he makes his choice, is vanquished and taken prisoner. As prisoner he is brought before the victor, to whom he foolishly presumes to offer his services on the same terms as were extended to him before the battle. Would not the victor say to him: My friend, you are now my prisoner; there was indeed a time when you could have chosen differently, but now everything is changed.[1]

All men and women are in the unenviable position of the captured knight. They had a choice and they made the wrong choice. There is no way in which a person out of his own resources can unmake this decision.

The Protestant faith shares, with many sensitive views of the human situation, the awareness of the desperate predicament in which all human beings find themselves. But, important as this insight is, it is only part of the story. The Protestant faith asserts that God became a human being in Jesus Christ in order to bridge the gap which humanity established through its revolt. God became a human being in Jesus Christ in order to save the race. This translation of God into human form is called the "incarnation." It is a translation of God into human language. Without this incarnation God would be utterly incomprehensible to people. He must speak to them with words and symbols they can understand. Since they cannot understand God as *God*, God must translate himself into their terms so that they may understand God as a *human being*. This is what happened in Jesus Christ. Here God speaks to us in our language. This is not the sophisticated language of philosophy and of theology. He has chosen to speak the simple language of action and words understandable to children and childlike minds and yet beyond the comprehension of even the most profound. This is the message of Christmas. In a sense even the smallest child can get some meaning out of the baby in the manger who was Christ the Lord, worshiped by shepherds, wise men, and angels. He who cannot be contained by the universe is now in the arms of Mary and he who upholds with his power everything that is has become a baby—this message transcends all philosophical speculation.

Classical Protestantism asserts with one voice that Jesus Christ is both "very God of very God" and truly human subject to all the frailties and temptations of other human beings. As true man and true God he is the mediator between God and humanity. For the Protestant faith this term is reserved for Christ. As the Apostle Paul says: "For there is one God, and there is one mediator between God and men, the man Christ Jesus" (1 Tim. 2:5). While some people may consider other human beings as possible "mediators," on this point classical Protestantism is adamant. There is only one mediator, and he is Jesus Christ. He alone can translate God into our language; he alone can restore the relationship which the revolt of men and women has destroyed. For he is not only the teacher but above all the Savior.

The Humanity of Christ

It is important to understand what is meant when the Protestant faith asserts that Christ is truly human, for there have been times in the history of the Christian church when his humanity has been called into question. In the early church there were many people who denied Christ's humanity. They claimed that he was God but denied that he was a human being. To buttress their claims, these people, who were called Docetists, asserted that Jesus' body was not a true body but merely looked like a body. They said that God merely *appeared* in human form. As early as the end of the first century Ignatius, Bishop of Antioch, wrote against those who denied the humanity of Jesus Christ: "Be deaf therefore when anyone speaks to you apart from Jesus Christ, who was of the family of David, and of Mary, who was truly born, both ate and drank, who was truly persecuted under Pontius Pilate, was truly crucified and died."[2]

Against the Docetists and all others who deny the humanity of Christ the Protestant faith asserts that Jesus Christ was human, just as truly a human being as any one of us. He was conceived, was born, grew from infancy to manhood, was hungry and thirsty, was tired and sad, wept and rejoiced, suffered and died. For the Protestant faith Jesus Christ is a person who was born when Quirinius was governor of Syria and who died under Pontius Pilate. He was bound in history and time; he was limited in knowledge. We read in the New Testament that Jesus said concerning the end of the world: "But of that day and hour no one knows, not even the angels of heaven, nor the Son, but the Father only" (Matt. 24:36). This, say Protestant theologians, demonstrates that Jesus' humanity was so complete that it included such limitations as his knowledge of the future. However, this must not be understood as merely a piece of interesting information. Rather, this very humanity of Jesus Christ is a challenge and call to discipleship for the Christian. This is how the Apostle Paul interprets it:

> Have this mind among yourselves, which you have in Christ Jesus, who, though he was in the form of God, did not count equality with God a thing to be grasped, but emptied himself,

taking the form of a servant, being born in the likeness of men. And being found in human form he humbled himself and became obedient unto death, even death on a cross. (Phil. 2:5–8)

Not merely speculation but action, not merely thought but life, is the significance of Christ's humanity.

All this means that for the Protestant faith Jesus Christ is no abstract philosophical ideal but a real historical person. He is as real and historical as any other person who ever walked on this earth. He is no "ghost," no "poetic symbol," no "vision," but flesh of our flesh and blood of our blood. The humanity of Christ is also demonstrated in his relationship to the Father. He learns, he prays, he obeys, he is tempted and struggles, and finally exclaims, "Father, into thy hands I commit my spirit!" (Luke 23:46).

According to the Protestant faith there is no pretense about any of these expressions of Jesus' humanity. His temptations are not play-acting; they are real temptations, as real as any other human temptations. Protestants take much comfort from these temptations of Christ because they illuminate our own temptations. Because God became a human person in Jesus Christ, the Protestant faith asserts, temptation is not alien to him; in Jesus Christ God has shared even our temptations with us.

And the man Jesus Christ truly suffers. His suffering is not a show, a game of "let's pretend." It is the most real suffering imaginable. What makes the Lenten season so profoundly moving is that we see God share our human suffering. He is no mere spectator of the human tragedy. It is not a show which God is watching. Rather, the human tragedy is experienced by God in Jesus Christ. He suffers with us; he suffers in us. Christ shares not only humanity's physical suffering, when he is beaten and bleeding on the way to the Cross. He shares even our spiritual suffering, our loneliness and our despair. This is the meaning of Gethsemane. Here we see Jesus plead with his disciples that they should stay with him in that terrible night before his arrest, trial, and execution. He wants them to stay awake with him, to keep him company, to comfort him in these difficult hours. But the disciples fall asleep, and in these last hours Jesus is left all alone. He is not the conquering hero who knows exactly what he wants to do and how to do it, but a troubled man who knows anxiety and despair. This is what we read in the Gospel according to St. Matthew:

> And taking with him Peter and the two sons of Zebedee, he began to be sorrowful and troubled. Then he said to them, "My soul is very sorrowful, even to death; remain here and watch with me." And going a little farther he fell on his face and prayed, "My father, if it be possible, let this cup pass from me; nevertheless, not as I will, but as thou wilt." And he came to the disciples and found them sleeping. . . . (Matt. 26:37–40)

Here we meet a man who knows what trouble is and who needs companionship in his troubles. This is the most profound conviction of the Protestant faith and it is movingly expressed in some of the hymns of the church and also in the Negro spirituals when they sing, "Nobody knows the trouble I've seen—nobody knows but Jesus!"[3] Here we find a profound awareness characteristic of the Protestant faith of the reality and the depth of the suffering and despair which Jesus experienced and which he shared with all people. No human suffering, no human anxiety, is alien to him.

This is perhaps most profoundly expressed in the word from the Cross: "My God, my God, why hast thou forsaken me?" (Mark 15:34). Here Jesus experiences in his person the profound separation of each human being from God which is the result of sin and leads to the catastrophe of human life. For the Protestant faith this means that nobody is ever so forsaken by God that his experience is not shared by God himself in the man Jesus Christ, and this includes even the ultimate human experience, the experience of death itself. Jesus Christ suffered, was crucified, died, and was buried! Because Jesus Christ is a real human person, nothing human is alien to God.

Because of Christ's humanity all he does is relevant to us. In the New Testament we are not confronted by a hero of Greek mythology, a being which is half human and half divine. The Greeks, indeed, had many such hybrid beings. Achilles and Hercules, for example, were not truly human nor truly divine, but somewhere in between, a peculiar blend of humanity and divinity. Against all

164

these figures of Greek antiquity the Protestant faith asserts that Jesus Christ was a real human being. He is the son of Mary, our brother and our example.

The Divinity of Christ

But this is only one side of the story. Complementary to it and equally important is the assertion of the divinity of Christ. The same Jesus Christ who is a real human being is also truly God. This confession has many and inexhaustible implications. For the Protestant faith it means that when Jesus Christ speaks, God speaks. In him we meet God the Creator, the Lord, the Judge, the Father. For the Protestant faith there is no other way to meet God than in Jesus Christ. Apart from Christ we cannot know God. Apart from Christ God remains for us always the unknown God, the hidden God. In Christ we meet him face to face. In Christ God reveals himself to men and women.

It is in the very proclamation of Christ that we find described his unique relationship to the Father. "All things have been delivered to me by my Father; and no one knows the Son except the Father, and no one knows the Father except the Son and any one to whom the Son chooses to reveal him" (Matt. 11:27). Or we read in John 14:9, 11: "He who has seen me has seen the Father. . . . Believe me that I am in the Father and the Father in me. . . ." It is Jesus Christ himself who makes these claims, according to the New Testament. After his resurrection Jesus said to the disciples: "Where two or three are gathered in my name, there am I in the midst of them" (Matt. 18:20). And a little later we read in the same Gospel: "All authority in heaven and on earth has been given to me. . . . lo, I am with you always to the close of the age" (Matt. 28:18, 20).

The New Testament is full of the faith in Jesus Christ as true God. In Col. 1:17 we read about him: "He is before all things, and in him all things hold together." In the book of Revelation the Christ proclaims: "I am the Alpha and the Omega, . . . who is and who was and who is to come, the Almighty" (Rev. 1:8). In other words, according to the proclamation of the Bible and thus as an integral part of the Protestant faith the human being Jesus, the

165

Christ, is at the same time the eternal God. In Heb. 13:8, the Apostolic Church proclaims: "Jesus Christ is the same yesterday and today and for ever"—thus confessing that this man Jesus Christ is at the same time the Immutable God.

In this context the statements in the Gospel of John concerning the eternal Christ must be understood:

> In the beginning was the Word, and the Word was with God and the Word was God. He was in the beginning with God; all things were made through him, and without him was not anything made that was made. (John 1:1–3)

For the Protestant faith this is not idle theological speculation concerning some abstract and theoretical proposition about Jesus Christ. On the contrary, it is the language of worship which adores the Savior. The Christian church knows him as free from the chains of time and space. His omnipotence and omnipresence are not logically derived from some theory concerning the nature of God; they are, rather, the way in which the Almighty Lord has always and everywhere confronted his people.

The fact that Jesus Christ is true God suffuses and permeates everything that has been said about his humanity. At the same time the fact that Jesus Christ is a real human being gives relevance to the worshipful confession of his divinity, making it a call to faith and love.

Therefore the church sings:

> Thou art the King of Glory, O Christ;
> Thou art the everlasting Son of the Father.
> When thou tookest upon thee to deliver man:
> Thou didst humble thyself to be born of a virgin.
> When thou hadst overcome the sharpness of death:
> Thou didst open the kingdom of heaven to all believers.
> (From the *Te Deum Laudamus*)

Indeed Christ did humble himself, but even in this humiliation, this voluntary giving up of the exercise of his divine power, the Protestant faith confesses that Christ was truly God. Simone Weil saw this when she wrote:

166

Christ healing the sick, raising the dead, etc., that is the humble, human, almost low part of his mission. The supernatural part is the sweat of blood, the unsatisfied longing for human consolation, the supplication that he might be spared, the sense of being abandoned by God. The abandonment at the supreme moment of the crucifixion, what an abyss of love on both sides! "My God, my God, why hast thou forsaken me?" There we have the real proof that Christianity is something divine.[4]

The Christian church will speak of this Christ as having power to forgive sins and raise the dead. He is the object of faith and worship with the Father and the Holy Spirit. As the Gospel of John quotes Jesus: "I am the way, and the truth, and the life; no one comes to the Father, but by me" (John 14:6). Classical Protestantism has been unanimous in the assertion that Jesus Christ is true God, the second person of the Holy Trinity.

Luther's explanation of the Second Article of the Apostles' Creed is this: "I believe that Jesus Christ, true God, begotten of the Father from eternity, and also true man, born of the Virgin Mary, is my Lord." This is basically the faith of the mainstream of Protestantism everywhere. However, it must be added that it is impossible to dissociate the message of Christ from the Christ who proclaims this message. It is the person of Christ, the fact that he is God speaking to people, which gives validity to the message. At the same time the message is in conformity with the messenger. It is a fitting message corresponding to the source.

For the Protestant faith it is impossible to accept the message without accepting him who proclaimed it. There have always been people who have liked what Christ had to say but who did not want to yield to him who said it. While wanting to adopt the truths proclaimed by Christ, they rejected the claims which Christ made about himself in connection with these truths. But the message cannot be separated from the spokesman. If the spokesman is a megalomaniac, a man who suffers from some mental disorder which makes him think he is the son of God, then it is neither intelligent nor safe to accept his message. This is the dilemma of those who like the message but do not accept the messenger.

Whenever Christians have given up the faith in the person of Christ, they have discarded faith in his message soon afterward. Without the authority of the person of Christ his message is of little value.

It is equally impossible to accept the Christ without accepting his message. This too has been tried. There have always been some people who have been fascinated by the idea of Christ, over-whelmed by the speculative grandeur of Christology, the doctrine of Christ, but who have ignored what Christ said or did. These people have been most willing to believe statements and proposi-tions about Christ's humanity and divinity but have not seemed equally ready to follow him, obey him, and be his disciples.

Classical Protestantism has always emphasized that the Christ and his gospel are inseparable. The validity of the gospel depends upon the authority of the Christ, and the authority of the Christ in the life of the Christian depends upon the willingness of the Chris-tian to let the gospel transform his life. It is as futile to say "yes" to Christ and "no" to his gospel as it is to say "yes" to his gospel and "no" to the Christ. Although both of these confused responses have been tried, classical Protestantism has insisted that the "yes" to the gospel depends upon the "yes" to the Christ and that "yes" to the Christ must find expression in a "yes" to his gospel.

In the light of what has now been said about the divinity of Christ, is it really possible to maintain his true humanity? Does not the fact of his holiness and sinlessness detract from his true man-hood? The Letter to the Hebrews states that he is "holy, blameless, unstained, separated from sinners, exalted above the heavens" (Heb. 7:26). St. Paul writes that Christ "knew no sin" (2 Cor. 5:21). The First Letter of Peter refers to him symbolically as "a lamb without blemish or spot" (1 Pet. 1:19). And in the Gospel of John we read that Jesus challenged his opponents to convict him of sin (John 8:46). Grounded in the biblical witness the classical Protestant faith proclaims that Jesus Christ is sinless. He is not in revolt against God—his life is a life of obedience, surrender, and fel-lowship with the Father. But rather than detracting from his hu-manity this holiness makes Jesus Christ the *true* human person. Men and women in revolt against God are false human beings, people cut off from their roots. To see what God wants all people to be, one must look at Jesus Christ, the true human person.

This is what theologians of the Christian church have meant when they called Jesus Christ the second Adam. He is the alternative to Adam. The Apostle Paul expressed it this way:

> For as by a man came death, by a man has come also the resurrection of the dead. For as in Adam all die, so also in Christ shall all be made alive. (1 Cor. 15:21, 22)

Humanity knows now not only what the pattern of estrangement and revolt against God is like and will lead to; it knows also what the pattern of obedience to God is like and will lead to. Through Christ another alternative has come into human history. Christ has made the pattern of obedience and fellowship possible.

If a Protestant were to try to define what the human life is supposed to be, he would not point to any Christian, be he ever so outstanding; he would point to Christ, in whom the human possibilities under God have been fully revealed. This is what it means that Jesus Christ is "the second Adam." In him we see humanity at its best. Jesus Christ is what human beings should be and can be according to God's holy will.

No Protestant discussion of the person of Christ would be complete without a reference to the climactic event of his earthly life, the resurrection. The resurrection of Christ is the deed of God which explains to the Christian the origin and destiny of the church. If Christians did not believe in the resurrection, if Christ had not been raised from the dead—then all the things said initially about the tragedy of human existence would still be true. Christ's death would be the murder of another Socrates, a good man who was killed by an evil age. This would still only show that "you can't win," that "the dice are loaded." Life would still be only the tale told by the idiot full of sound and fury, signifying nothing.

But we are confronted by the fact of the Christian church, which has proclaimed from the very beginning that God raised Jesus Christ from the dead. In other words, the crooked politicians and the corrupt ecclesiastical dignitaries who had Christ crucified were not victorious. The Cross is not the end—it is merely the beginning.

To a world which claimed that it had killed Christ the early Christians answered that Christ lives. They did not merely say that, they were willing to die for it. They knew it to be true, because they had experienced it in person. The fact that Christ had overcome death took away all the terror from death and made the Christians who believed in the resurrection invincible.

Every effort was made to destroy this message and to hush it up, for it had a demoralizing effect on the Roman Empire. If your power is built on the fact that you can exterminate people, then your power will be undermined if people learn that although you may be able to kill them, they will live again. This "good news" of the early Christians was the kind of message which could not be suppressed by force. Every effort was made—thousands and hundreds of thousands were killed throughout the centuries to suppress the message that death has no power. But for every Christian who was killed, others who saw him die without fear were converted to Christianity, so that the early Christians could say, "The blood of the martyrs is the seed of the church!"

The faith in the resurrection of Christ explains the existence of the Christian church. Without this faith the Christian church would never have come into being, and should it ever lose this faith it will not last very long. The resurrection and the message of Christ are mutually interdependent. The resurrection is God's confirmation of the gospel. This is why the Apostle Paul says:

> If Christ has not been raised, your faith is futile and you are still in your sins. . . . But in fact Christ has been raised from the dead, the first fruits of those who have fallen asleep. (1 Cor. 15:17, 20)

While it is generally admitted that the resurrection of Christ is the crowning event of his life, some Christians would put equal stress upon his miraculous birth. In view of the fact that neither the Apostle Paul nor the Gospel of John even mentions the circumstances of his birth, such an emphasis seems unjustified. The tendency among some Christians to make the belief in the virgin birth into a theological shibboleth is unfortunate because it has effectively obscured the meaning of the church's proclamation that Jesus Christ was born of the Virgin Mary. Yet it is part of the faith of an overwhelming majority of all Christians that this birth was extraordinary and different from all other human births. Most Protestants believe that in a unique sense God was the author of the human life of Jesus. Since this doctrine has become controversial among Protestants in the nineteenth and twentieth centuries, it might be in order to try to explain what this doctrine does and does not mean.

For the Protestant faith the doctrine of the virgin birth does not imply a depreciation of sex, nor is it an attempt to provide a spectacular beginning for Jesus' life. If we remember the temper of the times in which Jesus was born, we will note that a virgin giving birth to a child was not particularly spectacular; in that age such events were considered quite possible. This was a prescientific age and the law of cause and effect was not held to be insurmountable. If the early Christians wanted to invent a spectacular origin for Christ, the virgin birth appears to have been a fairly unauspicious choice. According to Greek mythology Pallas Athene, a goddess of the Greeks, had jumped fully armed out of the head of Zeus. This was indeed a spectacular beginning, and in comparison with this type of story current in the Hellenistic world the virgin mother in the stable surrounded by shepherds does not seem very extravagant.

Rather than a proof of the divinity of Christ, the doctrine of the virgin birth is for the Protestant faith, at least for the many Protestants who take this doctrine seriously, a part of the emphasis on the central significance of "by grace alone," which we discussed at the very beginning. We said then, and we repeat now, that one of Protestantism's main theses is the assertion that men and women are saved and brought into fellowship with God through God's action and not because of anything they can do. The doctrine of the virgin birth underlines this sovereign grace of God. It proclaims that God gives the Savior to the human race. Christ is God's gift to mankind. Humanity cannot claim to have saved itself in Jesus Christ. God saved people in Jesus Christ "by grace alone," and this fact is safeguarded by the doctrine of the virgin birth.

For almost all Christians, however, the doctrine of the virgin birth is the result of faith in Christ and not its cause. Protestants, even those Protestants who greatly stress the importance of the virgin birth, will insist that they believe in the virgin birth because they believe in Christ and not that they believe in Christ because of the virgin birth. Belief in the virgin birth is the result of faith in Christ rather than its condition!

Ultimately the person of Christ is for the Protestant faith a secret of God's grace. No theological statement can exhaustively describe what is essentially an experience of the Christian individual within the Christian community. If one listens carefully to the words of the Christmas hymns of the church, one can gain some insight into the nature of the Christian faith as faith in Christ. For adoration and worship are the only adequate response to God's gift. A Christmas hymn by Charles Wesley may sometimes communicate the faith better than any amount of theological analysis. Thus the church sings:

> Hark! The herald Angels sing, "Glory to the newborn King;
> Peace on earth and mercy mild, God and sinners reconciled!"
> Joyful all ye nations rise, Join the triumph of the skies,
> With th' angelic host proclaim, "Christ is born in Bethlehem."
> Hark! the herald Angels sing, "Glory to the new-born King."
>
> Christ, by highest heaven adored, Christ the everlasting Lord;
> Late in time behold him come, Off-spring of a virgin's womb!
> Veiled in flesh, the God-head see, Hail th' incarnate Deity!
> Pleased as Man with men to appear, Jesus our Immanuel here!
>
> Hail, the heavenly Prince of Peace, Hail the Sun of Righteousness!
> Light and life to all he brings, Risen with healing in his wings.
> Mild he lays his glory by, Born that Man no more may die:
> Born to raise the sons of earth; Born to give them second birth.
>
> Come, Desire of nations, come, Fix in us thy humble home;
> O, to all thyself impart, Formed in each believing heart!
> Hark! the herald Angels sing, "Glory to the new-born King;
> Peace on earth, and mercy mild, God and sinners reconciled!"

Very briefly and very simply, and yet very profoundly, this is the Protestant faith as far as the person of Christ is concerned.

The Work of Christ

What does the Protestant faith teach about the work of Christ? According to the teaching of classical Protestantism the work has been divided into three parts: the work of prophet, priest, and king. Christ's work is prophetic because he proclaims uniquely and definitively the will and purpose of God for humanity. No other proclamation can possibly surpass or replace the proclamation of God in Jesus Christ. Christ is the definitive and final expression of God's will for people; he is not merely a stage in the self-disclosure of God, he himself is the self-disclosure of God.

This assertion has significant implications. It makes it impossible for Protestants to expect greater revelations or other revelations which will contradict or surpass the revelation in Christ. There are religious groups who accept all revelations as partially valid, and all religions as true. For them Christ is one of many inspired prophets who communicates some partial information about God. This position cannot be taken by the Protestant faith. The Protestant faith claims: "No one has ever seen God; the only Son, who is in the bosom of the Father, he has made him known" (John 1:18). The Protestant faith asserts that Christ and his teachings are the standard or criterion by which all religious truth must be measured. Compared with the proclamation of Christ all other proclamations are of secondary importance. Christ gives the ultimate interpretation and revelation of God's will.

Next, what is the priestly work of Christ according to the Protestant faith? Perhaps this question is best answered with the quotation from Isaiah 53 which was cited before: The priestly office was fulfilled when "he has borne our griefs and carried our sorrows; . . . he was wounded for our transgressions, he was bruised for our iniquities; upon him was the chastisement that made us whole, . . . the Lord has laid on him the iniquity of us all" (Isa. 53:4–6).

This idea, that through Christ's death on the Cross the abyss that separates the human race from God has been bridged, is known as the doctrine of the atonement. The atonement for humanity is Christ's work as priest. There are numerous passages in the New Testament which describe this aspect of the work of Christ. In Romans we read: "For if while we were enemies we were reconciled to God by the death of his Son, much more, now that we are reconciled, shall we be saved by his life" (Rom. 5:10). Perhaps the most profoundly simple passage expressing this doctrine of the atonement is the following:

> Beloved, let us love one another; for love is of God, and he who loves is born of God and knows God. He who does not love does not know God; for God is love. In this the love of God was made manifest among us, that God sent his only Son into the world, so that we might live through him. In this is love, not that we loved God but that he loved us and sent his Son to be the expiation for our sins. Beloved, if God so loved us, we also ought to love one another. (1 John 4:7–11)

There are innumerable other passages in which this notion of expiation, of Christ being the "ransom" and the reconciler between God and humankind, is expressed. That the Christian church in general and the Protestant faith in particular teaches that men and women are reconciled with God through the work of Christ, particularly his death on the Cross, is evident. However, how this atonement is to be interpreted is less evident. That Christ reconciles God and the sinner is universally accepted by Christians. That he accomplishes this reconciliation through his death on the Cross is also generally agreed upon. The question that remains is how this death on the Cross is effective.

Essentially three interpretations of the atonement have been offered in the past two thousand years. Since the Protestant faith has been influenced by all three, they all deserve our attention.

The oldest interpretation of the atonement has been called the *Christus Victor* interpretation. Here the conflict in which the human being is involved is seen as a conflict between the forces of God and the forces of evil. The human being is in the middle. But as a result of sin he is now a victim and prisoner in the power of Satan. Christ defeats Satan on the Cross and frees people from the power of evil, which has held them in bondage. Christ's death on the

Cross is the victory of God over Satan, which releases people from his power. This interpretation of the atonement was first suggested by the great Christian theologian Ignatius. In its full sharpness it was stated by Rufinus of Aquileia as follows:

> The purpose of the Incarnation . . . was that the divine virtue of the Son of God might be as it were a hook hidden beneath the form of human flesh . . . to lure on the prince of this age [devil] to a contest; that the Son might offer him his flesh as a bait and that then the divinity which lay beneath might catch him and hold him fast with its hook. . . . Then, as a fish when it seizes a baited hook not only fails to drag off the bait but is itself dragged out of the water to serve as food for others; so he that had the power of death seized the body of Jesus in death, unaware of the hook of the divinity concealed therein. Having swallowed it, he was caught straightway; the bars of hell were burst, and he was, as it were, drawn up from the pit, to become food for others.[5]

This view, picturesque and crude as it is, reveals a strong dualism. The atonement is seen as a struggle between good and evil, Christ and the devil. In this conflict the Cross becomes the great defeat of the forces of evil because in their encounter with Jesus Christ they overreach themselves. The very nature of these forces is to kill those who are separated from God because they have become the slaves of Satan, but they have no right to kill the sinless Christ. By killing him they lose everything.

Here the atonement takes place against the background of a cosmic struggle. In a sense a cosmocentric view of the priestly offce of Christ, it operates with what we could call a limited dualism. Dualism is that view of reality which insists that everything must be explained against the background of a cosmic struggle between the forces of good and the forces of evil. Absolute dualism makes these forces coequal. They are two gods eternally at war with each other. The human race and its world are in the middle in this struggle, with the option to choose one side or the other. This absolute dualism can be found in Persian religion, where Ormuzd or Ahura Mazda, the good god, is opposed by Ahirman, the evil spirit.

However, Christian dualism is never that absolute. Even the powers of evil are not independent of God, for they derive their power ultimately from the one and only God. Absolute evil would be sheer nothing. As Augustine stated it: "Everything which has form, insofar as it has form, and everything which has not yet form, insofar as it is capable of receiving form, holds what it has from God."[6] But, while an absolute dualism is inconsistent with the Christian faith in God as Creator, limited dualism has been a permanent part of Christian teaching. The powers of evil are known as real powers. But these powers are defeated through Christ's death on the Cross. It is a victory over death and sin and devil, and Christ is the victor. An old Easter hymn puts it:

> The strife is o'er, the battle done;
> Now is the Victor's triumph won;
> Now be the song of praise begun,
> Alleluia!
> The powers of death have done their worst,
> But Christ their legions hath dispersed;
> Let shouts of holy joy outburst!
> Alleluia![7]

And Luther sings in one of his Easter hymns:

> It was a strange and dreadful strife
>   When Life and death contended;
> The victory remained with Life,
>   The reign of death was ended;
> Stripped of power, no more he reigns,
> An empty form alone remains,
>   His sting is lost forever!
>   Alleluia![8]

Christus Victor is, indeed, a valid and persistent element in the Protestant faith's understanding of the priestly work of Christ.

The most familiar interpretation of the atonement and Christ's priestly work, however, is known as the *satisfaction* interpretation. In his famous book *Cur Deus Homo?* Anselm of Canterbury wrote:

> The problem is, how can God forgive man's sin? To clear our thought let us first consider what sin is, and what satisfaction for sin is. . . . To sin is to fail to render God His due. What is due to God? Righteousness, or rectitude of will. He who fails to render this honor to God, robs God of that which belongs to

Him, and dishonors God. This is sin. . . . And what is satisfaction? It is not enough simply to restore what has been taken away; but in consideration of the insult offered, more than what was taken away must be rendered back.

Let us consider whether God could properly remit sin by mercy alone without satisfaction. So to remit sin would be simply to abstain from punishing it. And since the only possible way of correcting sin, for which no satisfaction has been made, is to punish it; not to punish it, is to remit it uncorrected. But God cannot properly leave anything uncorrected in His Kingdom. Moreover, so to remit sin unpunished would be treating the sinful and the sinless alike, which would be incongruous to God's nature. And incongruity is injustice.

It is necessary, therefore, that either the honor taken away should be repaid, or punishment should be inflicted. Otherwise one of two things follows—either God is not just to Himself, or He is powerless to do what He ought to do. A blasphemous supposition. The satisfaction ought to be in proportion to the sin. . . . And thou hast not yet duly estimated the gravity of sin. . . . Thou canst not make satisfaction for it, unless thou payest something greater than the whole creation. All that is created, that is, all that is not God, cannot compensate the sin.

And Anselm continues:

Satisfaction cannot be made unless there be some One able to pay to God for man's sin something greater than all that is beside God. . . . Now nothing is greater than all that is not God, except God Himself. None therefore can make this satisfaction except God. And none ought to make it except man. . . . If, then, it be necessary that the kingdom of heaven be completed by man's admission, and if man cannot be admitted unless the aforesaid satisfaction for sin be first made, and if God only *can*, and man only *ought* to make this satisfaction, then necessarily one must make it who is both God and man.

He must have something to offer greater than all that is below God, and something that He can give to God voluntarily, and not as in duty bound. Mere obedience would not be a gift of this kind; for every rational creature owes this obedience as a duty to God. But *death* Christ was in no way bound to suffer, having never sinned. So death was an offering that He could make as of free will, and not of debt.

Now one who could freely offer so great a gift to God

clearly ought not to be without reward. . . . But what reward could be given to one who needed nothing—One who craved neither gift nor pardon? . . . If the Son chose to make over the claim He had on God to man, could the Father justly forbid Him doing so, or refuse to man what the Son willed to give him?

What greater mercy can be conceived than that God the Father should say to the sinner—"Receive my only Son, and offer Him for thyself," while the Son Himself said—"Take me, and redeem thyself"?

And what greater justice than that One who receives a payment far exceeding the amount due, should, if it be paid with the right intention, remit all that is due?[9]

Here we have the satisfaction interpretation of the atonement in its oldest and most concise form. Sin offends God's justice; if it were not punished, justice would be overthrown. Through Christ's death on the Cross God shows his mercy and his justice at the same time.

The satisfaction interpretation, though first developed in this rigorous form by Anselm, has, of course, its roots in New Testament teaching. Many times Jesus' death is described as propitiation for man's sin. He is called "the Lamb of God that taketh away the sins of the world." In classical Protestantism this satisfaction theory plays an important part. The Protestant faith emphasizes, however, the fact that *God* reconciles, that *God* satisfies, that *God* reestablishes the relationship with people which they have destroyed by their sin. While Anselm's interpretation permitted the human being to offer Christ to God, the Protestant faith insists that it is God, not the human person, who reconciles fallen humanity by sacrificing his son.

Perhaps the Protestant understanding of this priestly work of Christ could be illustrated with a rather simple story. Let us assume that there was once in some foreign country a tribe of people who were destroying their tribal existence through excessive drink. Everybody was brewing his own beverages and consuming them thirstily. Eventually no work was done and the tribe began to disintegrate. The chief finally decided something had to be done. Only very severe punishment would stop this road to destruction. He proclaimed that the next person who brewed some of this strong drink would be punished severely—fifty lashes over his back with a bull whip. This severity stopped the rioting. Slowly the village recovered and the tribe went back to work. And then, one day, there was another drunken riot. The chief tried to find out who had brewed the drink, but nobody wanted to tell him. Finally, he discovered that it was his old mother who had been responsible. What was he to do? If he did not punish her, he had lost the right to punish anybody else. Chaos would return and the tribe would be doomed to destruction. If he punished her, the old woman would not survive, and he would be responsible for the execution of his own mother. Well, when the hour of judgment approached and his mother was brought before him, the chief found her guilty as charged. But instead of having her punished, he stepped from his throne and ordered the executioner to give him the fifty lashes. In this way justice was preserved and his mother's life was saved. This is, of course, a rather superficial illustration, but it may help illustrate what is the basic concern of the interpretation of the atonement which emphasizes the justice of God. It is important to keep in mind that for the Protestant faith it is God and God alone who does the reconciling. He does it through his death on the Cross. And he does it once and for all. It is an accomplished fact. God, the Protestants say, has indeed reconciled the world unto himself; it is now only a question of who will believe in what God has done. The sacrifice does not have to be repeated in any form or manner. For people do not sacrifice Christ to God; God has sacrificed himself for people. This is an important emphasis in the Protestant interpretation of the atonement as satisfaction for human sin.

As we called the first interpretation of the priestly office of Christ "cosmocentric," because it sees the atonement against the background of a cosmic struggle between the forces of death and sin against the forces of life and love, so might we label the Anselmian interpretation "theocentric." It is God who reconciles the world unto himself.

The third interpretation of the atonement, commonly associated with the medieval theologian Peter Abelard, is known as the *moral influence* interpretation. According to Abelard the significance of Christ's atoning death lies in the example it provides to the sinful human race. It reveals God's love and shows Christ to be our teacher and model. The result of such example and teaching is to produce faith and love in the believers. The forgiveness of sins is based upon the love aroused in the believer by Christ's teaching and example. Abelard put it:

> But to us it seems that by this means we are justified in the blood of Christ and reconciled to God; that through this particular favor manifested toward us, that his Son assumed our nature and persisted even until death in instructing us both by word and by example, he has very strongly drawn us to himself through love, so that, inflamed by this great benefaction of divine grace, true love now shrinks not from the endurance of anything whatsoever.[10]

Abelard's interpretation of the atonement was immediately attacked in the Middle Ages as reducing the work of Christ to the work of a teacher. In the form in which Abelard suggested it, classical Protestantism would also reject it categorically, since it placed the emphasis on what people would do under the moral influence of the life of Christ. This view was anthropocentric, since it saw the meaning of the atonement in the transformation of the moral behavior of the human race. Yet, while classical Protestantism rejected this point of view, those later Protestants who saw in Jesus the great teacher who guides us to a better life through his inspired example found in Peter Abelard an early precursor.

If we want to summarize the understanding of the atonement of Christ as held by the mainstream of Protestantism, we should say that it accepts both the Christus Victor interpretation and the satisfaction interpretation of Anselm as complementary to each other. This means that each has to be seen in the light of the other. Thus the Protestant faith is certainly less crudely dualistic than Rufinus and less obviously legalistic than Anselm. The emphasis is here as everywhere else upon God's work in Jesus Christ. The atonement is Christ's priestly work; it is not human beings who reconcile themselves to God but God who reconciles men and women to himself. This is the dominating and significant emphasis of the Protestant faith, here and everywhere else. Abelard's view represents a valid, though definitely and dangerously partial, insight into the nature of the atonement. Certainly people are involved in the atonement. The Christian faith is never a spectator sport, and the atonement can never be merely a cosmic battle or a transaction within God. What God has done on the Cross must make a difference in the life of the believers. Abelard's view is a valid element, which is preserved in the Protestant faith. The insistence that sanctification is a necessary consequence of justification means that human beings are involved in the drama of the atonement. The atonement is bound to make a difference in their lives. What Christ has accomplished on the Cross makes it possible for men and women to live the new life in Christ.

The Cross, therefore, is in the center of the Protestant proclamation. It is not possible to state the classical Protestant faith apart from its message. For the central message of Protestantism is what God has done for men and women on the Cross and what they can now do through God's power thus made available to them.

In the Cross God's love is revealed. It is not Jesus' love which changes the Father's mind. It is not the man Jesus Christ who turns the wrath of God away from sinful humanity. The Protestant faith insists that the Father sent the Son into the world to reconcile God and people and to defeat the powers of darkness. The Cross is not human sacrifice to God, but God sacrificing himself for the sake of the human race.

The Cross reveals the love of God so profoundly and dramatically that it makes faith possible. It reveals the importance of the law and the seriousness of sin as revolt against the order and structure established by God. The Cross proclaims and preserves the holiness of God's law, while at the same time revealing his boundless and overwhelming love. This means that it is impossible for those who take the Protestant faith seriously to take the sinful revolt of human beings against God lightly. The Cross makes it apparent that God cannot forgive sin as an indulgent parent may forgive an offense. Forgiveness which is merely indulgence would subvert the order and structure of the universe. To understand what is at stake one could compare justice and mercy as it confronts people in the ordering of human society. Because of the obvious and profound deficiencies in our criminal justice system it has been suggested, and some people advocate vociferously, that it might be a good idea not to punish crimes. Since it appears that criminals do not generally become better through punishment and a crime cannot be undone by punishment, some say that we might as well abolish all prisons and courts and thus save a great deal of money. This is the indulgent-parent approach to crime, which advocates letting bygones be bygones and showing mercy instead of punishing the offender. If most people do not approve of such a procedure it may be that, knowing themselves, they realize that people are often deterred from illegal actions by the fear of punishment. This is, of course, not a very high motive; however, it helps to keep some sort of order in our human world. The evidence seems to indicate that people are not willing to obey the law because it is good for them; rather, they obey because punishment will follow disobedience. Since this has at times been questioned by learned people, let us look, for example, at the laws concerning speeding and drunken driving on the statute books of most states.

Of course, people should obey these laws because they are good for them. Punishment does not make people better. By paying a fine for speeding or going to jail for drunken driving, a person does not improve his character. Granted all that, the fact remains that speeding and drunken driving can be controlled by rigid law enforcement. The more strictly the law is enforced, the greater chance that I might get caught and be punished, the more carefully I will drive. In other words, although law enforcement may not make me truly better, it makes me behave in a manner which is safer for me and for my fellow human beings. We have all no doubt observed what happens when a police car enters a stream of traffic. Cars slow down, and drivers meticulously observe the traffic laws. It is doubtful whether anybody has become better because of the appearance of this police car, but everyone's behavior—poorly motivated as it may be—has become safer for everyone concerned. It is a truism that rigid law enforcement is necessary to achieve greater safety on the roads.

There is nothing commendable about a policeman who lets his friends go free when they break the law. Likewise, a judge is not exhibiting love or charity when, because of political pressure, he acquits offenders brought before him. The result is that the inter-

THE DOCTRINE OF CHRIST

ests of criminals are more carefully protected than those of society and its law-abiding citizens. In fact, this kind of "law enforcement," which makes justice a joke under the mantle of mercy, is the surest way to chaos and anarchy.

There is likewise nothing praiseworthy about parents who do not restrain the destructive and antisocial impulses of their children, who bring up juvenile delinquents and claim that it is their love and mercy which keep them from punishing and restraining antisocial behavior. Ignoring the structures which maintain life and make society function is not mercy or love but sheer irresponsibility. It is against this background that Protestant assertions about the Cross must be understood. Through the Cross the holiness of God's law is preserved. This law protects all people and makes the life of society possible. At the same time the Cross also reveals God's boundless love.

Jesus Christ as the mediator between God and humanity suffers for us under the judgment. He takes upon himself all human sin, even to the moment of despair on the Cross. His priestly work is to reestablish the broken tie between God and the human race without doing violence to God's justice, which upholds the universe, or God's love, which gives it meaning.

Simone Weil has put it:

> When the whole universe weighs upon us, there is no other counterweight possible but God himself—the true God, for in this case false gods cannot do anything, not even under the name of the true one. Evil is infinite in the sense of being indefinite; matter, space, time. Nothing can overcome this kind of infinity except the true infinity. That is why on the balance of the cross a body which was frail and light, but which was God, lifted up the whole world. "Give me a point of leverage and I will lift up the world." This point of leverage is the cross. There can be no other. It has to be at the intersection of the world and that which is not the world. The cross is this intersection.[11]

In summary, there are many different elements for the Protestant faith in Christ's atoning work on the Cross which are all valid and complementary to each other. The Cross is *sacrifice*, in that it is

God's sacrifice for the sake of people. The Cross is *punishment,* in that it reveals the seriousness of the offense against the divine law. It contains elements of *satisfaction.* In Paul's words: "Christ redeemed us from the curse of the law, having become a curse for us . . ." (Gal. 3:13). But the Cross is also *example.* Jesus said to his disciples, "If any man would come after me, let him deny himself and take up his cross and follow me" (Matt. 16:24). And finally the Cross is *victory.* It is the sign of triumph over the forces that separate men and women from God. It demonstrates that suffering and death can, through the grace of God, become meaningful and lead to peace and joy and life. For the Protestant faith all these elements of the atoning work of Christ are valid. Far from being mutually exclusive, they complement and supplement each other. For all the theories of the atonement are formulations in human language of the divine act which transcends all formulations. It is the divine act which saves, rather than its description, be it ever so precise. The Protestant faith in its classical expressions is a Cross-centered faith. Thus it can be said that the theology of classical Protestantism is always the theology of the Cross.

It would, however, be an error to assume that Protestantism claims to be able to exhaust the meaning of the atonement and of the Cross by means of any or all of the interpretations here presented. After all is said and done, the Cross remains God's *mystery.* As the great mystery of the love of God for people it is in the center of the Protestant faith.

The third office of Christ as defined by the theologians of Protestantism is his royal office. With the Apostles' Creed the Protestant faith asserts that Christ "sitteth at the right hand of God the Father." This is, of course, not a geographical description but symbolic language expressing the faith that, through Christ, God the Father rules the universe. Or, as the Apostle Paul puts it: "That at the name of Jesus every knee should bow, in heaven and on earth and under the earth" (Phil. 2:10). Christ is King, indeed, and he rules everywhere.

For this reason Protestants like to speak of the "lordship of Christ." This means that when confronted by Christ the believer knows that he is face to face with him who has "all authority in heaven and on earth" (Matt. 28:19). In the words of Karl Barth, the famous Swiss Protestant theologian:

> He [God] rules his people and cosmos as this man is at his right hand, i.e., as he is the concretion and manifestation of his power and righteousness. . . . His kingdom and lordship and dominion are concretely the kingdom and lordship and dominion of this man exalted by him to fellowship with his being and work; of the man in whom he, God, humbling himself in his Son, became a servant.[12]

For Protestantism this faith in Christ's work as King is based upon the biblical witness. The Gospels are unanimous in their report that people "were amazed, so that they questioned among themselves, saying, 'What is this? A new teaching! With authority he commands even the unclean spirits, and they obey him'" (Mark 1:27).

This royal authority of Christ is also expressed in the words which the New Testament uses for the proclamation of Jesus. He proclaims the "good news." When John the Baptist sends his disciples to Jesus to ask, "Are you he who is to come, or shall we look for another?" Jesus' answer is: "Go and tell John what you hear and see: the blind receive their sight and the lame walk, lepers are cleansed and the deaf hear, and the dead are raised up, and the poor have good news preached to them" (Matt. 11:3–5).

Jesus *teaches*. But this is teaching with a difference. As the New Testament reports: "When Jesus finished these sayings, the crowds were astonished at his teaching, for he taught them as one who had authority, and not as their scribes" (Matt. 7:28, 29). For he speaks as the Father has taught him (John 8:28).

And Jesus *preaches*. The Greek word literally means to "cry or proclaim as a herald." It is the authoritative proclamation of the King which is here described: "And he went about all Galilee, teaching in their synagogues and preaching the gospel of the kingdom and healing every disease and every infirmity among the people" (Matt. 4:23).

But this *proclaiming of the good news*, this *teaching with authority*, this *preaching the gospel of the kingdom* are not merely the articulation of words but the expression of royal power. They reveal Christ as the King who rules the destiny of the human race.

While the Gospels bear witness to the fact that Jesus Christ is King, they are not alone in this proclamation. "Christ is King," is the confession which unites the entire Christian community. This confession separates Protestant Christians from all those who may believe in other rulers. The Protestant faith proclaims that Christ has been King from all eternity. The book of Revelation refers to him as "Lord of lords and King of kings" (Rev. 17:14 and 19:16), and in the Gospel of John, Jesus prays: "Father, glorify thou me in thy own presence with the glory which I had with thee before the world was made" (John 17:5). And he rules his church now. In the holy Christian church Christ rules over all believers. He is present as the ruler of his people today, for he has promised, "Lo, I am with you always, to the close of the age" (Matt. 28:20). He makes those who believe in him into a new nation, a new people. "But you are a chosen race, a royal priesthood, a holy nation, God's own people . . ." (1 Pet. 2:9).

The Protestant faith asserts that Christ rules directly and in person: "Where two or three are gathered in my name, there am I in the midst of them." He is personally and really present in the Lord's Supper. This is the central and distinguishing emphasis which is derived from faith in Christ as Lord and King.

Finally, Christ is King because his eternal kingdom is, according to the Protestant faith, the ultimate destiny of the universe. This kingdom has begun but is not completed. It has been described in one of the most famous passages of the New Testament:

> When the Son of man comes in his glory, and all the angels with him, then he will sit on his glorious throne. Before him will be gathered all the nations, and he will separate them one from another as a shepherd separates the sheep from the goats, and he will place the sheep at his right hand, but the goats at the left. Then the King will say to those at his right hand, "Come, O blessed of my Father, inherit the kingdom prepared for you from the foundation of the world; for I was hungry and you gave me food, I was thirsty and you gave me drink, I was a stranger and you welcomed me, I was naked and you clothed me, I was sick and you visited me, I was in prison,

and you came to me." Then the righteous will answer him, "Lord, when did we see thee hungry and feed thee, or thirsty and give thee drink? And when did we see thee a stranger and welcome thee, or naked and clothe thee? And when did we see thee sick or in prison, and visit thee?" And the King will answer them, "Truly, I say to you, as you did it to one of the least of these my brethren, you did it to me." (Matt. 25:31–40)

This kingdom of glory is the profound aspiration of the Protestant faith. Thus, Protestants will speak of themselves as a pilgrim people of God, that is, a people who are marching toward a future kingdom. This has been brilliantly described in a great Protestant classic, John Bunyan's *Pilgrim's Progress*. In various forms this is a universal hope of Protestantism. In several periods in church history Protestants have expected this kingdom in the very near future. Christians in the early church and again at the time of the Reformation, for example, hoped that the end of this world and Christ's kingdom of glory were impending. In a somewhat different sense liberal Protestantism in the early part of this century expected the kingdom could be attained through the conversion of the world to the social gospel of Christ. A popular hymn of the period by William Pierson Merrill gives expression to this aspiration:

Rise up, O men of God!
Have done with lesser things;
Give heart and soul and mind and strength
To serve the King of kings.
Rise up, O men of God!
His kingdom tarries long;
Bring in the day of brotherhood,
And end the night of wrong.

Rise up, O men of God!
The church for you doth wait,
Her strength unequal to her task;
Rise up and make her great!
Lift high the Cross of Christ!
Tread where his feet have trod;
As brothers of the Son of Man,
Rise up, O men of God![13]

Even though most Protestants may be less confident today that it is in their power to bring in the kingdom of glory, many Protestants expect the manifestation of Christ as King in their lifetime. The eager expectation of Christ's kingdom is an essential part of the Protestant faith.

NOTES

1. Søren Kierkegaard, *Philosophical Fragments*, trans. David F. Swenson (Princeton, N.J.: Princeton University Press, 1942), p. 11.

2. *Ignatius to the Trallians*, IX/I, *The Apostolic Fathers*, trans. Kirsopp Lake (Cambridge: Harvard University Press, Loeb Classical Library, 1945), p. 211.

3. Cf. also: *Service Book and Hymnal of the Lutheran Church in America*, Hymn No. 500, stanzas 1–3.

4. Simone Weil, *Gravity and Grace* (New York: G. P. Putnam's Sons, 1952), p. 139.

5. Henry S. Bettenson, *Documents of the Christian Church* (New York: Oxford University Press, 1954), p. 49.

6. "De vera religione," XVIII, 35–36, in Erich Przywara, *An Augustine Synthesis* (New York: Harper Torchbook, 1958), p. 123.

7. *Service Book and Hymnal of the Lutheran Church in America*, Hymn No. 90, stanza 1.

8. Ibid., No. 98, stanza 2.

9. Bettenson, *Documents*, pp. 196 ff.

10. Reinhold Seeberg, *Textbook of the History of Doctrines*, trans. Charles E. Hay (2 vols.; Philadelphia: Lutheran Publication Society, 1905), I, 71.

11. Weil, *Gravity and Grace*, p. 146.

12. Karl Barth, *Church Dogmatics*, trans. G. W. Bromiley (Edinburgh: T. & T. Clark, 1958), vol. IV, part 2, p. 155.

13. *Service Book and Hymnal of the Lutheran Church in America*, No. 541. Words by permission of *The Presbyterian Outlook*.

Chapter 7

THE HOLY SPIRIT
AND THE CHURCH

In our discussion of the Protestant faith, we have now come to the Holy Spirit and the church. While the atonement is the work of Christ, the appropriation of this work of Christ by the individual believer is the work of the Holy Spirit. Through the power of the Holy Spirit the Christian is brought to faith in Christ. In his explanation of the Third Article of the Apostles' Creed, Luther says:

> I believe that I cannot by my own reason or strength believe in Jesus Christ my Lord, or come to him; but the Holy Spirit has called me through the gospel, enlightened me with his gifts, and sanctified and preserved me in the true faith; in like manner as he calls, gathers, enlightens and sanctifies the whole Christian church on earth, and preserves it in union with Jesus Christ in the true faith; in which Christian church he daily forgives abundantly all my sins, and the sins of all believers, and at the last day will raise up me and all the dead, and will grant everlasting life to me and to all who believe in Christ.[1]

The Holy Spirit

This explanation of the creed shows that the task of the Holy Spirit is no minor task; the Holy Spirit is not, so to speak, an afterthought in Protestantism, although one might get this idea from much of contemporary Protestant worship. In classical Protestantism, the Holy Spirit is God at work in all human beings, saving and transforming them according to his purpose. Of Luther, Professor Regin Prenter has said:

The concept of the Holy Spirit completely dominates Luther's theology. In every decisive matter, whether it be the study of Luther's doctrine of justification, of his doctrine of the sacraments, of his ethics, or of any other fundamental teaching, we are forced to take into consideration this concept of the Holy Spirit.[2]

Congregationalists and Anglicans, Methodists and Presbyterians have written hymns in praise of the Holy Spirit. According to the Protestant faith the doctrine of the Holy Spirit is deeply rooted in the proclamation of the early church. The New Testament abounds in references to the Holy Spirit and his power:

"If you love me you will keep my commandments and I will pray the Father, and he will give you another Counselor, to be with you for ever, even the Spirit of truth, whom the world cannot receive, because it neither sees him nor knows him; you know him for he dwells with you, and will be in you." (John 14:15–17)

And the Apostle Paul says: "It is the Spirit himself bearing witness with our spirit that we are children of God" (Rom. 8:16).

According to the Protestant faith, this Holy Spirit is God. As the Father is God and the Son is God so the Spirit is God. When Ananias in the Acts of the Apostles lies to the Apostles and to the Holy Spirit, Peter says: "You have not lied to men but to God" (Acts 5:4). And the Holy Spirit is person. The whole Christian church and the Protestant faith assert that the Holy Spirit is not merely a divine "force" or divine "truth," but, rather, that the personal God confronts people personally in the Holy Spirit. Karl Barth puts it:

According to the New Testament, the Holy Spirit is one of the objects of faith. The Creed too declares in conformity with the New Testament: I believe in the Holy Ghost. The Holy Spirit, object of faith, is also an object of prayer: We must not only pray that we may receive the Holy Spirit. We must pray to him.[3]

Although this may appear to be quibbling, the insistence on the part of classical Protestantism that the Holy Spirit is a person to whom we can pray protects the Protestant faith against the tendency of human beings to identify themselves with God. In mysticism, especially in its Oriental forms, divine force is understood in such impersonal terms that the result is the self-identification of the individual with God. Humanity and God run into each other, and it becomes ever more difficult to see where humanity ends and God begins. Humanity is God and God is humanity. This is impossible within biblical Christianity because of the insistence upon the Holy Spirit as person. He is not divine energy, he is not some undefined divine force; rather, he is the third person of the Trinity and he meets human beings personally. The meeting with the Holy Spirit is for the Protestant faith a personal encounter. Again it is an I-thou relationship rather than infiltration or emanation. Edward Cooper sings: "Eternal Spirit! By whose breath the soul is raised from sin and death, Before thy throne we sinners bend: To us thy quickening power extend."[4]

And in Whitfield's collection of 1757, we find this hymn: "Come, Holy Comforter, thy sacred witness bear, In this glad hour! Thou who Almighty art, Now rule in every heart, And ne'er from us depart, Spirit of power!"[5]

The Holy Trinity

On the basis of what we have said so far, we can now conclude that the Protestant faith asserts that there is one God in three persons, Father, Son, and Holy Spirit. This is known as the doctrine of the Holy Trinity. Perhaps no other hymn is more popular than the so-called doxology: Praise God, from whom all blessings flow; Praise him, all creatures here below; Praise him above, ye heavenly host; Praise Father, Son, and Holy Ghost!" Although few Protestants are able to give a detailed definition of the doctrine of the Trinity, faith in God as Father, Son, and Holy Spirit is part of the common Protestant heritage.

Protestants believe in the Holy Trinity because the one God, the God of Abraham and Isaac and Jacob, as the Old Testament likes to call him, has revealed himself in Scripture as Father, Son, and Holy Spirit. This experience of the Trinity points to the eternal

Trinity; God was always three in one. This means that although the Son became man in Jesus Christ this is not an evolution in God, but from all eternity God was Father, Son, and Holy Spirit. This assertion of the eternity of the Trinity safeguards the Christian understanding of God against all pantheistic and mystical notions which tend to make God dependent upon humanity.

The doctrine of the Trinity is an attempt to express the reality of God and guard it against certain **obvious** and historical misunderstandings. In its developed form it has been stated in defense of the Christian faith against efforts to change and misinterpret it. It asserts the reality of the creative tension in God. Aristotle's God, we are told, is the unmoved mover, eternally beholding his own perfection—"and his thinking is a thinking on thinking." Christians confess that God is a living God—not the abstract keystone of a philosophical system.

Thus the I-thou relationship, which is the basis of all relationships between God and human beings and their relationship with each other, is a reflection or image of the primary I-thou relationship in the very being of God. The doctrine of the Trinity testifies to the eternal encounter in the one living God, Father, Son, and Holy Spirit.

On the one hand, by confessing the Trinity the Protestant faith rejects two prevalent interpretations as inadequate and false. One is *Unitarianism*, the assertion that there is one God, but only one, rather than three persons. The Son is not God and neither is the Holy Spirit. This view was rejected very early in the history of the Christian church, and the Protestant faith has unanimously joined in this rejection. Even such an inclusive organization of Christians as the World Council of Churches does not, therefore, include the Unitarians. The other interpretation removing this tension in God is known as *Sabellianism*, which was also rejected early in the history of the Christian church. Sabellianism asserts that there is one God and that the Father, Son, and Holy Spirit are three modes in which this one God appears. It is as if one would look at the sun through red and blue and yellow glasses and thus see three different suns or see the sun in three different colors. This view has also been rejected because it denies the living encounter in God.

On the other hand, the doctrine of the Trinity protects the Protestant faith against any form of three theism. There are not three gods, but only one. Each person in the godhead is coeternal with the two other persons.

Probably no aspect of the Protestant faith so far discussed in these pages seems as strange as the discussion of the Trinity. And yet, although the definitions may appear abstruse and complicated, the underlying reality is rather simple. The Protestant faith asserts that there is one God and that Father, Son, and Holy Spirit are God. In the defense of these basic assertions of the Christian faith, the admittedly complicated formulation of the doctrine of the Trinity became a necessity.

This doctrine helped a good deal to preserve the early Christian church from the fate of the Oriental religions which had been amalgamated into the general religious chaos of the Hellenistic world. The doctrine of the Trinity does not dispel the mystery of God. It does not explain God. It is an effort on the part of the Christian church to protect its witness to God against misinterpretation and perversion. The theologians of the early church who had a hand in defining these doctrines were not interested in mere speculation. They were not professors of philosophy or even theology—actually they were veterans of persecution who had often demonstrated their willingness to live and die for their faith. They insisted on this definition of the Trinity because they saw in it the only way to preserve all the confessions of the Christian faith about God. However, in order to understand this attitude we ought to keep in mind that these confessions appear in the context of worship and adoration. As Horatius Bonar sings: "Glory be to God the Father! Glory be to God the Son! Glory be to God the Spirit! God Eternal, Three in One!"[6] It is impossible to understand any assertion of the Protestant faith and, most especially, the confession of the Trinity, apart from the worshiping and praying community which makes the confession. The doctrine of the Trinity is for the Protestant faith not abstract metaphysical speculation—but adoration and worship of the God who has revealed himself in his Word: Father, Son, and Holy Spirit!

The Church

In our discussion of the Protestant faith, we have now come to the doctrine of the church and its task. The Christian church is specifically the product of the Holy Spirit. The day of Pentecost, the day on which, according to the Acts of the Apostles, the Holy Spirit was given to the early Christians, is the birthday of the church, for it is through the Holy Spirit that the risen Christ creates the church. But what is the church according to the Protestant faith? It is the witnessing community, the people of God proclaiming its faith in its King to each other and to all the world.

If we want to understand the Protestant doctrine of the church, it will be helpful to keep in mind the principle of complementarity which we have used frequently to interpret the Protestant faith. For most assertions concerning the church have to be made by making a number of statements which may appear contradictory but which taken together give the most adequate description of the church.

First, the church is both an institution and a fellowship. The assertion that it is an institution is necessary in order to convey the insight that here is a reality which transcends all individuals. It is made up of individuals but no individual is the church. The reality of the church surpasses all individuals and is greater than the sum of all individuals. In other words, the Protestant faith claims that here the sum total is more than the sum of its parts; the church is more than the addition of individual members. It transcends and comprehends the individual members. But, at the same time, the Protestant faith asserts that the church is fellowship and communion. Never merely institution, it is people, the people of God living together in a personal fellowship. Whenever the church is merely institution, organization, machinery—apart from people—it is no longer truly church. And whenever the church is only a collection of individuals who like each other, who meet because they like each other—it is no longer church. Both extremes are temptations to the Protestant faith. It would not be too difficult to give examples of Protestant churches which have much more in common with a well-run corporation like the General Motors Corporation than with the New Testament church. Sometimes machinery for machinery's sake accumulates, and when the church meets, it seems like a stockholders' meeting. The Protestant faith would assert that a church which is merely an efficiently run corporation designed for the preservation of its organizational life is no longer a Protestant church. Conversely, when the church becomes a group of like-minded individuals who have a good time together, who belong to the same race, the same nationality, the same income group, the same educational level, sometimes the same family—a group of individuals who meet because they enjoy each other's company—we see another aberration from the Protestant concept of the church.

Secondly, the church is a means and a goal at the same time. It is a means to an end. Through the church the gospel of Christ is proclaimed. Through the church, men and women are confronted by Christ. It is God's tool and instrument for the proclamation of his Word and the administration of the sacraments. Through the church, Christian love becomes effective in the missionary efforts, the relief work, the deeds of charity of the community. God uses the church, say the Protestants, so that his message of salvation might be proclaimed to all people. Here the church is a means to an end, the proclamation of the Christian faith.

If one studies the life of the typical American Protestant church, it is not hard to see the instrumental character of the community. Through the church the insights of the Christian faith are made available to the immediate community in which the church is established and also to people in those parts of the country where there may be no churches and in foreign lands where the Christian message would otherwise not be proclaimed. Through the church men, women, and children everywhere are given the opportunity to worship God. From this point of view it is not difficult to see how the church functions as a means to an end and as a tool and instrument in the hands of God.

However, the Protestant faith makes the complementary assertion that the church is an end, a goal, and the purpose of God's plan with humanity. The proclamation of the message creates a community of believers, a people of God, which is an end in itself. In the New Testament word, it makes people members of the body of Christ. According to the Protestant faith the purpose of human existence is to be grafted into the body of Christ. While it is not difficult to see the church as a means to an end, it is generally harder for the average Protestant to understand how this church is also the product and objective of the divine will. Yet, the Protestant faith asserts that if these tasks of teaching and preaching and serving are taken seriously, God creates a fellowship of love and worship. When people love God with all their being and the neighbor as themselves, the kingdom of God is among them. For the Protestant faith the love and service which is part of the life in and for the church is not merely a way to God, it *is* fellowship with God. This life of fellowship with God, which is the ultimate purpose of human existence, is not entirely in the future; it is at least partially anticipated in the present. To be sure, as the Apostle Paul says: "Now we see in a mirror dimly, but then face to face. Now I know in part; then I shall understand fully . . ." (1 Cor. 13:12). However, even now we see! The Protestant faith claims that in every deed done in the service of God, in every word spoken through the power of God's love, in every thought that goes through a human mind under the influence of the Holy Spirit, there is a foretaste, an anticipation, of the ultimate fulfillment. It is therefore an error, according to the Protestant faith, to see in the church merely a tool of God's purpose, an instrument which will eventually be cast away. It is rather an instrument which God is perfecting. The church is the great creative effort of the Creator of heaven and earth and the Savior of the human race.

The church is means as well as end, tool as well as product, yet these functions are complementary and must not be disjoined. Whenever the church is merely a means to an end it is no longer the church at all. Sometimes this happens. The church may become a means to build a better community, to reduce juvenile delinquency, to send relief to hungry people abroad, or to safeguard the American way of life. Whenever the life of the church exhausts itself in being a means to ever-so-worthy ends, it is no longer the church of Christ. The church is also failing if it is merely an end in itself. Sometimes churches act as if they were resting places of people who have arrived. When Christians sit quietly in their corner or in their church "content to let the world go by," they no longer can be considered the Christian church. The church of Christ according to the Protestant faith is not a mutual-admiration society of those who consider themselves perfect Christians. It can never be a static gathering of those who merely observe and criticize human society from a safe haven. Only when the church is both means and end, tool and product, is it truly the church of Christ according to the Protestant faith.

Thirdly, the Protestant faith asserts that the church is both the proclamation of God and the people of God. Here again it is necessary to maintain both assertions as complementary to each other. The church is a proclaiming church, a community with a message. When we read the New Testament, we are impressed by the urgency of the message which this church proclaims in season and out of season. The church has been defined as a witnessing community, and this witness is of the essence. If this witness is lost, what is left is not the church but a social club, sometimes, indeed, an a-social club. No other community, no other institution, depends as much on what it proclaims as the Christian church. Take away the message of Christ and of the Cross, discussed in detail in previous chapters, and buildings, budgets, membership lists, and able leadership cannot make up for it. According to the Protestant faith, the church depends on its proclamation. The church is where the proclamation is or, perhaps in even simpler terms, the church is where the Word is—and where the Word is not proclaimed, there is only machinery, stone and bricks, but no church. But it is of the greatest importance not to lose sight of the other half of the assertion. The church is the people of God. The Word is not disembodied, it is spoken by people and for people, it is a living Word. It remakes and transforms living people. The church is people— women and men who have heard this Word, obey this Word, and who are transformed by this Word. The Protestant faith claims, therefore, that the church must be judged by the life it produces. This is the new life in Christ. This is how Jesus Christ describes this new possibility: "I came that they may have life, and have it abundantly" (John 10:10). And the Apostle Paul asks in the same vein:

> Do you not know that all of us who have been baptized into
> Christ Jesus were baptized into his death? We were buried
> therefore with him by baptism into death, so that as Christ was
> raised from the dead by the glory of the Father, we too might
> walk in newness of life. (Rom. 6:3, 4)

And we can also read:

> And this is the testimony, that God gave us eternal life, and this
> life is in his Son. He who has the Son has life; he who has not
> the Son has not life. (1 John 5:11)

A philosophical system may stand on the coherence or persua-
siveness of its propositions. A philosopher may be personally a
scoundrel, a thief, and a murderer; this does not affect the validity
of the theories which he has uttered. They stand on their own
merits and are neither proved by his charm nor disproved by his
obnoxious behavior. The church is otherwise. It is not a collection
of propositions or sayings; but a people transformed by the Word,
the people of God. There is a vital link between the life and
thought of Christian people, according to the Protestant faith. In
the church this vital connection must be obvious. The church is
both proclamation of God and people of God. This can also be
expressed by saying that the church is both Word and flesh. Just as
in Jesus Christ, the Word became flesh, so, in dependence upon this
incarnation of God, the Word must ever become flesh in the
church. This means that the Word must grasp men and women so
that they live their faith in love. The Protestant faith insists that it
is not sufficient to tell the story of God's incarnation in Jesus
Christ; this story must bear fruit in the life of the church, so that
the Christian can say with the Apostle Paul: "It is no longer I who
live, but Christ who lives in me . . ." (Gal. 2:20).

The link between life and thought explains also the famous distinction between the invisible and the visible church. The Protestant faith almost universally uses these two terms to express the
belief that the church as an ecclesiastical institution, the empirical
church, is not coextensive with the church as the people of God. As
there was a Judas even among the twelve disciples of Jesus, Protestants would say that mere membership in the visible church does

not guarantee membership in the kingdom of God. And the reverse statement would be almost as widely accepted: The mere fact that a person does not belong to any particular ecclesiastical organization does not necessarily exclude him from membership in the kingdom of God. If Judas is the spectacular example of the member who did not truly belong, the thief on the Cross, who died on Jesus' side and to whom Jesus said, "Truly, I say to you, today you will be with me in Paradise" (Luke 23:43), is an equally spectacular example of a person who belonged to Christ although he was never baptized or formally a disciple.

It would be an error to assume from these two examples that the Protestant faith considers membership in the visible church irrelevant and immaterial. On the contrary, the church is in a sense always visible—but visible to faith. In the creed most Protestants will say that they "believe in one holy universal church." It is part of the Protestant faith to see the true church of Christ in the motley collection of "butchers and bakers and candlestick makers" who make up the visible church. The invisible church does not exist apart from the visible church, but within it. It would indicate a serious misunderstanding of the Protestant faith to claim that it teaches an invisible church to which people can belong apart from the visible church. It rather teaches that the church of Christ is the people of God, and "The Lord knows those who are his" (2 Tim. 2:19). Whenever the notion of the visible and the invisible church is used as an excuse by an individual to separate himself from the visible church, the rejection of this excuse by Protestantism has been universal and sometimes scathing. The great Protestant evangelist Dwight L. Moody was once told by a person who had not joined a church that he could not do so because there were too many hypocrites in the church. Moody looked at him for a while and then said, "Friend, don't mind that; there is always room for one more." The Protestant faith sees the reality of the church as visible and invisible. The invisible church is visible to faith and the visible church is invisible—as the church of Christ—to unbelief. Here, too, it is dangerous to dissolve the complementarity of the two assertions.

The church is not merely a message or merely a fellowship, but a fellowship with a message and a message which creates a fellow-ship. Both are essential for the understanding of the Protestant faith when it speaks about the church. Here the oldest of the Protestant definitions of the church may be illuminating. Article VII of the Augsburg Confession states: "The Church is the congregation of saints, in which the Gospel is rightly taught and the sacraments rightly administered." The fellowship, which is the congregation of saints, the message, which is the true proclamation of the gospel, and the right administration of the sacraments are of the essence of the church. Similar definitions can be found in almost all Protestant confessions.

This brings us to a discussion of the common characteristics of the church, the characteristics generally accepted by the Protestant faith. First of all, the Protestant faith asserts that the church is both *militant* and *triumphant*. This is an ancient distinction that de-scribes the church in this world as the militant church, the church at war with the powers of evil, which obstruct the purpose of God. The church must always be "militant." It cannot be at rest in this world as long as there is injustice and hate, conflict and strife. Anybody who is even superficially familiar with the Protestant faith and the Protestant churches in America knows that its prophetic leaders have often been in the forefront in the fight for justice and a better life for all, sometimes to the great annoyance of some of their more conservative members. It is obvious that sometimes the causes were poorly conceived and the goals were not attained, but regardless of setbacks and failures, the Protestant faith sees in the church a fighting force which tries to bring about changes for the better in the world. From the establishment of the republic to the abolition of slavery and the struggle for social justice and against racism, the Protestant faith has supplied inspiration and leadership. This participation in the struggle against evil is colorfully expressed in Julia Ward Howe's famous "Battle Hymn of the Republic":

> Mine eyes have seen the glory of the coming of the Lord;
> He is trampling out the vintage where the grapes of wrath
>   are stored;
> He hath loosed the fateful lightning of his terrible swift sword:
>   His truth is marching on.

He has sounded forth the trumpet that shall never call retreat;
He is sifting out the hearts of men before his judgment-seat;
O be swift, my soul to answer him; be jubilant, my feet!
  Our God is marching on.
In the beauty of the lilies Christ was born across the sea,
With a glory in his bosom that transfigures you and me:
As he died to make men holy, let us die to make men free,
  While God is marching on.[7]

The militancy of the Protestant faith is not reserved for enemies without. Protestants historically have been always ready to fight the enemy within the gates as well as the enemies outside. This is one of the reasons for the many divisions within Protestantism. The Protestant faith insists that the fight must be carried into the midst of the church, when good reason exists to believe that the enemy has infiltrated. While this militancy has been divisive, it has also been corrective. Evil has not remained unpunished, and the most severe and acute criticism of Protestantism's failures has come from its own ranks.

But while the Protestant faith interprets the church as militant, it also speaks of the church triumphant. These are "the saints who from their labors rest." It is that part of the church which is no longer fighting but which, according to the Protestant faith, participates in the triumph which was won for the whole church on the Cross. For the church consists not only of those few Christians who happen to live on this earth at one particular time but of all believers from the beginning of the world to its end. For this reason the author of Hebrews writes: "Since we are surrounded by so great a cloud of witnesses, let us also lay aside every weight and the sin which clings so closely, and let us run with perseverance the race that is set before us" (Heb. 12:1). The church militant lives supported and encompassed by the church triumphant. The concept *church*, however, includes both realities: the church still involved in battle and the church which even now participates in God's victory.

Furthermore, the church is *one*. This seems a very strange assertion coming from people so obviously divided as Protestants are. Yet in spite of their many denominations they will by and large be united in the claim that the church is one. The obvious divisions in the ecclesiastical organization of the empirical church do not affect the ultimate unity. The church is in fact one because Christ is one: "There is one body and one Spirit, just as you were called to the one hope that belongs to your call, one Lord, one faith, one baptism, one God and Father of us all, who is above all and through all and in all" (Eph. 4:4–6). This is the source of the church's unity, which is not dependent upon a unified organization. There seems to be no evidence that the Christian church was ever organizationally one. Such unity was apparently of no concern to the early Christians. For them the oneness of the church is the oneness in faith, hope, and love. The Apostle Paul indicates that there were divisions in the church of Corinth (1 Cor. 1:10–17). No superorganization controlled the various Christian groups in the earliest centuries of church history. Soon there were Armenian, Indian, Syrian, and Coptic churches. In 867 the church of the Roman Empire was divided into an Eastern and a Western church. In 1054 A.D. Pope Leo IX excommunicated the patriarch of Constantinople, Michael Cerularius, who quite naturally returned the anathema a little later. This major division took place almost five hundred years before Luther and has never been healed. And, of course, long before the better-known Protestants, there were Protestants such as John Wycliffe and John Hus who preferred faithfulness to the Bible to organizational unity. Now, in spite of all these acknowledged divisions—and the Protestant faith does not deny or ignore these divisions—Protestants assert that the church is one. It was Luther who stated in 1520 against the claims of the Roman leadership that "the Moscovites, the White Russians, the Greeks, the Bohemians and many others, believe as we do, baptize as we do and preach as we do."[8] Although there was no organizational unity, the oneness of the church transcended the disunity of the churches. The unity of the church, according to the Protestant faith, has its roots in the oneness in Christ. It is founded upon the common Lord of the Christians, not their common organization. To assure the oneness of the church, the Protestant faith relies on the one Lord. Where this Christ is Lord, the church is one and united. Protestants are therefore generally suspicious of those who insist that organizational unity is the condition for the oneness of the church. The church is one because Christ is one. For this reason all movements toward organizational unity are for Protestants to be justified on pragmatic grounds. No amount of human efficiency and organizational skill will ever improve on the unity which Christians already have.

With all other Christians the Protestant faith asserts the holiness of the church. The church is *holy* because it shares in the holiness of Christ, its head. This does not mean for the Protestant faith that the members or leaders of the church automatically possess a special holiness which should exempt them from the common duties and obligations which are the responsibilities of other citizens. Protestants have been ready and willing to assume all their civic duties. Even the exemption of the clergy from military service is hardly in line with the Protestant understanding of the holiness of the church. This holiness does not imply that the message of the church is invalidated because of moral lapses of individual members or leaders of the church. With most of Christendom the great majority of Protestants take the side of Augustine in the Donatist controversy. The Donatists asserted that the preaching and the administration of the sacraments by people who were living in sin invalidated what they did. For example, a person baptized by a priest who had committed a murder would not truly be baptized. Against this position the ancient church, and with it the Protestant faith, asserts that the holiness of the church is not dependent upon the holiness of the members—although this is very desirable—but rather on the holiness of the Christ who is the head of the church. In the words of St. Augustine:

> Wherefore, anyone who is on the devil's side cannot defile the sacrament, which is of Christ. . . . When Baptism is administered in the words of the gospel, however great be the perverseness of either minister or recipient, the sacrament itself is holy on his account whose sacrament it is.[9]

And the church is *universal*. In his Epistle to the Galatians, the Apostle Paul writes:

> For as many of you as were baptized into Christ have put on
> Christ. There is neither Jew nor Greek, there is neither slave
> nor free, there is neither male nor female; for you are all one in
> Christ Jesus. (Gal. 3:27, 28)

The universality of the church means to the Protestant faith that it
includes all kinds and conditions of men and women. Most Protestants would say that being a man or woman is not religiously
significant. One is not closer to God by belonging to one sex or the
other. Similarly, one's nationality or race has no theological significance. The church of Christ is not "white" or "black," "American"
or "European," and such distinctions must not be allowed to divide
the church. In other words, the church of Christ is by definition
"integrated," and while hell may indeed be segregated, the Protestant faith asserts that heaven is not! Similarly, all social distinctions
are meaningless in the universal church. Although Protestantism in
America has undoubtedly tended to organize along ethnic and social lines,[10] the assertion of the universality of the church makes
this type of organization not only useless but actually godless. To
the degree to which the living Christ is the Lord of the Protestant
churches, the universality of the church will also be realized. This
is the reason why the conflict over racial justice in the churches is
of such profound significance. While in other institutions segregation may be harmful or expensive, in the church segregation is
subversive to its very nature. A medical school which advocates
segregation may remain a good medical school, but a church which
does the same ceases to be the church.

The church is furthermore *apostolic*. This means for Protestants
that the church is based upon the preaching and teaching of the
Apostles. The church is where the *kerygma* is, that is, where the
witness to the Christ given by the Apostles and evangelists can be
found. Most Protestants are highly suspicious of those efforts
which try to establish the authenticity of the church upon some two-
thousand-year supergenealogy, although some few Protestants are
actually engaged in efforts to base the validity of their Christian
proclamation upon an uninterrupted chain of ecclesiastical dignitaries dating back to the Apostles. The mainstream of Protestantism seems to have little use for this so-called apostolic succession,

204

but rather insists that the church must have the apostolic preaching. The "faith which was once for all delivered to the saints" must be apostolic. If this is the case, most Protestants will pay little attention to the hierarchical genealogies. But if this apostolic proclamation is absent, no genealogy can possibly make up for it.

Once the church has been defined in the manner here described, the Protestant faith can also say that *outside the church there is no salvation*. It does not mean, as has been said before, that any human institution has exclusive rights to Christ. It does mean that salvation implies incorporation in the body of Christ and citizenship in the people of God. That such inclusion is essential and can occur apart from organizations and institutions is part of the Protestant faith.

But what about the organization of the church? Does the Protestant faith have anything to say concerning the manner in which the churches have been or should be organized? Actually, three basic patterns have appeared and been adopted by Protestantism. They are somewhat similar to the familiar patterns of ancient political philosophy: monarchy, aristocracy, and democracy. The pattern of church government most similar to monarchy is the episcopal pattern. Many Protestants have organized their churches in this manner. In Protestantism, however, the bishop is usually elected rather than appointed, although there are also important Protestant churches where the bishop is appointed by some lay authority, frequently the crown. The pattern of church government most similar to aristocracy is the presbyterian pattern. Here a body of selectmen, both laymen and clergy, rules the church. The pattern most similar to democracy is the congregational form of government. The church is here controlled locally and by all the members in good standing. Any larger association of churches has only as much power as has been delegated to it by the individual congregations.

The episcopal, the presbyterian, and the congregational patterns can be found among Protestants. There is a tendency to claim that one or the other pattern is *the* pattern of the New Testament church. But it seems hard or even impossible to establish which was the exact pattern, if a universal pattern existed, in New Testament times. Few Protestants, however, would insist that any particular organization is of the essence of the church. The manner in which the institutional church is to be administered is for them a pragmatic concern and should be adjusted to the needs of the contemporary situation. Thus in one situation the congregational system may offer the best machinery for an effective church. In another situation an episcopal system might prove more efficient. But since it is Christ, the Lord, who saves, it is inconsistent with the basic proclamation of Protestantism to attribute saving significance to the administrative method chosen for the direction of the church.

Perhaps the most significant difference in the conception of the church that can be found in Protestantism has little to do with the episcopal, congregational, or presbyterian form of organization but rather concerns what has been called the "inclusive" or "exclusive" view of the church. Certain Protestant churches tend to emphasize that the church in the world is inclusive. This means that it includes both the true believers and the hypocrites. It is impossible for human beings to tell them apart, and we must therefore wait until the Lord of the church himself separates those who belong to him and those who do not. This position is taken by the Protestant defenders of the established church or a folk church. Such Protestant churches can be found today in Scotland, to a certain extent in England and in the Scandinavian countries, in Finland, Sweden, Norway, and Denmark. In the United States the Puritan fathers were advocates of the idea of "establishment," and historically there have been various establishments in this country. It is significant that followers of the congregationalist as well as the presbyterian and the episcopal patterns of church organization have at times advocated the establishment of their churches. The favorite parable of those who support this inclusive view of the church is the parable of the wheat and the tares:

> The kingdom of heaven may be compared to a man who sowed good seed in his field; but while men were sleeping, his enemy came and sowed weeds among the wheat, and went away. So when the plants came up and bore grain, then the weeds appeared also. And the servants of the householder came and said

to him, "Sir, did you not sow good seed in your field? How then has it weeds?" He said to them, "An enemy has done this." The servants said to him, "Then do you want us to go and gather them?" But he said, "No; lest in gathering the weeds you root up the wheat along with them. Let both grow together until the harvest; and at harvest time I will tell the reapers, Gather the weeds first and bind them in bundles to be burned, but gather the wheat into my barn." (Matt. 13:24–30)

A little later Jesus tells a very similar parable when he says:

Again, the kingdom of heaven is like a net which was thrown into the sea and gathered fish of every kind; when it was full, men drew it ashore and sat down and sorted the good into vessels but threw away the bad. (Matt. 13:47, 48)

The other point of view considers the church a "gathered people," a "holy minority," and adherents of this view make every effort to separate the true believers from the unbelievers even now. This point of view has perhaps been most clearly expressed by Menno Simons, a leader of the Mennonites:

Christ's church consists of the Chosen of God, his saints and beloved who have washed their robes in the blood of the Lamb, who are born of God and led by Christ's Spirit, who are in Christ and Christ in them, who hear and believe his word, live in their weakness according to his commandments and in patience and meekness follow in his footsteps, who hate evil and love the good, earnestly desiring to apprehend Christ as they are apprehended of him. For all who are in Christ are new creatures, flesh of his flesh, bone of his bone and members of his body. . . . Some of the parables, as of the net in which the good and bad fishes are caught; of the wise and foolish virgins and their lamps; of the wedding of the king's son and the guests, and of the threshing floor with wheat and chaff, although the Lord spoke them in allusion to the church, yet they were not spoken for the purpose that the church should knowingly and willfully accept and suffer open transgressors in its communion; because in that case, Christ and Paul would differ in doctrine, for Paul says that such should be disciplined and avoided. But they were spoken because many intermingle with the Christians in a Christian semblance, and place themselves under the Word and its sacraments who in fact are no Christians, but are hypocrites and dissemblers before their God.[11]

Historically, Lutherans, Anglicans, Presbyterians, and Congregationalists have tended toward the inclusive view of the church, while Mennonites, Baptists, and Methodists have tended toward the exclusive view. However, in the peculiar denominational pattern of the American church these distinctions are no longer particularly meaningful, and all Protestant churches have adopted a more voluntary pattern than was the case with the established Protestant churches of Europe. This adjustment to the conditions of the New World was made easy by the relative unimportance of the organizational pattern of the church for the Protestant faith.

The relationship of *the* church and the churches in Protestant thought is particularly significant since in recent decades Protestants have been involved in a fairly comprehensive process of examining the reasons for their diversities and discovering the basis for greater cooperation and unity. These examinations have led to the development of agencies through which many Protestant churches in the world as well as in the United States have worked together in various areas in which the church must express its concern. Much of the relief, for example, which Protestants have offered to the needy of the world since World War II has been given through cooperative agencies which represented most of the major Protestant denominations in America. The most famous agencies for such inter-Protestant cooperation are probably the NCCUSA, the National Council of the Churches of Christ in the United States of America, and the WCC, the World Council of Churches. The latter also includes prominently the representatives of various Greek and Russian Orthodox traditions. The areas in which the WCC has been working are the following:

(1) A group has been engaged in studies of *faith and order*, discussing the subject under the heading "Our Oneness in Christ and Our Disunity as Churches." Representatives of the various Protestant and Orthodox traditions have studied together and explained to each other the meaning of the church. This process is still going on and is one of the most significant developments in contemporary Christendom.

(2) *Evangelism* has been summarized as "the mission of the church to those outside her life." By mutual consultation Protes-

tants have attempted to understand their responsibility for the proclamation of the gospel to the whole world.

(3) A third area in which the WCC has given leadership and
has supplied a forum for discussion for Protestantism is the field of
social questions. Protestants have discussed with each other the
implications of the social revolution going on all over the world for
their various churches and for the church.

(4) *International affairs* is a fourth concern of the WCC, difficult and controversial as any discussion of international affairs is
bound to be if the participants represent people on both sides of the
various "curtains" which have divided the world. Protestant and
Orthodox Christians have asked themselves, "What is the responsibility of Christians in the struggle for world community?" The
answers they have found have hardly pleased everybody, but the
very fact that the questions were asked has awakened Protestants
to some of their political responsibilities.

(5) The discussion of *intergroup relations* is an effort to study
the church's responsibility in racial and ethnic tensions. While
some individual Protestants have been leaders in the fight for
greater justice in the relationship between the races, the WCC attempts to call all churches to responsible participation in this
struggle.

(6) The sixth area of concern of the WCC, *the laity*, centers
around the responsibility of the Christian in his daily work. Working together, Protestants are trying to find ways to implement in
daily life their common faith in the priesthood of all believers.

These six concerns of the WCC indicate that many Protestants
are seriously involved with the problems which confront the Protestant faith in the world today. They apparently realize that they will
have to work together to make an impact commensurate with the
scope of the problems. Not all Protestants cooperate in these joint
efforts. Even those who do not cooperate, however, are indirectly
influenced by this twentieth-century development.

In recent years Protestants have begun to discuss frankly many
of the nontheological factors which have separated the various
Protestant denominations from each other. It is obvious that especially here in the United States many divisions among Protestants,

one could almost say most divisions, have their roots in sociology rather than theology. For example, it would be difficult to see why there should be more than one Lutheran church—were it not for the fact that some Lutherans came originally from Sweden and others from Norway, some from Germany and others from Denmark. Similarly, many divisions among Calvinists are traceable to differences in the country of origin of the ancestors of the present members of these churches. Furthermore, the Civil War split many churches, and some of these schisms have still not been healed. Another nontheological factor which has proven disruptive is income bracket and social status. It seems that, in American Protestantism, a tendency has developed to assemble together according to the members' place in the social structure.

Since the reason for the existence of different denominations is often found to be national background, history, or sociological status, it seems obvious that efforts should be made to overcome these rifts. Attempts to unite Protestants into larger denominations crossing the nontheological divisions have been characteristic of contemporary Protestantism.

In the discussion of the Protestant faith, one must be careful to separate these nontheological factors from "faith." For the Protestant faith, the church is not identical with the churches, but the church does not exist apart from the churches. The church and the churches exist in creative tension. But this tension can only be creative if it is understood. Today the Protestant faith is seriously attempting to understand all the aspects of this tension in order to overcome sterile aspects and to utilize those that contribute to greater vitality.

The Significance of the Word and the Sacraments for the Protestant Faith

The task of the church is to be the witnessing community. This means that the church must proclaim the apostolic witness concerning Jesus Christ, the Son of God, the Savior. For the Protestant faith the proclamation of the church is thus bound to the witness of

Scripture; it is essentially and primarily the exposition of Scripture. In other words, whatever the Protestant faith claims that it has to say to people today or in the past or in the future must be related to the events experienced and proclaimed by the early Christians. The message of the Protestant faith is inescapably bound up with these events of the first century; with the birth, life, death, and resurrection of Christ. Take these events away, ignore them, and the Protestant faith has nothing to say. This is not idle conjecture because, actually, in the history of Protestantism there have been times and places when the Protestant faith was separated from this *kerygma*, from the proclamation of the Christ event, from what we have called previously "holy history." The resulting proclamation was always irrelevant and fruitless. During the period of rationalism in Germany, for example, an effort was made by some preachers to proclaim a useful message to the world—apart from the Christ event and apart from what we have called the *kerygma* and the message of the early church.

The results were sometimes amusing, frequently boring, always utterly irrelevant. For example, while rationalism flourished, a minister of a country parish might begin his Christmas sermon by reading the Christmas Gospel which mentions the fact that at Jesus' birth there was no room in the inn and that he was born in a stable (Luke 2:1 ff.). At this point the preacher would launch forth into a discussion of the advantages of feeding animals in a stable in the winter time over keeping them out in the open air. For almost an hour his farm audience would have to listen to his more or less expert opinion on this fascinating agricultural problem. Such sermons represented an effort to get away from the so-called supernatural or irrational elements of the Christmas story and make its lessons useful to the parishioner. If it happened to be Easter, the minister might read the story of the women who got up early to go to the tomb of Jesus and found the tomb empty (cf. John 20:1 ff.). At this point the preacher would hold forth on the advantages of getting up early in the morning. He would explain how this makes for a longer day in which to accomplish one's tasks and how "early to bed and early to rise keeps a man healthy, wealthy, and wise." This, then, would be the Easter sermon.

Of course, not only the late seventeenth and early eighteenth centuries suffered from this peculiar understanding of the Christian proclamation. It has always been a temptation in Christendom to separate the proclamation from the person whom the Christians are supposed to proclaim. Historically, Christians have at times proclaimed interesting philosophical views, sage moral advice, and brilliant oratorical masterpieces. Indeed, almost every concern has at some time or other been proclaimed by Christians as the Christian faith. Breathing exercises, health fads, sexual and dietary idiosyncrasies, racial and political prejudices, and other substitutes have all been preached in Christian churches and from Christian pulpits as the Christian message. But if classical Protestantism is used to supply the standards for the evaluation of the Protestant proclamation, one discovers that in Luther and Calvin, for example, preaching is always the proclamation of God's deeds for human beings as recorded in the Old or the New Testament. It is always followed by an explanation and application of the meaning of these events, their significance for the listeners, whoever they might be.

Perhaps the following illustration will help to show how this was done. In one of Luther's Christmas sermons, as quoted by Professor Bainton in his book *Here I Stand*, we read:

> How unobtrusively and simply do those events take place on earth that are so heralded in heaven! On earth it happened in this wise: There was a poor young wife, Mary of Nazareth, among the meanest dwellers of the town, so little esteemed that none noticed the great wonder that she carried. She was silent, did not vaunt herself, but served her husband, who had no man or maid. They simply left the house. Perhaps they had a donkey for Mary to ride upon, though the Gospels say nothing about it, and we may well believe that she went on foot. The journey was certainly more than a day from Nazareth in Galilee to Bethlehem, which lies on the farther side of Jerusalem. Joseph had thought, "When we get to Bethlehem, we shall be among relatives and can borrow everything." A fine idea that was! Bad enough that a young bride married only a year could not have had her baby at Nazareth in her own house instead of making all that journey of three days when heavy with child! How much worse that when she arrived there was no room for her!

The inn was full. No one would release a room to this pregnant woman. She had to go to a cow stall and there bring forth the Maker of all creatures because nobody would give way. Shame on you, wretched Bethlehem! The inn ought to have been burned with brimstone, for even though Mary had been a beggar maid or unwed, anybody at such a time should have been glad to give her a hand. There are many of you in this congregation who think to yourselves: "If only I had been there! How quick I would have been to help the Baby! I would have washed his linen. How happy I would have been to go with the shepherds to see the Lord lying in the manger!" Yes, you would! You say that because you know how great Christ is, but if you had been there at that time you would have done no better than the people of Bethlehem. Childish and silly thoughts are these! Why don't you do it now? You have Christ in your neighbor. You ought to serve him, for what you do to your neighbor in need you do to the Lord Christ himself. The birth was still more pitiable. No one regarded this young wife bringing forth her first-born. No one took her condition to heart. No one noticed that in a strange place she had not the very least thing needful in childbirth. There she was without preparation: no light, no fire, in the dead of night, in thick darkness. No one came to give the customary assistance. The guests swarming in the inn were carousing, and no one attended to this woman. I think myself if Joseph and Mary had realized that her time was so close she might perhaps have been left in Nazareth. And now think what she could use for swaddling clothes—some garment she could spare, perhaps her veil—certainly not Joseph's breeches, which now are on exhibition at Aachen.

Think, women, there was no one there to bathe the baby. No warm water, nor even cold. No fire, no light. The mother was herself midwife and maid. The cold manger was the bed and the bathtub. Who showed the poor girl what to do? She had never had a baby before. I am amazed that the little one did not freeze. Do not make of Mary a stone. For the higher people are in the favor of God, the more tender they are.

Let us then meditate upon the Nativity just as we see it happening in our own babies. Behold Christ lying in the lap of his young mother. What can be sweeter than the Babe, what more lovely than the mother! What fairer than her youth! What more gracious than her virginity! Look at the Child, knowing nothing. Yet all that is belongs to him, that your conscience should not fear but take comfort in him. Doubt nothing. To me

> there is no greater consolation given to mankind than this, that
> Christ became man, a child, a babe, playing in the lap and at
> the breast of his most gracious mother. Who is there whom this
> sight would not comfort? Now is overcome the power of sin,
> death, hell, conscience, and guilt, if you come to this gurgling
> Babe and believe that he is come, not to judge you, but to
> save.[12]

We have given this quotation at such length in order to illustrate
how the proclamation of classical Protestantism is bound up with
Scripture. It is expository in that it explains the Scriptures and their
message to the church. This quotation from Luther, however,
should also show that such proclamation is not merely the retelling
of past events but also the living witness to the present generation
on the basis of the Christ event. The Word as proclaimed by the
church is not ancient history but a relevant witness to the men and
women of today. It is supposed to speak to their situation and
make the events of holy history speak meaningfully to their own
lives. There is nothing particularly Christian about a boring sermon, although it is indubitably true that a good many sermons are
boring. The Protestant faith claims that the Word if truly preached
is always meaningful, that it is a "means of grace," that is, a way in
which God reaches people. For this reason the sermon occupies a
central place in Protestant worship. Through the Word of God, as
it is preached by the minister and proclaimed by the entire Christian community, God speaks to people today.

His message is primarily the good news, the gospel of his deeds for
humanity in Jesus Christ. Secondarily, this message is the exhorta-
tion to discipleship, the explanation of what it means to trust in the
gospel. But the sermon is primarily means of grace, that is, that its
main function is to tell what God has done for people and then
indicate what these people can do in grateful reply.

It is the result of an inadequate proclamation of the Protestant
faith if one sometimes gets the impression that the Protestant sermon is only supposed to show people how evil they are and to tell
them that they should try to do better. Looking at the preaching of
classical Protestantism, one must conclude that this negative
preaching is not Protestant at all. It represents a mistaken under-

standing of the proclamation of the Word as a means of grace. The primary function of the sermon is to tell the good news, to proclaim the *kerygma*, to recount God's deeds for humanity. This is the reason why the proclamation of the Word is indeed means of grace.

An examination of the proclamation of the Word as means of grace further reveals that such preaching is subject to the same tensions which have repeatedly become apparent as the key to the understanding of the Protestant faith. Two complementary statements have to be made simultaneously, for this proclamation is at the same time human word *and* the Word of God.

The sermon is human word; indeed it is the word of one particular man or woman. This individual may be very eloquent or rather inarticulate. Actually, it does not matter how eloquent he is, for according to the Protestant faith God can use the eloquence of the eloquent and the stammering of the inarticulate speaker as a vehicle of his grace. The effectiveness of the preaching does not ultimately depend upon the fluency of the speaker. What matters is that the Holy Spirit must use the words to address the listener. Church history is full of reports which illustrate how great orators like St. Ambrose of Milan have been vehicles of the Holy Spirit and also how simple, unlearned revival preachers have been used in the same manner. As far as the Protestant faith is concerned, it does not even have to be a member of the clergy who becomes the medium of God's address. The Sunday school teacher who explains the Bible to her pupils, the parent who leads a family in devotions may become instruments of God's grace through the power of the Holy Spirit. For such proclamation can always become the Word of God. God uses it to speak to the human heart. The power of the Holy Spirit addresses people through human words. But it is important to remember that God does not abolish the human being he so uses. It is still a human being through which the Word of God reaches other people. Thus the proclamation of the Word is simultaneously human and divine.

What is the relationship of the sacraments to this proclamation? For most Protestants the sacraments are a uniquely effective type of the ministry of the Word. The sacraments are not some other form of proclamation in addition or superior to the proclamation of the Word. On the contrary, in the sacraments the Word is proclaimed in a uniquely effective manner. The sacraments are, in the phrase of Augustine, *verbum visibile*, visible word. Words are means of communication. We use words to tell other people what we think and want and hope. But it is possible to use other means of communication to convey these innermost feelings. These other means of communication are visible words. The most obvious example that comes to mind is the kiss. Whether a parent kisses his child or a man kisses the woman he loves, we are dealing with a visible word, an action that "speaks louder than words." This action may convey our meaning more effectively and more profoundly than any number of words.

There are other visible words. Let us assume you have received the news that your best friend has lost his mother. You know that he was very close to her and loved her very much. Now, the first time you meet him, you may not know what to say. Everything that comes to mind seems platitudinous, meaningless, and empty. So you may just take his hand and grasp it firmly and look at him. It is quite possible that such an action may convey your sympathy as effectively, perhaps more effectively, than any number of well-chosen words.

In 1945, just after World War II, there was a meeting of Protestant churchmen in Geneva. Among the men invited were Bishop Eivind Berggrav and the German pastor, Martin Niemoeller. Berggrav was a Norwegian who had just spent a long time in a Nazi prison in Norway. Pastor Niemoeller was much worried about how he would be able to meet this man who had suffered so much from the Nazis. How would he react to a German? As soon as Niemoeller came into the room, old Bishop Berggrav went up to him and embraced him. This was an action that spoke louder than words; it was a true *verbum visibile*, a visible word.

For classical Protestantism, the sacraments are such divine actions, mediated through the church, by which God speaks to people. Protestants are unanimous in their assertion that the visible words are no more effective by the mere fact that they are uttered than any other words. If words of comfort and help are to do you some good, you must believe them. So the Protestant faith asserts that the sacraments proclaim God's saving Word to believers, to those who do not harden their hearts to the message, and their saving power, not their validity, is dependent upon the faith of the recipient. The efficacy of the means of grace, both Word and sacraments, is similar to the efficacy of a check. The validity of the check does not depend on the faith of the recipient in its soundness. Yet, unless the recipient trusts in the signature, he will not deposit and use it. Thus a perfectly good check could be discarded because the person to whom it was issued did not believe in it. Faith, while unable to make the check valid, can make it worthless. Similarly, the means of grace, while objectively valid, may become useless to the person who refuses to accept them in faith.

However, while all Protestants agree that the means of grace are received in faith, the exact understanding of the sacraments tends to divide Lutheran Christians from Christians of the Reformed tradition, for example, Presbyterians, Congregationalists, and Baptists. In this controversy the Episcopalians and the Methodists are hard to classify. Their tradition allows for great breadth in the interpretation of the sacraments, so that some hold views very similar to the Lutheran position, while others accept a Reformed interpretation.

The difference between the Lutheran understanding of the sacraments and the Reformed understanding is that the former would emphasize the objective effectiveness of the sacraments, while the latter would interpret the sacraments more as symbolic actions. These differences will become clearer a little later, when the sacrament of Baptism and the sacrament of the Lord's Supper are discussed.

Of both sacraments, however, it can be said that as divinely instituted actions they guard the Protestant faith against a false intellectualism. The God of the Bible is a God who acts. It is always important to distinguish the Christian God from the unmoved mover of the philosophers. Aristotle's unmoved mover could not possibly establish sacraments. The God of the Bible does. Thus the sacraments demonstrate again that the God whom the Protestant faith proclaims is no mere intellect, power, or even morality, but a personal God who acts in history. Furthermore, the sacraments as physical actions, involving the physical elements of water, bread, and wine, guard the Protestant faith against a false spiritualism which depreciates matter. As has been shown before, the God of the Bible is the God of spirit *and* matter. Christians insist that he created matter. The sacraments, with their use of the material to convey God's grace to people, emphasize the significance of matter and thus protect the Protestant faith against a false spiritualism which would make matter evil and somehow opposed to God.

But what is the specific function of the sacraments in the Protestant faith? The first important assertion of Protestantism is that there are only two sacraments: Baptism and the Lord's Supper. Other Christians have more sacraments; they are Confirmation, Penance, Extreme Unction, Holy Orders, and Matrimony, in addition to Baptism and the Lord's Supper. The reason for the smaller number of sacraments administered by Protestants is that only Baptism and the Lord's Supper are described by the Protestant definition of a sacrament as an action instituted by Christ, using an earthly element and conveying grace. The Protestant conviction that a sacrament must be instituted by Christ means that Christ himself must have told his followers to use the sacrament. Furthermore, the sacrament must use a physical element like water or bread and wine and promise to convey grace. The churches of the Reformation claim that only Baptism and the Lord's Supper meet these specifications. Marriage, for example, is accepted as an extremely important divine order by all Christians, but, since it was this also in Old Testament times and even among those people who have never heard of Christianity, it cannot be said to have been instituted by Christ. Therefore, for Protestants, marriage is not a sacrament.

Baptism, however, is clearly an action instituted by Christ, using an earthly element and conveying grace. Baptism describes through action the meaning of membership in the church of Christ. It expresses purification, since water has always been used for washing. In Baptism it is used to express the washing away of sin. Especially when immersion is practiced, it clearly expresses death and the new life, the immersion expressing the dying of the old man or woman and the rising out of the water expressing the birth of the new person.

Baptism is for most Protestants an act of God, mediated through the church. It is the Word of God in action. Baptism is, so to speak, the seal of God's love applied to the person being baptized. Just as a seal expresses the power and authority of the person whose seal is being affixed, so Baptism expresses the power and authority of God, whose seal it is.

Baptism could also be described as the kiss of God applied to the person being baptized. A kiss is an expression of love. Most Protestants would say in applying this figure to Baptism that, when a father kisses his baby, this kiss is an expression of love whether the baby fully understands the meaning of the kiss or not. What matters is the love of the father expressed in the kiss rather than the comprehension of the baby who receives the kiss. Thus a child may be baptized in early infancy.

However, infant Baptism is one of the most controversial subjects among Protestants, and there are many Protestants of the Baptist tradition who will insist that Baptism is not really Baptism unless the person being baptized clearly understands what Baptism implies. He must have acknowledged his allegiance to Christ.

The attitude toward infant or adult Baptism depends largely upon the sacramental understanding of Baptism. Those Protestant churches which emphasize that Baptism is really an act of God, an act in which God shows his love and mercy to human beings in a visible word, will practice infant Baptism. Those Protestant churches who see in Baptism essentially an opportunity to confess the Christian faith and an expression of this confession will emphasize adult Baptism.

The Baptism of children has its antecedent in the Old Testament rite of circumcision. This operation was supposed to establish and express the covenant relationship between God and his people. It was performed on all male infants on the eighth day after birth. For most Protestants, Baptism establishes the covenant relationship for the people of the New Covenant, where there is neither male nor female, neither Jew nor Greek (Gal. 3:28). It is therefore to be applied to all.

Those who insist on adult Baptism object that infant Baptism is a meaningless rite, which has often merely superstitious connotations and thus counteracts the very message of the Christian gospel. While this is certainly often the case, the advocates of infant Baptism assert that its abuses and misunderstandings should lead not to its abolition but to a clearer teaching concerning its true meaning.

Protestants, especially in America, are thoroughly divided on the subject of Baptism. Yet they are almost universally agreed that all Christians ought to be baptized, either in infancy or when they are able to express the desire themselves. But, while all Christians ought to be baptized, most Protestants hold that not the lack but the contempt of Baptism separates a human being from God. Unbaptized persons, be they infants or adults, are committed to the mercy of God.

All that is necessary for a valid Baptism are the words of institution:

> Go therefore and make disciples of all nations, baptizing them in the name of the Father and of the Son and of the Holy Spirit, teaching them to observe all that I have commanded you; and lo, I am with you always, to the close of the age. (Matt. 28:19, 20)

And with these words is the application of water in the name of the Father and of the Son and of the Holy Spirit. Although many Protestants do not believe that emergency baptisms are necessary, those who do insist that in an emergency a Baptism can be performed by anyone. It is not even necessary that the person performing the Baptism be a Christian.

The second sacrament, and the only other sacrament accepted by Protestants, is the Lord's Supper. It has many other names; sometimes it is called Holy Communion, or the Holy Eucharist. Christ established the sacrament for the forgiveness of sins of the believers. The institution of this sacrament is described in the Gospel of Matthew in the following words:

Now as they were eating, Jesus took bread, and blessed, and broke it, and gave it to the disciples and said, "Take, eat; this is my body." And he took a cup, and when he had given thanks he gave it to them, saying, "Drink of it, all of you; for this is my blood of the covenant, which is poured out for many for the forgiveness of sins. I tell you I shall not drink again of this fruit of the vine until that day when I drink it new with you in my Father's kingdom." (Matt. 26:26–29)

The Old Testament antecedent of the Lord's Supper is the Jewish feast of the Passover. In the spring of every year the Jews, celebrating their deliverance from Egypt, recall how Pharaoh permitted the Jewish people to leave after the Lord had slain the first-born in every Egyptian family but passed over the Jewish homes, where the blood of the sacrificial lamb was placed on the door-posts. Jesus seems to have instituted the Lord's Supper in connection with a Passover celebration with his disciples. For the Protestant faith, Jesus is the Passover lamb of the Christians. In the Gospel of John we read, "The next day [John] saw Jesus coming toward him, and said, 'Behold, the Lamb of God, who takes away the sin of the world!'" (John 1:29). The book of Revelation is full of allusions to Christ as the Lamb of God.

While the Lord's Supper is an expression of the divine love and mercy and of the communion of the Christian church with its Lord, it is also the sacrament which divides Christians most deeply. One could almost say that the Lord's Supper is the most controversial subject in the Christian faith. Understood differently by Protestants and Roman Catholics, it has also led to considerable disagreement among Protestants.

To discuss in detail the various positions in regard to the Lord's Supper is beyond the scope of this volume, yet the four basic positions can be described quite easily. They are usually known as (1) transubstantiation; (2) real presence; (3) symbolic presence; (4) memorial. What do these different terms mean?

The official teaching of the Western Church at the time of the Reformation and of the Roman Catholic Church to this day is called transubstantiation. This means that, after the priest has con-

221

secrated the elements of the Eucharist, the substance of the bread has changed into the body of Christ and the substance of the wine has changed into the blood of Christ. In order to understand what this means, one must keep in mind that this doctrine assumes the soundness of the Aristotelian distinction between substance and accidents. According to this philosopher everything consists of substance and accidents. A dog, for example, may have certain "accidents"—it may be white, have four legs, two eyes, a certain weight, and so forth. These characteristics are called "accidents" because the animal would still be a dog even if it lost one eye or one leg, or were dyed a different color, or changed its weight. But in addition to these accidents a dog has a "substance"—its "dogness," so to speak. If this changes, it would no longer be a dog, but something else. Now according to Aristotle the same could be said about an apple or a watch—or any other object. All have accidents and a substance. For example, an apple may be red, but if it were yellow it would still be an apple. Chalk may be white and round, but, if it were blue and square, it would still be chalk. But what has all this to do with the doctrine of transubstantiation? Simply this: It teaches that after the consecration of the elements, the accidents of the wine and the bread remain. In other words, the wine still looks like wine and smells like wine and tastes like wine, for these are accidents. But the *substance* has changed. Instead of the substance of wine it is now the substance of blood, and instead of the substance of bread the bread is now the substance of flesh. This is the meaning of the doctrine of transubstantiation. This is the one extreme of the various positions concerning the Lord's Supper taken by Christians.

On the other extreme we find the memorial view of the Lord's Supper. Most Christians who hold this position are those who have been called "left-wing Protestants." They assert that the elements are in no way affected by anything that is said or done at Holy Communion. The Lord's Supper is entirely a memorial feast. Christians come together to remember what Jesus did for them two thousand years ago. Just as Americans may come together on the Fourth of July in order to remember the Fourth of July, 1776, so

Christians meet at the Lord's table to remember the first Lord's Supper and what this event has meant to the church ever since.

Most Protestants' understanding of the Lord's Supper is somewhere between the doctrine of transubstantiation on the one hand and the memorial view on the other. Calvinists believe in the symbolic presence of Christ in the Lord's Supper. This is how Calvin himself describes the significance of the Lord's Supper:

> After God receives us into his family, and not only so as to admit us among his servants, but to number us with his children—in order to fulfill the part of a most excellent father, solicitous for his offspring, he also undertakes to sustain and to nourish us as long as we live; and not content with this, he has been pleased to give us a pledge, as a further assurance of this never-ceasing liberality. For this purpose, therefore, by the hand of his only begotten Son, he has favored his church with another sacrament, a spiritual banquet, in which Christ testifies himself to be the bread of life, to feed our souls for a true and blessed immortality. . . . Now, the only food of our souls is Christ; and to him, therefore, our heavenly Father invites us, that being refreshed by a participation of him, we may gain fresh vigor from day to day, till we arrive at the heavenly immortality. And because this mystery of the secret union of Christ with believers is incomprehensible by nature, he exhibits a figure and image of it in visible signs, peculiarly adapted to our feeble capacity; and, as it were, by giving tokens and pledges, renders it equally as certain to us as if we beheld it with our eyes.[13]

Calvin believed that this sacrament was so important that it should be celebrated "at least once in every week."

The Lutherans and most Anglicans believe in the real presence of Christ with the elements of the Lord's Supper. The Christ, "through whom all things were made and in whom all things hold together," to use the New Testament phrase, is believed to be present everywhere and in everything.

> For in him all things were created, in heaven and on earth, visible and invisible, whether thrones or dominions or principalities or authorities—all things were created through him and for him. He is before all things and in him all things hold together. (Col. 1:16, 17)

It is this Christ who is truly present for the believer in the sacrament of Holy Communion. He allows himself to be found here because he has given his word that in these elements human beings may find him. Luther says:

> What is the Sacrament of the Altar? It is the true Body and Blood of our Lord Jesus Christ, under the bread and wine, given unto us Christians to eat and to drink, as it was instituted by Christ himself. . . . What is the benefit of such eating and drinking? It is pointed out in these words: Given and shed for you for the remission of sins. Through these words, the remission of sin, life and salvation are given unto us in the Sacrament; for where there is remission of sins, there is also life and salvation.

And then Luther continues by asking:

> How can bodily eating and drinking produce such great benefits? The eating and drinking, indeed, do not produce them, but the words: Given and shed for you for the remission of sins. For besides the bodily eating and drinking, these words are the chief thing in the sacrament; and he who believes them, has what they say and declare, namely, the "remission of sins."[14]

While the overwhelming majority of Protestants accept and use the sacraments of Baptism and the Lord's Supper, some Protestants, for example, the Quakers, do not use any sacraments at all. Although they admit that such practices were at one time used in the church, they claim that they were only "the shadows of better things" and they "cease in such as have obtained the substance."[15]

Although this short discussion by no means exhausts the complexity of the Protestant teaching concerning the sacraments, it may show that probably no other area of the Protestant faith is so full of conflict and disagreement as this particular field. The very sacrament which Protestants believe was instituted to establish and express the unity of the Christian people has in fact caused innumerable divisions. This has been for many Protestants a sure sign that evil not only is a force outside the church but has deeply infiltrated its ranks.

The Ministry

Closely associated with the means of grace, the Word and the sacraments, are the people to whom the church has entrusted the administration of these means, the ministers. To Protestants the ministry is a functional office, not a sacrament. Some Christians believe that a person who has been ordained to the ministry will always be a priest; ordination puts an indelible mark on him. He can become an unfaithful and evil priest, but he will always stand in a special relationship to God. Since ordination is for them a sacrament, one can never lose this mark. For the Protestant faith the ministry is a functional office instituted by God for the sake of the church. While God uses the ministry for the proclamation of his message and the guidance and care of his people, a person is a minister only as long as he exercises the functions of the ministry. Classical Protestantism immediately rejected the notion of the *character indelibilis*, the indelible mark which ordination imprints on the minister. A person who exercises the functions of the ministry, who has a call from God and the church, is a minister. If he or she starts doing something else and gives up the functions of the ministry, no longer preaches and administers the sacraments—he may still be a very fine Christian, but he is no longer a minister in the eyes of Protestants.

Being a minister does not place a person any closer to God than other Christians. The minister can approach God by virtue of being a priest. But this is true of every other Christian, for according to the Bible and the Protestant faith all believers are priests and have direct access to God without any mediation except the mediation of Christ. The minister, or pastor, serves an essential function of the church—he preaches, he administers the sacraments, he administers the discipline of the church—but all these are functions of the church. The minister is a servant of God in the church, no closer to God than any other equally faithful Christian and fellow priest in the priesthood of all believers.

For most Protestants this understanding of the ministry as a functional office makes the form and particular organization of the ministry of secondary importance. The ministry is instituted by God in many forms, assert the Protestants:

> And his gifts were that some should be apostles, some prophets, some evangelists, some pastors and teachers, for the equipment of the saints, for the work of the ministry, for building up the body of Christ. . . . (Eph. 4:11, 12)

The various titles such as bishop and presbyter are used interchangeably in the New Testament. As far as the Protestant faith is concerned, these terms make little difference, but the following words will apply to all who seek to serve the church in any office of leadership:

> If any one aspires to the office of bishop, he desires a noble task. Now a bishop must be above reproach, married only once, temperate, sensible, dignified, hospitable, an apt teacher, no drunkard, not violent but gentle, not quarrelsome, and no lover of money. He must manage his own household well, keeping his children submissive and respectful in every way; for if a man does not know how to manage his own household how can he care for God's church? (1 Tim. 3:1)

The care for God's church is the primary task of the ministry. The Protestant faith considers all other aspects of the ministry as secondary to it. There is little concern with the specific manner of selection and appointment to this office. Most Protestants, however, would agree with Calvin, who said:

> Though there is no express precept for the imposition of hands [in ordination], yet since we find it to have been constantly used by the apostles, such a punctual observance of it by them ought to have the force of a precept with us. And certainly this ceremony is highly useful both to recommend to the people the dignity of the ministry, and to admonish the person ordained that he is no longer his own master, but devoted to the service of God and the church.[16]

NOTES

1. *The Book of Concord*, ed. Theodore G. Tappert (Philadelphia: Fortress Press, 1959), I, 367.

2. Regin Prenter, *Spiritus Creator*, trans. John M. Jensen (Philadelphia: Fortress Press, 1953), p. ix.

3. Karl Barth, *The Faith of the Church*, trans. Gabriel Vahanian (New York: Meridian Press, Inc., Living Age Books, 1958), p. 130.

4. *The Hymnal*, The Protestant Episcopal Church in the U.S.A. (New York: Church Pension Fund, 1920), No. 206.

5. Ibid., No. 209.

6. *Service Book and Hymnal of the Lutheran Church in America*, No. 139.

7. Ibid., No. 356.

8. *Luther's Works* (Weimar Ausgabe), vol. 6, 287 (*Von dem Papsttum in Rom*, 1520).

9. St. Augustine, "De baptismo," in Henry S. Bettenson, *Documents of the Christian Church* (New York: Oxford University Press, 1954), pp. 109 ff.

10. Cf. Helmut R. Niebuhr, *The Social Sources of Denominationalism* (New York: Meridian Press, Inc., Living Age Books, 1957).

11. Harold S. Bender, *Menno Simons' Life and Writings* (Scottdale, Pa.: Mennonite Publishing House, 1944), as quoted in Fosdick, H. E., *Great Voices of the Reformation* (New York: Random House, 1952), pp. 316, 317.

12. Roland H. Bainton, trans., *Here I Stand* (Nashville: Abingdon, 1950), pp. 355 ff. Copyright 1950 by Pierce & Smith. By permission of Abingdon Press.

13. John Calvin, *Institutes of the Christian Religion* (Philadelphia: Presbyterian Board of Education, 1936), book IV, 17, I, vol. II, pp. 641–642.

14. "Small Catechism," *Book of Concord*, I, 374.

15. Robert Barclay, "Apology for the Quakers" (1678). See Appendix.

16. Calvin, *Institutes*, book IV, 3, 16, vol. II, p. 331.

Chapter 8

ESCHATOLOGY

No description of the Protestant faith would be complete without a discussion of the subject of eschatology. The word itself comes from the Greek word for "the furthest," "the last." Thus eschatology deals with the ultimate destiny of humanity and the world.

As the teaching concerning the end, the last things, the goal of life and history, eschatology is a part of all religions. Every major religious movement has something to say about humanity's ultimate destiny. Thus Buddhists teach about Nirvana and the ancient Greeks believed in Hades. The ultimate goal of existence is of concern not only to Protestants but to all people.

This is most strikingly demonstrated by the great secular religions of our time. Communism and fascism in all their forms have well-developed eschatologies. They have a great deal to say about the ultimate outcome of history. Some of the fascination which these pesudo-religions exert upon people today is apparently the result of this very concern with eschatology. They appeal because they claim to be "the wave of the future" and because they assert that they are able to foretell what the future will bring. This is clearly expressed in some of the Fascist and Communist songs. The notorious *"Horst Wessel Lied,"* the hymn of the Nazi movement, spoke about the *last* battle and promised that the future would belong to the *Führer.* Similarly the Communist "International" calls the workers to the *last* fight. Communism predicts that after the revolution the state will disappear and the classless paradise will dawn. It would seem that the success of communism in so many parts of the world is hardly the result of its economic theories, which few people read and even fewer understand, but rather the result of its eschatology. Its promise of a glorious future is attractive and easily understood.

But the eschatology of the great secular movements of our time is utterly different from the biblical eschatology of the Protestant faith. Protestant eschatology derives its uniqueness from the fact that it sees the ultimate destiny of human beings and the world as dependent upon their relationship to God, Father, Son, and Holy Spirit.

Some of the subjects with which Christian eschatology concerns itself are those which Protestants have considered the most stirring aspects of their faith. It deals with death, resurrection, judgment, life after death, and God's eternal kingdom. Its appearance at the end of a description of the Protestant faith must not be construed as a value judgment. Without its particular eschatology the Christian faith would not be Christian at all. Thus eschatology is actually the keystone of everything that has been said so far rather than a more or less superfluous final chapter.

At the beginning of this book we stated that the Protestant faith is derived from the confession that God was in Christ reconciling the world unto himself. Eschatology is the explication of this confession in regard to the future. It asserts that the future as well as the past is the Lord's. It is just as impossible to escape God in time as it is impossible to escape him in space. The Psalmist says about space:

> If I ascend to heaven, thou art there! If I make my bed in Sheol, thou art there! If I take the wings of the morning and dwell in the uttermost parts of the sea, even there thy hand shall lead me, and thy right hand shall hold me. (Ps. 139:8–10)

In the book of Revelation the Lord makes the very same assertion in regard to time: "I am the Alpha and the Omega, the first and the last, the beginning and the end" (Rev. 22:13). Christian eschatology speaks from the perspective of time about this sovereign majesty of God as revealed in Jesus Christ.

The Kingdom of God

If the sovereignty of God over time is taken seriously, the kingdom of God is seen as the purpose and goal of history. It is the realm where *God* rules in power and glory, and thus it is utterly different from all human Utopias which glorify human beings. In this kingdom the powers of evil have been destroyed and can no longer disrupt God's plan for humanity. Satan, who is often called the prince of this world, has been overcome on the Cross, but it is in the coming kingdom that this defeat of the evil powers will be apparent to all. The coming kingdom is reserved for God's people. Only those who are the subjects of the King will inherit his kingdom.

This kingdom of God has always been the hope of Christian people. The New Testament is dominated by this expectation, as are the writings of some of the greatest theologians in the history of the Christian church. But while this hope has been uppermost in the minds of Christians at certain times and in certain places, there have been other periods in which this hope has not been so vital a part of the Christian life. Within the Protestant faith the expectation of the kingdom of God has ranged from a position as the central doctrine to one of marginal concern largely buried in the textbooks on theology.

Whenever eschatology was in the forefront of Protestant thinking, certain books of the Bible were studied with particular zeal. The two books which have always been the favorites of eschatological ages are the book of Daniel in the Old Testament and the book of Revelation in the New Testament. The reason is obvious: both deal with the future and the outcome of history, and both are written in periods of persecution and distress.

A study of church history indicates that eschatology becomes a burning concern of Christians whenever people are no longer sure that the foundations upon which their society is built are sound. In ages of great turmoil and confusion and in countries which have experienced revolution and catastrophe, eschatological thought begins to dominate the thinking of the church.

Protestant Christians have therefore differed widely in their

230

understanding of the significance of eschatology. On the one hand those movements which are generally described as modernism or liberalism have been largely noneschatological in their outlook. Orthodoxy and fundamentalism, on the other hand, while taking eschatology more seriously, have tended to separate it from the totality of the Christian message and sometimes to pervert it through wild and materialistic speculation. Today many Protestant theologians place eschatology in the center of their theology. Some Protestants, however, are still slightly uncomfortable with this subject. Caught between the humanistic utopianism of the liberals and the materialistic speculations of the fundamentalists, they have not been able to make full use of the Christian assertion that the coming Christ is the hope of the world.

While certain shifts in the emphasis on eschatology can be easily understood in the light of the changing pressures upon the church, it must be said that a complete disregard of the Christian hope for the coming of God's kingdom would actually abolish the Protestant faith. The prayer "Thy kingdom come" cannot be abandoned without abandoning the faith itself.

Death and Time

But what are some of the specific assertions which the Protestant faith makes about the "last things"? What does it have to say about death and time? Classical Protestantism accepts the reality of death. Death is not an illusion which can be banished by wishful thinking. Because it is *the* fact which faces every human being, it must be taken seriously. Every effort to ignore it will only lead to self-deception. Classical Protestantism has little use for the elaborate modern efforts to devise methods which make it possible for men and women to deceive themselves about the reality of death. The illusion of modern people that they will live forever misleads them in regard to the seriousness of their predicamant. Protestantism must point out to those lulled into a false security by the flood of statistics concerning life expectancy that regardless of the real accomplishments of the medical profession, the mortality rate remains a constant one hundred percent. It does not ultimately matter that we may be able to reduce the percentage of people who die from heart disease or cancer. Finally, when all the figures are added up, they will invariably show that all people die. The Protestant faith takes this fact very seriously.

But, while death is a fact of human existence, it is not the last word. In a sense it is the first word that must be said about humanity. From the moment we are born, we move toward death. In the words of the German philosopher Martin Heidegger, our existence is a "being unto death." It is this fact which gives urgency and significance to our life. Time is not merely the endless repetition of identical moments; it has an end. Endless time could not be wasted. But human time is not endless; it ends in death. Thus what happens while it lasts is of the utmost significance.

Especially because death, according to the Protestant faith, is not the end at all, the life that ends in death receives ultimate importance. "It is appointed for men to die once, and after that comes judgment" (Heb. 9:27). This judgment after death is the result of the resurrection of the dead. Most religions base their hope for a life after death upon the somewhat vague notion of the immortality of the soul. But, while many Christians believe also in the immortality of the soul, this is not the category which the Bible uses to describe life after death. Immortality of the soul seems to rest the life after death in some indestructible part of the person, namely, his soul. Many who believe in it seem to think that people possess some immortal quality which death cannot destroy.

Against this human being–centered notion of a life after death the Protestant faith asserts the biblical teaching of the resurrection of the body. This doctrine, which can be found in all the great creeds of Christendom, grounds the Christian faith in an eternal life in fellowship with God in God's creative sovereignty rather than in any particular quality in human nature. While the emphasis on the immortality of the soul seems to suggest that there is something in humanity which is of necessity immortal, the doctrine of the resurrection asserts that the God who created human beings in the first place can recreate them in the second place.

We are here in this world. This is a fact which we cannot deny.

We had no choice about being placed in this world. God placed us here according to his purpose. Indeed, we will die, but who are we to say that the God who put us into this world cannot raise us from the dead, recreate us whenever and however he desires? According to the Protestant faith God desires to do so. This is his sovereign decision, no more and no less sovereign than the decision which places us in this world now. If we say that God cannot do it or that it is impossible or highly improbable, the Protestant faith asserts that our existence here and now is also logically impossible or at least highly improbable. But God has placed us in this world nevertheless. Look at us; we are here; we exist! Who are we to say that we will not exist again if the sovereign Creator so chooses?

The emphasis in the doctrine of the resurrection in the Protestant faith is entirely on *God's* creative power rather than on any innate quality of human beings which may prevent their extinction. Even the continuity between human life now and the new life in the world to come is guaranteed by God rather than by any human quality. The Gospel of Luke reports that when the disciples of Jesus had returned from a successful missionary journey during which they had been able to subdue the powers of evil, they were full of joy and gratitude. On this occasion Jesus said to them that while such authority over evil was indeed reason for gratitude they should rejoice rather because they were known by God. In the words of the New Testament: "Nevertheless do not rejoice in this, that the spirits are subject to you; but rejoice that your names are written in heaven" (Luke 10:20). In the language of the Bible the word *name* stands for the "I," the person. To know God's name is to know God personally. And if God knows my name, he knows me personally.

Because the believer is known by God, because he has encountered God and God has established a personal relationship with him, he has become a "thou" to God's "I" and has hope for eternal life. The Christian hope for eternal life is thus rooted in the nature of God rather than in the nature and equipment of human beings. This is the meaning of the Protestant doctrine of the resurrection of the body.

233

The Intermediate Stage

While the faith in the resurrection has always been a basic part of the Protestant faith, the state between the death of a person and his resurrection has been widely and inconclusively debated by theologians. The fundamental problem in all these discussions is the assumption that time is not only a category of the human mind but also a reality in God. The problem disappears, however, if one is prepared to take seriously the scriptural evidence that in God there is no time. He is "the same yesterday and today and for ever" (Heb. 13:8). Of him the Psalmist says: "For a thousand years in thy sight are but as yesterday when it is past, or as a watch in the night" (Ps. 90:4). The Second Letter of Peter states: "But do not ignore this one fact, beloved, that with the Lord one day is as a thousand years, and a thousand years as one day" (2 Pet. 3:8). Thus Jesus Christ can say to the thief on the Cross: "Truly, I say to you, today you will be with me in Paradise" (Luke 23:43). All this seems to indicate that it is an error to project human time into God and to subject God to the limitations of the human concept of time.

In line with the biblical witness it appears to be more accurate to assert that death means confrontation with the living God. Thus each person is confronted by eternity at the moment of his death and no longer subject to the limitations of human time. However, while this seems to be a solution for the problems which a crude understanding of time creates for the Protestant faith, it is by no means unanimously accepted by Protestants. Time and eternity have been much debated, but at present there is no common teaching to do justice to all points of view.

While the understanding of time in relation to God is controversial, Protestants unanimously and categorically reject the notion of purgatory as a state which is neither heaven nor hell in which the souls of men are purged and prepared for fellowship with God. Protestants have always rejected especially the idea that the prayers and offerings of the living can release souls imprisoned there. In fact, a question of this sort produced the occasion for the Reformation.

Since the Protestant faith insists that fellowship with God is solely the result of God's grace and not in any way dependent upon human merit, the notion of purgatory is incongruous to one of the fundamental axioms of this faith. Luther himself, who accepted the existence of a purgatory for a long time after the Reformation, finally abandoned it since he could not find any scriptural evidence for this doctrine.

The Millennium

Another controversial issue in the area of eschatology is the so-called millennium. This is a period of one thousand years at the end of history when, according to some, Christ will return to earth and rule the world with his saints. Millennialism is based on a somewhat obscure passage in the book of Revelation:

> Then I saw an angel coming down from heaven, holding in his hand the key of the bottomless pit and a great chain. And he seized the dragon, that ancient serpent, who is the Devil and Satan, and bound him for a thousand years, and threw him into the pit, and shut it and sealed it over him, that he should deceive the nations no more, till the thousand years were ended. After that he must be loosed a little while.
>
> Then I saw thrones, and seated on them were those to whom judgment was committed. Also I saw the souls of those who had been beheaded for their testimony to Jesus and for the word of God, and who had not worshiped the beast or its image and had not received its mark on their foreheads or their hands. They came to life again, and reigned with Christ a thousand years. (Rev. 20:1–4)

This quotation shows that we are dealing with a vision. The interpretation of such visions is never very easy and obviously gives great leeway to those who love to speculate. Some Protestants have become very much attached to these few verses and have exaggerated their significance out of all proportion to the total Christian message. They eagerly await the literal fulfillment of this prophecy of a thousand-year rule of the saints. However, like most literalists, they are somewhat selective about the passages they are going to take literally. For example, while this text seems to limit the rule to those who have been "beheaded for their testimony to Jesus and for the word of God," most millennialists teach that all true believers share in this rule.

Because of the obscurity of the passage there are a great many differences among Protestants who have made the millennium part of their faith. Classical Protestantism has rejected all these speculations. For the mainstream of the descendants of the Reformation the position of the Augsburg Confession is typical:

> Rejected, too, are certain Jewish opinions which are even now making an appearance and which teach that, before the resurrection of the dead, saints and godly men will possess a worldly kingdom and annihilate all the godless.[1]

Following Augustine, Luther and Calvin understood the millennium as a period of church history which began with Christ's victory over death. The left-wing Protestants generally interpreted it as a golden age at the end of history, either before (premillennialism) or after (postmillennialism) Christ's return. In the modernism of the nineteenth and twentieth centuries the millennial hope was transformed into the expectation of God's rule on earth through the application of Christian moral insights to the social order.

While the millennium has fascinated Christians through the ages, no consensus has ever been achieved. But it must be rejected as worthless and dangerous, whenever speculation concerning the coming rule of the saints leads Protestants to neglect their responsibilities to God and the neighbor here and now, on the basis of the principles of the Protestant faith.

Even this short review of the Protestant faith and eschatology shows that this is an area of great concern and tension. But in spite of the many real disagreements concerning various aspects of eschatology, Protestants do agree on the source of the ultimate Christian hope. God has created people for his purpose. He "desires all men to be saved and to come to the knowledge of the truth" (1 Tim. 2:4). He has called them to fellowship with him and service in his kingdom. This goal is achieved as the result of God's creative grace in Jesus Christ. It is a life which his people live eternally out of the power of his love with and for each other.

To the Protestant faith his eternal fellowship is a personal fellowship with a personal God, bestowed through a personal promise. The Protestant faith rejects the absorption of the individual "I" into some undifferentiated world soul. It asserts the life everlasting as a personal possession. both God + man

But, if God establishes a personal relationship with each human being, it must be possible to reject it. If forced on people it would not be the free relationship of God's "I" to their "thou." Such a forced fellowship would abolish human beings as human. For this reason the Protestant faith proclaims not only eternal salvation but also eternal damnation. Hell, permanent separation from God, is the result of the unlimited possibility of people to say "no" to God. People can resist the love of God forever, for the God of the Bible cannot and will not force his love upon anybody. For this reason most Protestants reject universalism, that is, the teaching that eventually all people will be saved.

? When taken seriously, universalism tends to detract from the importance of the decision to which all people are called when confronted by God. If universalism is accepted, then people are why not saved by some automatic process rather than by the free and sovereign grace of God. This free and sovereign grace of God according to Protestantism is the center of the biblical witness. Nevertheless there have always been voices in the Christian tradition and also in Protestantism who have clung to those statements in Scripture which hold out hope for salvation to everybody. Placing their confidence in the unfathomable grace of God, they pray that God's sovereign grace may overcome all obstacles.

Thus at the end of this study it is important to repeat what was said in the beginning. The Protestant faith in its classical expression glorifies the sovereign grace of God. It is God who creates, it is God who saves, it is God who preserves, it is God who alone guarantees eternal life. The underlying conviction of Protestantism concerning the "first things" as well as the "last things" is expressed most accurately in a hymn written by the Apostle Paul:

> What then shall we say to this? If God is for us, who is against us? He who did not spare his own Son but gave him up for us all, will he not also give us all things with him? Who shall bring any charge against God's elect? It is God who justifies; who is

237

to condemn? Is it Christ Jesus, who died, yes, who was raised from the dead, who is at the right hand of God, who indeed intercedes for us? Who shall separate us from the love of Christ? Shall tribulation, or distress, or persecution, or famine, or nakedness, or peril, or sword? As it is written, "For thy sake we are being killed all the day long; we are regarded as sheep to be slaughtered." No, in all these things we are more than conquerors through him who loved us. For I am sure that neither death, nor life, nor angels, nor principalities, nor things present, nor things to come, nor powers, nor height, nor depth, nor anything else in all creation, will be able to separate us from the love of God in Christ Jesus our Lord. (Rom. 8:31–39)

This, essentially, is the Protestant faith.

NOTES

1. *Augsburg Confession*, Article XVII, see Appendix.

APPENDIX

The Apostles' Creed

I believe in God the Father Almighty, Maker of heaven and earth.

And in Jesus Christ his only (begotten) Son our Lord; who was conceived by the Holy Ghost, born of the Virgin Mary; suffered under Pontius Pilate, was crucified, dead, and buried; he descended into hell; the third day he rose from the dead; he ascended into heaven; and sitteth at the right hand of God the Father Almighty; from thence he shall come to judge the quick and the dead.

I believe in the Holy Ghost; the holy catholic Church; the communion of saints; the forgiveness of sins; the resurrection of the body; and the life everlasting. Amen.

Philip Schaff, *The Creeds of Christendom*
(New York: Harper & Brothers, 1877), II, 45.

The Nicene Creed*

I believe in one God the Father Almighty; Maker of heaven and earth, and of all things visible and invisible.

And in one Lord Jesus Christ, the only-begotten Son of God, begotten of the Father before all worlds [God of God], Light of Light, very God of very God, begotten, not made, being of one substance [essence] with the Father; by whom all things were made; who, for us men and for our salvation, came down from heaven, and was incarnate by the Holy Ghost of the Virgin Mary, and was made man; and was crucified also for us under Pontius Pilate; he suffered and was buried;

---

* The Western additions, of which the *Filioque* is the most important, are enclosed in brackets.

and the third day he rose again, according to the Scriptures; and ascended into heaven, and sitteth on the right hand of the Father; and he shall come again, with glory, to judge both the quick and the dead; whose kingdom shall have no end.

And [I believe] in the Holy Ghost, the Lord and Giver of Life; who proceedeth from the Father [and the Son]; who with the Father and Son together is worshiped and glorified; who spake by the Prophets. And [I believe] one Holy Catholic and Apostolic Church. I acknowledge one Baptism for the remission of sins; and I look for the resurrection of the dead, and the life of the world to come. Amen.

Schaff, *Creeds*, II, 58.

The Athanasian Creed

1. Whosoever will be saved: before all things it is necessary that he holds the Catholic Faith:

2. Which Faith except everyone do keep whole and undefiled: without doubt he shall perish everlastingly.

3. And the Catholic Faith is this: That we worship one God in Trinity, and Trinity in Unity;

4. Neither confounding the Persons: nor dividing the Substance [Essence].

5. For there is one Person of the Father: another of the Son: and another of the Holy Ghost.

6. But the Godhead of the Father, of the Son, and of the Holy Ghost, is all one: the Glory equal, the Majesty coeternal.

7. Such as the Father is: such is the Son: and such is the Holy Ghost.

8. The Father uncreate [uncreated]: the Son uncreate [uncreated]: and the Holy Ghost uncreate [uncreated].

9. The Father incomprehensible [unlimited]: the Son incomprehensible [unlimited]: and the Holy Ghost incomprehensible [unlimited, or infinite].

10. The Father eternal: the Son eternal: and the Holy Ghost eternal.

11. And yet they are not three eternals: but one eternal.

12. As also there are not three uncreated: nor three incomprehensibles [infinites], but one uncreated: and one incomprehensible [infinite].

13. So likewise the Father is Almighty: the Son Almighty: and the Holy Ghost Almighty.

14. And yet they are not three Almighties: but one Almighty.

15. So the Father is God: the Son is God: and the Holy Ghost is God.

16. And yet they are not three Gods: but one God.

17. So likewise the Father is Lord: the Son Lord: and the Holy Ghost Lord.

18. And yet not three Lords: but one Lord.

19. For like as we are compelled by the Christian verity: to acknowledge every Person by himself to be God and Lord:

20. So are we forbidden by the Catholic Religion: to say, There be [are] three Gods, or three Lords.

21. The Father is made of none: neither created, nor begotten.

22. The Son is of the Father alone: not made, nor created, but begotten.

23. The Holy Ghost is of the Father and of the Son: neither made, nor created, nor begotten: but proceeding.

24. So there is one Father, not three Fathers: one Son, not three Sons: one Holy Ghost, not three Holy Ghosts.

25. And in this Trinity none is afore, or after another: none is greater, or less than another [there is nothing before, or after: nothing greater or less].

26. But the whole three Persons are coeternal, and coequal.

27. So that in all things, as aforesaid: the Unity in Trinity, and the Trinity in Unity, is to be worshiped.

28. He therefore that will be saved, must [let him] thus think of the Trinity.

29. Furthermore it is necessary to everlasting salvation: that he also believe rightly [faithfully] the Incarnation of our Lord Jesus Christ.

30. For the right Faith is, that we believe and confess: that our Lord Jesus Christ, the Son of God, is God and Man;

31. God, of the Substance [Essence] of the Father; begotten before the worlds: and Man, of the Substance [Essence] of his Mother, born in the world.

32. Perfect God: and perfect Man, of a reasonable soul and human flesh subsisting.

33. Equal to the Father, as touching his Godhead: and inferior to the Father as touching his Manhood.

34. Who although he be [is] God and Man; yet he is not two, but one Christ.

35. One; not by conversion of the Godhead into flesh: but by taking [assumption] of the Manhood into God.

36. One altogether; not by confusion of Substance [Essence]: but by unity of Person.

37. For as the reasonable soul and flesh is one man: so God and Man is one Christ;

38. Who suffered for our salvation: descended into hell [Hades, spirit-world]: rose again the third day from the dead.

39. He ascended into heaven, he sitteth on the right hand of the Father God [God the Father] Almighty.

40. From whence [thence] he shall come to judge the quick and the dead.

41. At whose coming all men shall rise again with their bodies;

42. And shall give account for their own works.

43. And they that have done good shall go into life everlasting: and they that have done evil, into everlasting fire.

44. This is the Catholic Faith: which except a man believe faithfully [truly and firmly], he cannot be saved.

Schaff, *Creed,* II, 66.

The Augsburg Confession

Articles of Faith and Doctrine

I. God

We unanimously hold and teach, in accordance with the decree of the Council of Nicaea, that there is one divine essence, which is called and which is truly God, and that there are three persons in this one divine essence, equal in power and alike eternal: God the Father, God the Son, God the Holy Spirit. All three are one divine essence, eternal, without division, without end, of infinite power, wisdom, and goodness, one creator and preserver of all things visible and invisible. The word "person" is to be understood as the Fathers employed the term in this connection, not as a part or a property of another but as that which exists of itself.

Therefore all the heresies which are contrary to this article are rejected. Among these are the heresy of the Manichaeans, who assert that there are two gods, one good and one evil; also that of the Valentinians, Arians, Eunomians, Mohammedans, and others like them; also that of the Samosatenes, old and new, who hold that there is only one person and sophistically assert that the other two, the Word and the Holy Spirit, are not necessarily distinct persons but that the Word signifies a physical word or voice and that the Holy Spirit is a movement induced in creatures.

II. ORIGINAL SIN

It is also taught among us that since the fall of Adam all men who are born according to the course of nature are conceived and born in sin. That is, all men are full of evil lust and inclinations from their mothers' wombs and are unable by nature to have true fear of God and true faith in God. Moreover, this inborn sickness and hereditary sin is truly sin and condemns to the eternal wrath of God all those who are not born again through Baptism and the Holy Spirit.

Rejected in this connection are the Pelagians and others who deny that original sin is sin, for they hold that natural man is made righteous by his own powers, thus disparaging the sufferings and merit of Christ.

III. THE SON OF GOD

It is also taught among us that God the Son became man, born of the virgin Mary, and that the two natures, divine and human, are so inseparably united in one person that there is one Christ, true God and true man, who was truly born, suffered, was crucified, died, and was buried in order to be a sacrifice not only for original sin but also for all other sins and to propitiate God's wrath. The same Christ also descended into hell, truly rose from the dead on the third day, ascended into heaven, and sits on the right hand of God, that he may eternally rule and have dominion over all creatures, that through the Holy Spirit he may sanctify, purify, strengthen, and comfort all who believe in him, that he may bestow on them life and every grace and blessing, and that he may protect and defend them against the devil and against sin. The same Lord Christ will return openly to judge the living and the dead, as stated in the Apostles' Creed.

IV. JUSTIFICATION

It is also taught among us that we cannot obtain forgiveness of sin and righteousness before God by our own merits, works, or satisfactions, but that we receive forgiveness of sin and become righteous before God by grace, for Christ's sake, through faith, when we believe that Christ suffered for us and that for his sake our sin is forgiven and righteousness and eternal life are given to us. For God will regard and reckon this faith as righteousness, as Paul says in Romans 3:21–26 and 4:5.

243

V. The Office of the Ministry

To obtain such faith God instituted the office of the ministry, that is, provided the Gospel and the sacraments. Through these, as through means, he gives the Holy Spirit, who works faith, when and where he pleases, in those who hear the Gospel. And the Gospel teaches that we have a gracious God, not by our own merits but by the merit of Christ, when we believe this.

Condemned are the Anabaptists and others who teach that the Holy Spirit comes to us through our own preparations, thoughts, and works without the external word of the Gospel.

VI. The New Obedience

It is also taught among us that such faith should produce good fruits and good works and that we must do all such good works as God has commanded, but we should do them for God's sake and not place our trust in them as if thereby to merit favor before God. For we receive forgiveness of sin and righteousness through faith in Christ, as Christ himself says, "So you also, when you have done all that is commanded you, say, 'We are unworthy servants'" (Luke 17:10). The Fathers also teach thus, for Ambrose says, "It is ordained of God that whoever believes in Christ shall be saved, and he shall have forgiveness of sins, not through works but through faith alone, without merit."

VII. The Church

It is also taught among us that one holy Christian church will be and remain forever. This is the assembly of all believers among whom the Gospel is preached in its purity and the holy sacraments are administered according to the Gospel. For it is sufficient for the true unity of the Christian church that the Gospel be preached in conformity with a pure understanding of it and that the sacraments be administered in accordance with the divine Word. It is not necessary for the true unity of the Christian church that ceremonies, instituted by men, should be observed uniformly in all places. It is as Paul says in Eph. 4:4, 5, "There is one body and one Spirit, just as you were called to the one hope that belongs to your call, one Lord, one faith, one baptism."

VIII. What the Church Is

Again, although the Christian church, properly speaking, is nothing else than the assembly of all believers and saints, yet because in this life many false Christians, hypocrites, and even open sinners remain among the godly, the sacraments are efficacious even if the priests who administer them are wicked men, for as Christ himself indicated, "The Pharisees sit on Moses' seat" (Matt. 23:2).

Accordingly the Donatists and all others who hold contrary views are condemned.

IX. BAPTISM

It is taught among us that Baptism is necessary and that grace is offered through it. Children, too, should be baptized, for in Baptism they are committed to God and become acceptable to him.

On this account the Anabaptists who teach that infant Baptism is not right are rejected.

X. THE HOLY SUPPER OF OUR LORD

It is taught among us that the true body and blood of Christ are really present in the Supper of our Lord under the form of bread and wine and are there distributed and received. The contrary doctrine is therefore rejected.

XI. CONFESSION

It is taught among us that private absolution should be retained and not allowed to fall into disuse. However, in confession it is not necessary to enumerate all trespasses and sins, for this is impossible. Ps. 19:12, "Who can discern his errors?"

XII. REPENTANCE

It is taught among us that those who sin after Baptism receive forgiveness of sin whenever they come to repentance, and absolution should not be denied them by the church. Properly speaking, true repentance is nothing else than to have contrition and sorrow, or terror, on account of sin, and yet at the same time to believe the Gospel and absolution (namely, that sin has been forgiven and grace has been obtained through Christ), and this faith will comfort the heart and again set it at rest. Amendment of life and the forsaking of sin should then follow, for these must be the fruits of repentance, as John says, "Bear fruit that befits repentance" (Matt. 3:8).

Rejected here are those who teach that persons who have once become godly cannot fall again.

Condemned on the other hand are the Novatians who denied absolution to such as had sinned after Baptism.

Rejected also are those who teach that forgiveness of sin is not obtained through faith but through the satisfactions made by man.

XIII. The Use of the Sacraments

It is taught among us that the sacraments were instituted not only to be signs by which people might be identified outwardly as Christians, but that they are signs and testimonies of God's will toward us for the purpose of awakening and strengthening our faith. For this reason they require faith, and they are rightly used when they are received in faith and for the purpose of strengthening faith.

XIV. Order in the Church

It is taught among us that nobody should publicly teach or preach or administer the sacraments in the church without a regular call.

XV. Church Usages

With regard to church usages that have been established by men, it is taught among us that those usages are to be observed which may be observed without sin and which contribute to peace and good order in the church, among them being certain holy days, festivals, and the like. Yet we accompany these observances with instruction so that consciences may not be burdened by the notion that such things are necessary for salvation. Moreover it is taught that all ordinances and traditions instituted by men for the purpose of propitiating God and earning grace are contrary to the Gospel and the teaching about faith in Christ. Accordingly monastic vows and other traditions concerning distinctions of foods, days, etc., by which it is intended to earn grace and make satisfaction for sin, are useless and contrary to the Gospel.

XVI. Civil Government

It is taught among us that all government in the world and all established rule and laws were instituted and ordained by God for the sake of good order, and that Christians may without sin occupy civil offices or serve as princes and judges, render decisions and pass sentence according to imperial and other existing laws, punish evildoers with the sword, engage in just wars, serve as soldiers, buy and sell, take required oaths, possess property, be married, etc.

Condemned here are the Anabaptists who teach that none of the things indicated above is Christian.

Also condemned are those who teach that Christian perfection requires the forsaking of house and home, wife and child, and the renunciation of such activities as are mentioned above. Actually, true perfection consists alone of proper fear of God and real faith in God, for the Gospel does not teach an outward and temporal but an inward and eternal mode of existence and righteousness of the heart. The Gospel does not overthrow civil authority, the state, and marriage but requires that all these be kept as true orders of God and that everyone, each according to his own calling, manifest Christian love and genuine good works in his station of life. Accordingly Christians are obliged to be subject to civil authority and obey its commands and laws in all that can be done without sin. But when commands of the civil authority cannot be obeyed without sin, we must obey God rather than men (Acts 5:29).

XVII. The Return of Christ to Judgment

It is also taught among us that our Lord Jesus Christ will return on the last day for judgment and will raise up all the dead, to give eternal life and everlasting joy to believers and the elect but to condemn ungodly men and the devil to hell and eternal punishment.

Rejected, therefore, are the Anabaptists who teach that the devil and condemned men will not suffer eternal pain and torment.

Rejected, too, are certain Jewish opinions which are even now making an appearance and which teach that, before the resurrection of the dead, saints and godly men will possess a worldly kingdom and annihilate all the godless.

XVIII. Freedom of the Will

It is also taught among us that man possesses some measure of freedom of the will which enables him to live an outwardly honorable life and to make choices among the things that reason comprehends. But without the grace, help, and activity of the Holy Spirit man is not capable of making himself acceptable to God, of fearing God and believing in God with his whole heart, or of expelling inborn evil lusts from his heart. This is accomplished by the Holy Spirit, who is given through the word of God, for Paul says in I Cor. 2:14, "Natural man does not receive the gifts of the Spirit of God."

In order that it may be evident that this teaching is no novelty, the clear words of Augustine on free will are here quoted from the third book of his *Hypognosticon*: "We concede that all men have a free will, for all have a natural, innate understanding and reason. However, this does not enable them to act in matters pertaining to God (such as loving God with their whole heart or fearing him), for it is only in the outward acts of this life that they have freedom to choose good or evil. By good I mean what they are capable of by nature: whether or not to labor in the fields, whether or not to eat or drink or visit a friend, whether to dress or undress, whether to build a house, take a wife, engage in a trade, or do whatever else may be good and profitable. None of these is or exists without God, but all things are from him and through him. On the other hand, by his own choice man can also undertake evil, as when he wills to kneel before an idol, commit murder, etc."

XIX. The Cause of Sin

It is taught among us that although almighty God has created and still preserves nature, yet sin is caused in all wicked men and despisers of God by the perverted will. This is the will of the devil and of all ungodly men; as soon as God withdraws his support, the will turns away from God to evil. It is as Christ says in John 8:44, "When the devil lies, he speaks according to his own nature."

XX. Faith and Good Works

Our teachers have been falsely accused of forbidding good works. Their writings on the Ten Commandments, and other writings as well, show that they have given good and profitable accounts and instructions concerning true Christian estates and works. About these little was taught in former times, when for the most part sermons were concerned with childish and useless works like rosaries, the cult of saints, monasticism, pilgrimages, appointed fasts, holy days, brotherhoods, etc. Our opponents no longer praise these useless works so highly as they once did, and they have also learned to speak now of faith, about which they did not preach at all in former times. They do not teach now that we become righteous before God by our works alone, but they add faith in Christ and say that faith and works make us righteous before God. This teaching may offer a little more comfort than the teaching that we are to rely solely on our works.

Since the teaching about faith, which is the chief article in the Christian life, has been neglected so long (as all must admit) while nothing but works was preached everywhere, our people have been instructed as follows:

We begin by teaching that our works cannot reconcile us with God or obtain grace for us, for this happens only through faith, that is, when we believe that our sins are forgiven for Christ's sake, who alone is the mediator who reconciles the Father. Whoever imagines that he can accomplish this by works, or that he can merit grace, despises Christ and seeks his own way to God, contrary to the Gospel.

This teaching about faith is plainly and clearly treated by Paul in many passages, especially in Eph. 2:8, 9, "For by grace you have been saved through faith; and this is not your own doing, it is the gift of God—not because of works, lest any man should boast," etc.

That no new interpretation is here introduced can be demonstrated from Augustine, who discusses this question thoroughly and teaches the same thing, namely, that we obtain grace and are justified before God through faith in Christ and not through works. His whole book, *De spiritu et litera*, proves this.

Although this teaching is held in great contempt among untried people, yet it is a matter of experience that weak and terrified consciences find it most comforting and salutary. The conscience cannot come to rest and peace through works, but only through faith, that is, when it is assured and knows that for Christ's sake it has a gracious God, as Paul says in Rom. 5:1, "Since we are justified by faith, we have peace with God."

In former times this comfort was not heard in preaching, but poor consciences were driven to rely on their own efforts, and all sorts of works were undertaken. Some were driven by their conscience into monasteries in the hope that there they might merit grace through monastic life. Others devised other works for the purpose of earning grace and making satisfaction for sins. Many of them discovered that they did not obtain peace by such means. It was therefore necessary to preach this doctrine about faith in Christ and diligently to apply it in order that men may know that the grace of God is appropriated without merits, through faith alone.

Instruction is also given among us to show that the faith here spoken of is not that possessed by the devil and the ungodly, who also believe the history of Christ's suffering and his resurrection from the dead, but we mean such true faith as believes that we receive grace and forgiveness of sin through Christ.

Whoever knows that in Christ he has a gracious God, truly knows God, calls upon him, and is not, like the heathen, without God. For the devil and the ungodly do not believe this article concerning the forgiveness of sin, and so they are at enmity with God, cannot call upon him, and have no hope of receiving good from him. Therefore, as has just been indicated, the Scriptures speak of faith but do not mean by it such knowledge as the devil and ungodly men possess. Heb. 11:1 teaches about faith in such a way as to make it clear that faith is not merely a knowledge of historical events but is a confidence in God and in the fulfillment of his promises. Augustine also reminds us that we should understand the word "faith" in the Scriptures to mean confidence in God, assurance that God is gracious to us, and not merely such a knowledge of historical events as the devil also possesses.

It is also taught among us that good works should and must be done, not that we are to rely on them to earn grace but that we may do God's will and glorify him. It is always faith alone that apprehends grace and forgiveness of sin. When through faith the Holy Spirit is given, the heart is moved to do good works. Before that, when it is without the Holy Spirit, the heart is too weak. Moreover, it is in the power of the devil, who drives poor human beings into many sins. We see this in the philosophers who undertook to lead honorable and blameless lives; they failed to accomplish this, and instead fell into many great and open sins. This is what happens when a man is without true faith and the Holy Spirit and governs himself by his own human strength alone.

Consequently this teaching concerning faith is not to be accused of forbidding good works but is rather to be praised for teaching that good works are to be done and for offering help as to how they may be done. For without faith and without Christ human nature and human strength are much too weak to do good works, call upon God, have patience in suffering, love one's neighbor, diligently engage in callings which are commanded, render obedience, avoid evil lusts, etc. Such great and genuine works cannot be done without the help of Christ, as he himself says in John 15:5, "Apart from me you can do nothing."

XXI. The Cult of Saints

It is also taught among us that saints should be kept in remembrance so that our faith may be strengthened when we see what grace they received and how they were sustained by faith. Moreover, their good works are to be an example for us, each of us in his own calling. So His Imperial Majesty may in salutary and godly fashion imitate the example of David in making war on the Turk, for both are incumbents of a royal office which demands the defense and protection of their subjects.

However, it cannot be proved from the Scriptures that we are to invoke saints or seek help from them. "For there is one mediator between God and men, Christ Jesus" (I Tim. 2:5), who is the only saviour, the only highpriest, advocate, and intercessor before God

(Rom. 8:34). He alone has promised to hear our prayers. Moreover, according to the Scriptures, the highest form of divine service is sincerely to seek and call upon this same Jesus Christ in every time of need. "If anyone sins, we have an advocate with the Father, Jesus Christ the righteous" (I John 2:1).

This is just about a summary of the doctrines that are preached and taught in our churches for proper Christian instruction, the consolation of consciences, and the amendment of believers. Certainly we should not wish to put our own souls and consciences in grave peril before God by misusing his name or Word, nor should we wish to bequeath to our children and posterity any other teaching than that which agrees with the pure Word of God and Christian truth. Since this teaching is grounded clearly on the Holy Scriptures and is not contrary or opposed to that of the universal Christian church, or even of the Roman church (insofar as the latter's teaching is reflected in the writings of the Fathers), we think that our opponents cannot disagree with us in the articles set forth above. Therefore, those who presume to reject, avoid, and separate from our churches as if our teaching were heretical, act in an unkind and hasty fashion, contrary to all Christian unity and love, and do so without any solid basis of divine command or Scripture. The dispute and dissension are concerned chiefly with various traditions and abuses. Since, then, there is nothing unfounded or defective in the principal articles and since this our confession is seen to be godly and Christian, the bishops should in all fairness act more leniently, even if there were some defect among us in regard to traditions, although we hope to offer firm grounds and reasons why we have changed certain traditions and abuses.

From Theodore G. Tappert, ed., and trans., *The Book of Concord*
(Philadelphia, Fortress Press, 1959).
© 1959 by Fortress Press and used with permission.

The Articles of Religion of the Protestant Episcopal Church*

I. Of Faith in the Holy Trinity

There is but one living and true God, everlasting, without body, parts, [or passions]; of infinite power, wisdom, and goodness; the

---

* The material included in brackets has been omitted in the Articles of Religion of the Methodist Church, which otherwise uses this statement of faith.

Maker, the Preserver of all things [both] visible and invisible. And in the unity of this Godhead there be three Persons, of one substance, power, and eternity; the Father, the Son, and the Holy Ghost.

II. OF THE WORD OR SON OF GOD, WHICH WAS MADE VERY MAN

The Son, which is the Word of the Father, [begotten from everlasting of the Father,] the very and eternal God, and of one substance with the Father, took Man's nature in the womb of the blessed Virgin, [of her substance:] so that the two whole and perfect Natures, that is to say, the Godhead and Manhood, were joined together in one Person, never to be divided, whereof is one Christ, very God, and very Man; who truly suffered, was crucified, dead, and buried, to reconcile his Father to us, and to be a sacrifice, not only for original guilt, but also for actual sins of men.

[III. OF THE GOING DOWN OF CHRIST INTO HELL

As Christ died for us, and was buried; so also is it to be believed, that He went down into Hell.]

IV. OF THE RESURRECTION OF CHRIST

Christ did truly rise again from death, and took again his body, with flesh, bones, and all things appertaining to the perfection of Man's nature; wherewith he ascended into Heaven, and there sitteth, until he return to judge all Men at the last day.

V. OF THE HOLY GHOST

The Holy Ghost, proceeding from the Father and the Son, is of one substance, majesty, and glory, with the Father and the Son, very and eternal God.

VI. OF THE SUFFICIENCY OF THE HOLY SCRIPTURES FOR SALVATION

Holy Scripture containeth all things necessary to salvation: so that whatsoever is not read therein, nor may be proved thereby, is not to be required of any man, that it should be believed as an article of Faith, or be thought requisite or necessary to salvation. In the name of the Holy Scripture we do understand those canonical books of the Old and New Testaments, of whose authority was never any doubt in the Church.

APPENDIX

Of the Names and Number of the Canonical Books

Genesis,	The First Book of Samuel,	The Book of Esther,
Exodus,	The Second Book of Samuel,	The Book of Job,
Leviticus,	The First Book of Kings,	The Psalms,
Numbers,	The Second Book of Kings,	The Proverbs,
Deuteronomy,	The First Book of Chronicles,	Ecclesiastes or Preacher,
Joshua,	The Second Book of Chronicles,	Cantica, or Songs of Solomon,
Judges,	The First Book of Esdras,	Four Prophets the greater,
Ruth,	The Second Book of Esdras,	Twelve Prophets the less.

[And the other Books (as Hierome saith) the Church doth read for example of life and instruction of manners; but yet doth it not apply them to establish any doctrine; such are these following:

The Third Book of Esdras,	Baruch the Prophet,
The Fourth Book of Esdras,	The Sons of the Three Children,
The Book of Tobias,	The Story of Susanna,
The Book of Judith,	Of Bel and the Dragon,
The rest of the Book of Esther,	The Prayer of Manasses,
The Book of Wisdom,	The First Book of Maccabees,
Jesus the Son of Sirach,	The Second Book of Maccabees.]

All the Books of the New Testament, as they are commonly received, we do receive, and account them Canonical.

VII. Of the Old Testament

The Old Testament is not contrary to the New: for both in the Old and New Testaments everlasting life is offered to Mankind by Christ, who is the only Mediator between God and Man, being both God and Man. Wherefore, they are not to be heard, which feign that the old Fathers did look only for transitory promises. Although the Law given from God by Moses, as touching Ceremonies and Rites, do not bind Christian men, nor the Civil precepts thereof ought of necessity to be received in any commonwealth; yet notwithstanding, no Christian man whatsoever is free from the obedience of the Commandments which are called Moral.

[VIII. Of the Creeds

The Nicene Creed, and that which is commonly called the Apostles' Creed, ought thoroughly to be received and believed: for they may be proved by most certain warrants of Holy Scripture.]

APPENDIX

IX. OF ORIGINAL OR BIRTH-SIN

Original sin standeth not in the following of Adam (as the Pelagians do vainly talk); but it is the fault and corruption of the Nature of every man, that naturally is engendered of the offspring of Adam; whereby man is very far gone from original righteousness, and is of his own nature inclined to evil, [so that the flesh lusteth always contrary to the Spirit; and therefore in every person born into this world it deserveth God's wrath and damnation. And this infection of nature doth remain, yea in them that are regenerated; whereby the lust of the flesh, called in Greek, *phronema sarkos* (which some do expound the wisdom, some sensuality, some the affection, some the desire, of the flesh) is not subject to the Law of God. And although there is no condemnation for them that believe and are baptized; yet the Apostle doth confess, that concupiscence and lust hath of itself the nature of sin.]

X. OF FREE WILL

The condition of Man after the fall of Adam is such, that he cannot turn and prepare himself, by his own natural strength and good works, to faith, and calling upon God. Wherefore we have no power to do good works pleasant and acceptable to God, without the grace of God by Christ preventing us, that we may have a good will, and working with us, when we have that good will.

XI. OF THE JUSTIFICATION OF MAN

We are accounted righteous before God, only for the merit of our Lord and Savior Jesus Christ by Faith, and not for our own works or deservings. Wherefore, that we are justified by Faith only, is a most wholesome Doctrine, and very full of comfort, [as more largely is expressed in the Homily of Justification].

XII. OF GOOD WORKS

Albeit that Good Works, which are the fruits of Faith, and follow after Justification, cannot put away our sins, and endure the severity of God's judgment; yet are they pleasing and acceptable to God in Christ, and do spring out [necessarily] of a true and lively Faith; insomuch that by them a lively Faith may be as evidently known as a tree discerned by the fruit.

254

[XIII. OF WORKS BEFORE JUSTIFICATION

Works done before the grace of Christ, and the Inspiration of his Spirit, are not pleasant to God, forasmuch as they spring not of faith in Jesus Christ; neither do they make men meet to receive grace, or (as the School-authors say) deserve grace of congruity: yea rather, for that they are not done as God hath willed and commanded them to be done, we doubt not but they have the nature of sin.]

XIV. OF WORKS OF SUPEREROGATION

Voluntary Works besides, over and above, God's Commandments, which they call Works of Supererogation, cannot be taught without arrogancy and impiety: for by them men do declare, that they do not only render unto God as much as they are bound to do, but that they do more for his sake, than of bounden duty is required: whereas Christ saith plainly, When ye have done all that are commanded to you, say, We are unprofitable servants.

[XV. OF CHRIST ALONE WITHOUT SIN

Christ in the truth of our nature was made like unto us in all things, sin only except, from which he was clearly void, both in his flesh, and in his spirit. He came to be the Lamb without spot, who, by sacrifice of himself once made, should take away the sins of the world; and sin (as Saint John saith) was not in him. But all we the rest, although baptized, and born again in Christ, yet offend in many things; and if we say we have no sin, we deceive ourselves, and the truth is not in us.]

XVI. OF SIN AFTER BAPTISM

Not every [deadly] sin willingly committed after [Baptism (Justification, Meth.)] is sin against the Holy Ghost, and unpardonable. Wherefore the grant of repentance is not to be denied to such as fall into sin after [Baptism (Justification, Meth.)]. After we have received the Holy Ghost, we may depart from grace given, and fall into sin, and by the grace of God, we may arise again, and amend our lives. And therefore they are to be condemned, which say, they can no more sin as long as they live here, or deny the place of forgiveness to such as truly repent.

[XVII. OF PREDESTINATION AND ELECTION

Predestination of Life is the everlasting purpose of God, whereby (before the foundations of the world were laid) he hath constantly decreed by his counsel secret to us, to deliver from curse and damnation those whom he hath chosen in Christ out of mankind, and to bring them by Christ to everlasting salvation, as vessels made to honor. Wherefore, they which be endued with so excellent a benefit of God, be called according to God's purpose by his Spirit working in due season: they through Grace obey the calling: they be justified freely: they be made sons of God by adoption: they be made like the image of his only begotten Son Jesus Christ: they walk religiously in good works, and at length, by God's mercy, they attain to everlasting felicity.

As the godly consideration of Predestination, and our Election in Christ, is full of sweet, pleasant, and unspeakable comfort to godly persons, and such a feeling in themselves the working of the Spirit of Christ, mortifying the works of the flesh, and their earthly members, and drawing up their mind to high and heavenly things, as well because it doth greatly establish and confirm their faith of eternal Salvation to be enjoyed through Christ, as because it doth fervently kindle their love toward God: So, for curious and carnal persons, lacking the Spirit of Christ, to have continually before their eyes the sentence of God's Predestination, is a most dangerous downfall, whereby the Devil doth trust them either into desperation, or into wretchlessness of most unclean living, no less perilous than desperation.

Furthermore, we must conceive God's promises in such wise, as they be generally set forth to us in Holy Scripture: and, in our doings, the Will of God is to be followed, which we have expressly declared unto us in the Word of God.

XVIII. OF OBTAINING ETERNAL SALVATION ONLY BY THE NAME OF CHRIST

They also are to be had accursed that presume to say, That every man shall be saved by the Law or Sect which he professeth, so that he be diligent to frame his life according to that Law, and the light of Nature. For Holy Scripture doth set out unto us only the Name of Jesus Christ, whereby man must be saved.]

XIX. OF THE CHURCH

The visible Church is a congregation of faithful men, in the which the pure Word of God is preached, and the Sacraments be duly ministered according to Christ's ordinance, in all those things that of necessity are requisite to the same.

[As the Church of Jerusalem, Alexandria, and Antioch, have erred; so also the Church of Rome hath erred, not only in their living and manner of Ceremonies, but also in matters of Faith.]

[XX. OF THE AUTHORITY OF THE CHURCH

The Church hath power to decree Rites or Ceremonies, and authority in Controversies of Faith: and yet it is not lawful for the Church to ordain anything that is contrary to God's Word written, neither may it so expound one place of Scripture, that it be repugnant to another. Wherefore, although the Church be a witness and a keeper of Holy Writ, yet, as it ought not to decree anything against the same, so besides the same ought it not enforce anything to be believed for necessity of Salvation.

XXI. OF THE AUTHORITY OF GENERAL COUNCILS

(The Twenty-first of the former Articles is omitted; because it is partly of a local and civil nature, and is provided for, as to the remaining parts of it, in other Articles.)]

XXII. OF PURGATORY

The Romish Doctrine concerning Purgatory, Pardons, Worshipping and Adoration, as well of Images as of Relics, and also Invocation of Saints, is a fond thing, vainly invented, and grounded upon no warranty of Scripture, but rather repugnant to the Word of God.

[XXIII. OF MINISTERING IN THE CONGREGATION

It is not lawful for any man to take upon him the office of public preaching, or ministering the Sacraments in the Congregation, before he be lawfully called, and sent to execute the same. And those we ought to judge lawfully called and sent, which be chosen and called to this work by men who have public authority given unto them in the Congregation, to call and send Ministers into the Lord's vineyard.]

XXIV. OF SPEAKING IN THE CONGREGATION IN SUCH A TONGUE AS THE PEOPLE UNDERSTAND

It is a thing plainly repugnant to the Word of God, and the custom of the primitive Church, to have public Prayer in the Church, or to minister the Sacraments, in a tongue not understood of the people.

XXV. OF THE SACRAMENTS

Sacraments ordained of Christ be not only badges or tokens of Christian men's profession, but rather they be certain sure witnesses, and effectual signs of grace, and God's good will toward us, by the which he doth work invisibly in us, and doth not only quicken, but also strengthen and confirm our Faith in him.

There are two Sacraments ordained of Christ our Lord in the Gospel, that is to say, Baptism, and the Supper of the Lord.

Those five commonly called Sacraments, that is to say, Confirmation, Penance, Orders, Matrimony, and Extreme Unction, are not to be counted for Sacraments of the Gospel, being such as have grown partly of the corrupt following of the Apostles, partly are states of life allowed in the Scriptures; but yet have not like nature of Sacraments with Baptism, and the Lord's Supper, for that they have not any visible signs or ceremony ordained of God.

The Sacraments were not ordained of Christ to be gazed upon, or to be carried about, but that we should duly use them. And in such only as worthily receive the same, they have a wholesome effect or operation; but they that receive them unworthily, purchase to themselves damnation, as Saint Paul saith.

[XXVI. OF THE UNWORTHINESS OF THE MINISTERS, WHICH HINDERS NOT THE EFFECT OF THE SACRAMENTS

Although in the visible Church the evil be ever mingled with the good, and sometimes the evil have chief authority in the Ministration of the Word and the Sacraments, yet forasmuch as they do not use the same in their own name, but in Christ's, and do minister by his commission and authority, we may use their Ministry, both in hearing the Word of God, and in receiving the Sacraments. Neither is the effect of Christ's ordinance taken away by their wickedness, nor the grace of God's gifts diminished from such as by faith, and rightly, do receive the Sacraments ministered unto them; which be effectual, because of Christ's institution and promise, although they be ministered by evil men.

Nevertheless, it appertaineth to the discipline of the Church, that inquiry be made of evil Ministers, and that they be accused by those that have knowledge of their offenses; and finally, being found guilty, by just judgment be deposed.]

XXVII. OF BAPTISM

Baptism is not only a sign of profession, and mark of difference, whereby Christian men are discerned from others that be not christened, but it is also a sign of Regeneration or New-Birth [whereby, as by an instrument, they that receive Baptism rightly are grafted into the Church; the promises of the forgiveness of sin, and of our adoption to be the sons of God by the Holy Ghost, are visibly signed and sealed; Faith is confirmed, and Grace increased by virtue of prayer unto God].

The Baptism of young Children is in any wise to be retained in the Church, [as most agreeable with the institution of Christ].

XXVIII. OF THE LORD'S SUPPER

The Supper of the Lord is not only a sign of the love that Christians ought to have among themselves one to another; but rather it is a Sacrament of our Redemption by Christ's death: insomuch as to such as rightly, worthily, and with faith, receive the same, the Bread which we break is a partaking of the Body of Christ; and likewise the Cup of Blessing is a partaking of the Blood of Christ.

Transubstantiation (or the change of the substance of Bread and Wine) in the Supper of the Lord, cannot be proved by Holy Writ; but is repugnant to the plain words of Scripture, overthroweth the nature of a Sacrament, and hath given occasion to many superstitions.

The Body of Christ is given, taken, and eaten, in the Supper, only after an heavenly and spiritual manner. And the means whereby the Body of Christ is received and eaten in the Supper, is Faith.

The Sacrament of the Lord's Supper was not by Christ's ordinance reserved, carried about, lifted up, or worshipped.

[XXIX. OF THE WICKED, WHICH EAT NOT THE BODY OF CHRIST IN THE USE OF THE LORD'S SUPPER

The Wicked, and such as be void of a lively faith, although they do carnally and visibly press with their teeth (as Saint Augustine saith) the Sacrament of the Body and Blood of Christ; yet in no wise are they partakers of Christ; but rather, to their condemnation, do eat and drink the sign or Sacrament of so great a thing.]

XXX. OF BOTH KINDS

The Cup of the Lord is not to be denied to the Lay-people: for both the parts of the Lord's Sacrament, by Christ's ordinance and com-mandment, ought to be administered to all Christian men alike.

XXXI. Of the One Oblation of Christ Finished upon the Cross

The Offering of Christ once made is that perfect redemption, propitiation, and satisfaction, for all the sins of the whole world, both original and actual; and there is none other satisfaction for sin, but that alone. Wherefore the sacrifices of Masses, in the which it was commonly said, that the Priest did offer Christ for the quick and the dead, to have remission of pain or guilt, were blasphemous fables, and dangerous deceits.

XXXII. Of the Marriage of Priests

Bishops, Priests, and Deacons are not commanded by God's Law, either to vow the estate of single life, or to abstain from marriage: therefore it is lawful for them, as for all other Christian men, to marry at their own discretion, as they shall judge the same to serve better to godliness.

[XXXIII. Of Excommunicate Persons, How They Are to Be Avoided

That person which by open denunciation of the Church is rightly cut off from the unity of the Church, and excommunicated, ought to be taken of the whole multitude of the faithful, as an Heathen and Publican, until he be openly reconciled by penance, and received into the Church by a Judge that hath authority thereunto.]

XXXIV. Of the Traditions of the Church

It is not necessary that Traditions and Ceremonies be in all places one, or utterly like; for at all times they have been divers, and may be changed according to the diversity of countries, times, and men's manners, so that nothing be ordained against God's Word. Whosoever, through his private judgment, willingly and purposely, doth openly break the Traditions and Ceremonies of the Church, which be not repugnant to the Word of God, and be ordained and approved by common authority, ought to be rebuked openly (that others may fear to do the like) as he that offendeth against the common order of the Church [and hurteth the authority of the Magistrate], and woundeth the consciences of the weak brethren.

Every particular [or national] Church hath authority to ordain, change, and abolish, Ceremonies or Rites [of the Church ordained only by man's authority], so that all things be done to edifying.

APPENDIX

[XXXV. OF THE HOMILIES

The Second Book of Homilies, the several titles whereof we have joined under this Article, doth contain a godly and wholesome Doctrine, and necessary for these times, as doth the former Book of Homilies, which were set forth in the time of Edward the Sixth; and therefore we judge them to be read in Churches by the Ministers, diligently and distinctly, that they may be understanded of the people.

Of the Names of the Homilies

1. Of the Right Use of the Church
2. Against Peril of Idolatry
3. Of Repairing and Keeping Clean of Churches
4. Of Good Works: First of Fasting
5. Against Gluttony and Drunkenness
6. Against Excess of Apparel
7. Of Prayer
8. Of the Place and Time of Prayer
9. That Common Prayer and Sacraments Ought to Be Ministered in a Known Tongue
10. Of the Reverend Estimation of God's Word
11. Of Alms-doing
12. Of the Nativity of Christ
13. Of the Passion of Christ
14. Of the Resurrection of Christ
15. Of the Worthy Receiving of the Sacrament of the Body and Blood of Christ
16. Of the Gifts of the Holy Ghost
17. For the Rogation-days
18. Of the State of Matrimony
19. Of Repentance
20. Against Idleness
21. Against Rebellion

(This Article is received in this Church, so far as it declares the Books of Homilies to be an explication of Christian doctrine, and instructive in piety and morals. But all references to the constitution and laws of England are considered as inapplicable to the circumstances of this Church; which also suspends the order for the reading of said Homilies in churches, until a revision of them may be conveniently made, for the clearing of them, as well from obsolete words and phrases, as from the local references.)

XXXVI. OF CONSECRATION OF BISHOPS AND MINISTERS

The Book of Consecration of Bishops, and Ordering of Priests and Deacons, as set forth by the General Convention of this Church in 1792, doth contain all things necessary to such Consecration and Ordering; neither hath it anything that, of itself, is superstitious and ungodly. And, therefore, whosoever, are consecrated or ordered according to said Form, we decree all such to be rightly, orderly, and lawfully consecrated and ordered.

261

XXXVII. Of the Power of the Civil Magistrates

The Power of the Civil Magistrate extendeth to all men, as well Clergy as Laity, in all things temporal; but hath no authority in things purely spiritual. And we hold it to be the duty of all men who are professors of the Gospel, to pay respectful obedience to the Civil Authority, regularly and legitimately constituted.]

XXXVIII. Of Christian Men's Goods, Which Are Not Common

The Riches and Goods of Christians are not common, as touching the right, title, and possession of the same; as certain [Anabaptists] do falsely boast. Notwithstanding, every man ought, of such things as he possesseth, liberally to give alms to the poor, according to his ability.

XXXIX. Of a Christian Man's Oath

As we confess that vain and rash Swearing is forbidden Christian men by our Lord Jesus Christ, and James his Apostle, so we judge, that Christian religion doth not prohibit, but that a man may swear when the Magistrate requireth, in a cause of faith and charity, so it be done according to the Prophet's teaching, in justice, judgment, and truth.

The Book of Common Prayer (New York: Morehouse-Gorham Co., 1938), pp. 603 ff.

The Westminster Shorter Catechism

Ques. 1. What is the chief end of man?

Ans. Man's chief end is to glorify God, and to enjoy him forever.

Ques. 2. What rule hath God given to direct us how we may glorify and enjoy him?

Ans. The Word of God, which is contained in the Scriptures of the Old and New Testaments, is the only rule to direct us how we may glorify and enjoy him.

Ques. 3. What do the Scriptures principally teach?

Ans. The Scriptures principally teach what man is to believe concerning God, and what duty God requires of man.

Ques. 4. What is God?

Ans. God is a Spirit, infinite, eternal, and unchangeable, in his being, wisdom, power, holiness, justice, goodness, and truth.

Ques. 5. Are there more Gods than one?

Ans. There is but one only, the living and true God.

Ques. 6. How many persons are there in the Godhead?

Ans. There are three persons in the Godhead: the Father, the Son, and the Holy Ghost; and these three are one God, the same in substance, equal in power and glory.

Ques. 7. What are the decrees of God?

Ans. The decrees of God are his eternal purpose according to the counsel of his will, whereby, for his own glory, he hath foreordained whatsoever comes to pass.

Ques. 8. How doth God execute his decrees?

Ans. God executeth his decrees in the works of creation and providence.

Ques. 9. What is the work of creation?

Ans. The work of creation is God's making all things of nothing, by the word of his power, in the space of six days, and all very good.

Ques. 10. How did God create man?

Ans. God created man, male and female, after his own image, in knowledge, righteousness, and holiness, with dominion over the creatures.

Ques. 11. What are God's works of providence?

Ans. God's works of providence are his most holy, wise, and powerful preserving and governing all his creatures, and all their actions.

Ques. 12. What special act of providence did God exercise toward man, in the estate wherein he was created?

Ans. When God had created man, he entered into a covenant of life with him, upon condition of perfect obedience; forbidding him to eat of the tree of knowledge of good and evil, upon pain of death.

Ques. 13. Did our first parents continue in the estate wherein they were created?

Ans. Our first parents, being left to the freedom of their own will, fell from the estate wherein they were created, by sinning against God.

Ques. 14. What is sin?

Ans. Sin is any want of conformity unto, or transgression of, the law of God.

Ques. 15. What was the sin whereby our first parents fell from the estate wherein they were created?

Ans. The sin whereby our first parents fell from the estate wherein they were created was their eating the forbidden fruit.

Ques. 16. Did all mankind fall in Adam's first transgression?

Ans. The covenant being made with Adam, not only for himself, but for his posterity, all mankind descending from him by ordinary generation sinned in him, and fell with him, in his first transgression.

Ques. 17. Into what estate did the fall bring mankind?

Ans. The fall brought mankind into an estate of sin and misery.

Ques. 18. Wherein consists the sinfulness of that estate whereinto man fell?

Ans. The sinfulness of that estate whereinto man fell consists in the guilt of Adam's first sin, the want of original righteousness, and the corruption of his whole nature, which is commonly called original sin; together with all actual transgressions which proceed from it.

Ques. 19. What is the misery of that estate whereinto man fell?

Ans. All mankind by their fall lost communion with God, are under his wrath and curse, and so made liable to all the miseries in this life, to death itself, and to the pains of hell forever.

Ques. 20. Did God leave all mankind to perish in the estate of sin and misery?

Ans. God, having out of his mere good pleasure, from all eternity, elected some to everlasting life, did enter into a covenant of grace, to deliver them out of the estate of sin and misery, and to bring them into an estate of salvation by a Redeemer.

Ques. 21. Who is the Redeemer of God's elect?

Ans. The only Redeemer of God's elect is the Lord Jesus Christ, who being the eternal Son of God became man, and so was, and continueth to be, God and man, in two distinct natures, and one person forever.

Ques. 22. How did Christ, being the Son of God, become man?

Ans. Christ, the Son of God, became man, by taking to himself a true body, and a reasonable soul, being conceived by the power of the Holy Ghost, in the womb of the Virgin Mary, and born of her, yet without sin.

Ques. 23. What offices doth Christ execute as our Redeemer?

Ans. Christ, as our Redeemer, executeth the offices of a Prophet, of a Priest, and of a King, both in his estate of humiliation and exaltation.

Ques. 24. How doth Christ execute the office of a Prophet?

Ans. Christ executeth the office of a Prophet, in revealing to us by his Word and Spirit, the will of God for our salvation.

Ques. 25. How doth Christ execute the office of a Priest?

Ans. Christ executeth the office of Priest, in his once offering up of himself a sacrifice to satisfy divine justice, and reconcile us to God, and in making continual intercession for us.

Ques. 26. How doth Christ execute the office of a King?

Ans. Christ executeth the office of a King, in subduing us to himself, in ruling and defending us, and in restraining and conquering all his and our enemies.

Ques. 27. Wherein did Christ's humiliation consist?

Ans. Christ's humiliation consisted in his being born, and that in a low condition, made under the law, undergoing the miseries of this life, the wrath of God, and cursed death of the cross; in being buried, and continuing under the power of death for a time.

Ques. 28. Wherein consisteth Christ's exaltation?

Ans. Christ's exaltation consisteth in his rising again from the dead on the third day, in ascending up into heaven, in sitting at the right hand of God the Father, and in coming to judge the world at the last day.

Ques. 29. How are we made partakers of the redemption purchased by Christ?

Ans. We are made partakers of the redemption purchased by Christ, by the effectual application of it to us by his Holy Spirit.

Ques. 30. How doth the Spirit apply to us the redemption purchased by Christ?

Ans. The Spirit applieth to us the redemption purchased by Christ, by working faith in us, and thereby uniting us to Christ in our effectual calling.

Ques. 31. What is effectual calling?

Ans. Effectual calling is the work of God's Spirit, whereby, convincing us of our sin and misery, enlightening our minds in the knowledge of Christ, and renewing our wills, he doth persuade and enable us to embrace Jesus Christ, freely offered to us in the gospel.

Ques. 32. What benefits do they that are effectually called partake of in this life?

Ans. They that are effectually called do in this life partake of justification, adoption, sanctification, and the several benefits which, in this life, do either accompany or flow from them.

Ques. 33. What is justification?

Ans. Justification is an act of God's free grace, wherein he pardoneth all our sins, and accepteth us as righteous in his sight, only for the righteousness of Christ imputed to us, and received by faith alone.

Ques. 34. What is adoption?

Ans. Adoption is an act of God's free grace, whereby we are received into the number, and have a right to all the privileges, of the sons of God.

Ques. 35. What is sanctification?

Ans. Sanctification is the work of God's free grace, whereby we are renewed in the whole man after the image of God, and are enabled more and more to die unto sin, and live unto righteousness.

Ques. 36. What are the benefits which in this life do accompany or flow from justification, adoption, and sanctification?

Ans. The benefits which in this life do accompany or flow from justification, adoption, and sanctification, are, assurance of God's love, peace of conscience, joy in the Holy Ghost, increase of grace, and perseverance therein to the end.

Ques. 37. What benefits do believers receive from Christ at death?

Ans. The souls of believers are, at their death, made perfect in holiness, and do immediately pass into glory; and their bodies, being still united to Christ, do rest in their graves till the resurrection.

Ques. 38. What benefits do believers receive from Christ at the resurrection?

Ans. At the resurrection, believers being raised up in glory, shall be openly acknowledged and acquitted in the day of judgment, and made perfectly blessed in the full enjoying of God to all eternity.

Ques. 39. What is the duty which God requireth of man?

Ans. The duty which God requireth of man is obedience to his revealed will.

Ques. 40. What did God at first reveal to man for the rule of his obedience?

Ans. The rule which God at first revealed to man, for his obedience, was the moral law.

Ques. 41. Wherein is the moral law summarily comprehended?

Ans. The moral law is summarily comprehended in the ten commandments.

Ques. 42. What is the sum of the ten commandments?

Ans. The sum of the ten commandments is, to love the Lord our God with all our heart, with all our soul, and with all our strength, and with all our mind; and our neighbor as ourselves.

Ques. 43. What is the preface to the ten commandments?

Ans. The preface to the ten commandments is in these words: I am the Lord thy God, which brought thee out of the land of Egypt, out of the house of bondage.

Ques. 44. What doth the preface to the ten commandments teach us?

Ans. The preface to the ten commandments teacheth us, that because God is the Lord, and our God and Redeemer, therefore we are bound to keep all his commandments.

Ques. 45. Which is the first commandment?

Ans. The first commandment is, Thou shalt have no other gods before me.

Ques. 46. What is required in the first commandment?

Ans. The first commandment requireth us to know and acknowledge God, to be the only true God; and to worship and glorify him accordingly.

Ques. 47. What is forbidden in the first commandment?

Ans. The first commandment forbiddeth the denying or not worshiping and glorifying the true God, as God, and our God; and the giving that worship and glory to any other which is due to him alone.

Ques. 48. What are we specially taught by these words, "before me," in the first commandment?

Ans. These words, "before me," in the first commandment, teach us that God, who seeth all things, taketh notice of, and is much displeased with, the sin of having any other God.

Ques. 49. Which is the second commandment?

Ans. The second commandment is, Thou shalt not make unto thee any graven image, or any likeness of any thing that is in heaven above, or that is in the earth beneath, or that is in the water under the earth; thou shalt not bow down thyself to them, nor serve them; for I the Lord thy God am a jealous God, visiting the iniquity of the fathers upon the children, unto the third and fourth generation of them that hate me, and showing mercy unto thousands of them that love me and keep my commandments.

Ques. 50. What is required in the second commandment?

Ans. The second commandment requireth the receiving, observing, and keeping pure and entire, all such religious worship and ordinances as God hath appointed in his Word.

Ques. 51. What is forbidden in the second commandment?

Ans. The second commandment forbiddeth the worshiping of God by images, or any other way not appointed in his Word.

Ques. 52. What are the reasons annexed to the second commandment?

Ans. The reasons annexed to the second commandment are, God's sovereignty over us, his propriety in us, and the zeal he hath to his own worship.

Ques. 53. Which is the third commandment?

Ans. The third commandment is, Thou shalt not take the name of the Lord thy God in vain: for the Lord will not hold him guiltless that taketh his name in vain.

Ques. 54. What is required in the third commandment?

Ans. The third commandment requireth the holy and reverent use of God's names, titles, attributes, ordinances, word, and works.

Ques. 55. What is forbidden in the third commandment?

Ans. The third commandment forbiddeth all profaning or abusing of any thing whereby God maketh himself known.

Ques. 56. What is the reason annexed to the third commandment?

Ans. The reason annexed to the third commandment is, that however the breakers of this commandment may escape punishment from men, yet the Lord our God will not suffer them to escape his righteous judgment.

Ques. 57. Which is the fourth commandment?

Ans. The fourth commandment is, Remember the Sabbath-day to keep it holy. Six days shalt thou labor, and do all thy work: but the seventh day is the Sabbath of the Lord thy God: in it thou shalt not do any work, thou, nor thy son, nor thy daughter, thy man-servant, nor thy maid-servant, nor thy cattle, nor thy stranger that is within thy gates; for in six days the Lord made heaven and earth, the sea, and all that in them is, and rested the seventh day: wherefore the Lord blessed the Sabbath-day and hallowed it.

Ques. 58. What is required in the fourth commandment?

Ans. The fourth commandment requireth the keeping holy to God such set times as he hath appointed in his Word; expressly one whole day in seven, to be a holy Sabbath to himself.

Ques. 59. Which day of the seven hath God appointed to be the weekly Sabbath?

Ans. From the beginning of the world to the resurrection of Christ, God appointed the seventh day of the week to be the weekly Sabbath; and the first day of the week, ever since, to continue to the end of the world, which is the Christian Sabbath.

Ques. 60. How is the Sabbath to be sanctified?

Ans. The Sabbath is to be sanctified by a holy resting all that day, even from such worldly employment and recreations as are lawful on other days; and spending the whole time in the public and private exercises of God's worship, except so much as is to be taken up in the works of necessity and mercy.

Ques. 61. What is forbidden in the fourth commandment?

Ans. The fourth commandment forbiddeth the omission, or careless performance, of the duties required, and the profaning the day by idleness, or doing that which is in itself sinful, or by unnecessary thoughts, words, or works about our worldly employments and recreations.

Ques. 62. What are the reasons annexed to the fourth commandment?

Ans. The reasons annexed to the fourth commandment are, God's allowing us six days of the week for our own employments, his challenging a special propriety in the seventh, his own example, and his blessing the Sabbath-day.

Ques. 63. Which is the fifth commandment?

Ans. The fifth commandment is, Honor thy father and thy mother:

that thy days may be long upon the land which the Lord thy God giveth thee.

Ques. 64. What is required in the fifth commandment?

Ans. The fifth commandment requireth the preserving the honor of, and performing the duties belonging to, every one in their several places and relations, as superiors, inferiors, or equals.

Ques. 65. What is forbidden in the fifth commandment?

Ans. The fifth commandment forbiddeth the neglecting of, or doing any thing against, the honor and duty which belongeth to every one in their several places and relations.

Ques. 66. What is the reason annexed to the fifth commandment?

Ans. The reason annexed to the fifth commandment is, a promise of long life and prosperity (as far as it shall serve for God's glory, and their own good) to all such as keep this commandment.

Ques. 67. Which is the sixth commandment?

Ans. The sixth commandment is, Thou shalt not kill.

Ques. 68. What is required in the sixth commandment?

Ans. The sixth commandment requireth all lawful endeavors to preserve our own life, and the life of others.

Ques. 69. What is forbidden in the sixth commandment?

Ans. The sixth commandment forbiddeth the taking away of our own life, or the life of the neighbor unjustly, or whatsoever tendeth thereunto.

Ques. 70. Which is the seventh commandment?

Ans. The seventh commandment is, Thou shalt not commit adultery.

Ques. 71. What is required in the seventh commandment?

Ans. The seventh commandment requireth the preservation of our own and our neighbor's chastity, in heart, speech, and behavior.

Ques. 72. What is forbidden in the seventh commandment?

Ans. The seventh commandment forbiddeth all unchaste thoughts, words, and actions.

Ques. 73. Which is the eighth commandment?

Ans. The eighth commandment is, Thou shalt not steal.

Ques. 74. What is required in the eighth commandment?

Ans. The eighth commandment requireth the lawful procuring and furthering the wealth and outward estate of ourselves and others.

Ques. 75. What is forbidden in the eighth commandment?

Ans. The eighth commandment forbiddeth whatsoever doth, or may, unjustly hinder our own, or our neighbor's wealth or outward estate.

Ques. 76. Which is the ninth commandment?

Ans. The ninth commandment is, Thou shalt not bear false witness against thy neighbor.

Ques. 77. What is required in the ninth commandment?

Ans. The ninth commandment requireth the maintaining and promoting of truth between man and man, and of our own and our neighbor's good name, especially in witness-bearing.

Ques. 78. What is forbidden in the ninth commandment?

Ans. The ninth commandment forbiddeth whatsoever is prejudicial to truth, or injurious to our own or our neighbor's good name.

Ques. 79. Which is the tenth commandment?

Ans. The tenth commandment is, Thou shalt not covet thy neighbor's house, thou shalt not covet thy neighbor's wife, nor his man-servant, nor his maid-servant, nor his ox, nor his ass, nor any thing that is thy neighbor's.

Ques. 80. What is required in the tenth commandment?

Ans. The tenth commandment requireth full contentment with our own condition, with a right and charitable frame of spirit toward our neighbor, and all that is his.

Ques. 81. What is forbidden in the tenth commandment?

Ans. The tenth commandment forbiddeth all discontentment with our own estate, envying or grieving at the good of our neighbor, and all inordinate motions or affections to any thing that is his.

Ques. 82. Is any man able perfectly to keep the commandments of God?

Ans. No mere man, since the fall, is able, in this life, perfectly to keep the commandments of God; but doth daily break them, in thought, word, and deed.

Ques. 83. Are all transgressions of the law equally heinous?

Ans. Some sins in themselves, and by reason of several aggravations, are more heinous in the sight of God than others.

Ques. 84. What doth every sin deserve?

Ans. Every sin deserveth God's wrath and curse, both in this life and that which is to come.

Ques. 85. What doth God require of us, that we may escape his wrath and curse, due to us for sin?

Ans. To escape the wrath and curse of God, due to us for sin, God requireth of us faith in Jesus Christ, repentance unto life, with the diligent use of all the outward means whereby Christ communicateth to us the benefits of redemption.

Ques. 86. What is faith in Jesus Christ?

Ans. Faith in Jesus Christ is a saving grace, whereby we receive and rest upon him alone for salvation, as he is offered to us in the gospel.

Ques. 87. What is repentance unto life?

Ans. Repentance unto life is a saving grace, whereby a sinner, out of a true sense of his sin, and apprehension of the mercy of God in

Christ, doth, with grief and hatred of his sin, turn from it unto God, with full purpose of, and endeavor after, new obedience.

Ques. 88. What are the outward and ordinary means whereby Christ communicateth to us the benefits of redemption?

Ans. The outward and ordinary means whereby Christ communicateth to us the benefits of redemption, are his ordinances, especially the Word, sacraments, and prayer; all which are made effectual to the elect for salvation.

Ques. 89. How is the Word made effectual to salvation?

Ans. The Spirit of God maketh the reading, but especially the preaching of the Word, an effectual means of convincing and converting sinners, and of building them up in holiness and comfort through faith unto salvation.

Ques. 90. How is the Word to be read and heard, that it may become effectual to salvation?

Ans. That the Word may become effectual to salvation, we must attend thereunto with diligence, preparation, and prayer; receive it with faith and love, lay it up in our hearts, and practice it in our lives.

Ques. 91. How do the sacraments become effectual means of salvation?

Ans. The sacraments become effectual means of salvation, not from any virtue in them, or in him that doth administer them, but only by the blessing of Christ, and the working of his Spirit in them that by faith receive them.

Ques. 92. What is a sacrament?

Ans. A sacrament is a holy ordinance instituted by Christ; wherein, by sensible signs, Christ and the benefits of the new covenant are represented, sealed, and applied to believers.

Ques. 93. Which are the sacraments of the New Testament?

Ans. The sacraments of the New Testament are Baptism and the Lord's Supper.

Ques. 94. What is Baptism?

Ans. Baptism is a sacrament, wherein the washing with water, in the name of the Father, and of the Son, and of the Holy Ghost, doth signify and seal our ingrafting into Christ and partaking of the benefits of the covenant of grace, and our engagement to be the Lord's.

Ques. 95. To whom is Baptism to be administered?

Ans. Baptism is not to be administered to any that are out of the visible Church, till they profess their faith in Christ, and obedience to him; but the infants of such as are members of the visible church are to be baptized.

Ques. 96. What is the Lord's Supper?

Ans. The Lord's Supper is a sacrament, wherein, by giving and receiving bread and wine, according to Christ's appointment, his death is showed forth, and the worthy receivers are, not after a corporal and carnal manner, but by faith, made partakers of his body and blood, with all his benefits, to their spiritual nourishment and growth in grace.

Ques. 97. What is required to the worthy receiving of the Lord's Supper?

Ans. It is required of them that would worthily partake of the Lord's Supper, that they examine themselves of their knowledge to discern the Lord's body, of their faith to feed upon him, of their repentance, love, and new obedience; lest coming unworthily, they eat and drink judgment to themselves.

Ques. 98. What is prayer?

Ans. Prayer is an offering up of our desires unto God, for things agreeable to his will, in the name of Christ, with confession of our sins, and thankful acknowledgment of his mercies.

Ques. 99. What rule hath God given for our direction in prayer?

Ans. The whole Word of God is of use to direct us in prayer, but the special rule of direction is that form of prayer which Christ taught his disciples, commonly called, the Lord's Prayer.

Ques. 100. What doth the preface of the Lord's Prayer teach us?

Ans. The preface of the Lord's Prayer, which is, "Our Father which art in heaven," teacheth us to draw near to God with all holy reverence and confidence, as children to a father, able and ready to help us; and that we should pray with and for others.

Ques. 101. What do we pray for in the first petition?

Ans. In the first petition, which is, "Hallowed be thy name," we pray that God would enable us and others to glorify him in all that whereby he maketh himself known, and that he would dispose all things to his own glory.

Ques. 102. What do we pray for in the second petition?

Ans. In the second petition, which is, "Thy kingdom come," we pray that Satan's kingdom may be destroyed, and that the kingdom of grace may be advanced, ourselves and others brought into it, and kept in it, and that the kingdom of glory may be hastened.

Ques. 103. What do we pray for in the third petition?

Ans. In the third petition, which is, "Thy will be done on earth as it is in heaven," we pray that God by his grace would make us able and willing to know, obey, and submit to his will in all things, as the angels do in heaven.

Ques. 104. What do we pray for in the fourth petition?

Ans. In the fourth petition, which is, "Give us this day our daily bread," we pray that of God's free gift we may receive a competent portion of the good things of this life, and enjoy his blessing with them.

Ques. 105. What do we pray for in the fifth petition?

Ans. In the fifth petition, which is, "And forgive us our debts as we forgive our debtors," we pray that God, for Christ's sake, would freely pardon all our sins; which we are the rather encouraged to ask, because by his grace we are enabled from the heart to forgive others.

Ques. 106. What do we pray for in the sixth petition?

Ans. In the sixth petition, which is, "And lead us not into temptation, but deliver us from evil," we pray that God would either keep us from being tempted to sin, or support and deliver us when we are tempted.

Ques. 107. What doth the conclusion of the Lord's Prayer teach us?

Ans. The conclusion of the Lord's Prayer, which is, "For thine is the kingdom, and the power and the glory forever, Amen," teacheth us to take our encouragement in prayer from God only, and in our prayers to praise him; ascribing kingdom, power, and glory to him; and in testimony of our desire and assurance to be heard, we say, Amen.

Schaff, *Creeds,* III, 676–700.

The Confession of the Society of Friends, Commonly Called Quakers

The First Proposition

CONCERNING THE TRUE FOUNDATION OF KNOWLEDGE

Seeing the height of all happiness is placed in the true knowledge of God ("This is life eternal, to know thee the only true God, and Jesus Christ whom thou hast sent"), the true and right understanding of this foundation and ground of knowledge is that which is most necessary to be known and believed in the first place.

The Second Proposition

CONCERNING IMMEDIATE REVELATION

Seeing "no man knoweth the Father but the Son, and he to whom the Son revealeth him"; and seeing the revelation of the Son is in and by the Spirit; therefore the testimony of the Spirit is that alone by which the true knowledge of God hath been, is, and can be only revealed; who as, by moving of his own Spirit, he converted the chaos of this world into that wonderful order wherein it was in the beginning, and created man a living soul, to rule and govern it, so by the revelation of the same Spirit he hath manifested himself all along unto the sons of men, both patriarchs, prophets, and apostles; which revelations of God by the Spirit, whether by outward voices and appearances, dreams, or inward objective manifestations in the heart, were of old the formal object of their faith, and remain yet so to be; since the object of the saints' faith is the same in all ages, though set forth under divers administrations. Moreover, these divine inward revelations, which we make absolutely necessary for the building up of true faith, neither do nor can ever contradict the outward testimony of the Scriptures, or right and sound reason. Yet from hence it will not follow that these divine revelations are to be subjected to examination, either of the outward testimony of the Scriptures or of the natural reason of man, as to a more noble or certain rule or touchstone; for this divine revelation and inward illumination is that which is evident and clear of itself, forcing, by its own evidence and clearness, the well-disposed understanding to assent, irresistibly moving the same thereunto; even as the common principles of natural truths move and incline the mind to a natural assent: as, that the whole is greater than its part; that two contradictory sayings cannot be both true, nor both false: which is also manifest, according to our adversaries' principle, who—supposing the possibility of inward divine revelations—will nevertheless confess with us that neither Scripture nor sound reason will contradict it: and yet it will not follow, according to them, that the Scripture or sound reason should be subjected to the examination of the divine revelations in the heart.

The Third Proposition

CONCERNING THE SCRIPTURES

From these revelations of the Spirit of God to the saints have proceeded the Scriptures of truth, which contain: 1. A faithful historical account of the actings of God's people in divers ages, with many singular and remarkable providences attending them. 2. A prophetical account of several things, whereof some are already past, and some yet to come. 3. A full and ample account of all the chief principles of the doctrine of Christ, held forth in divers precious declarations, exhortations, and sentences, which, by the moving of God's Spirit, were at several times, and upon sundry occasions, spoken and written unto some churches and their pastors: nevertheless, because they are only a declaration of the fountain, and not the fountain itself, therefore they are not to be esteemed the principal ground of all truth and knowledge, nor yet the adequate primary rule of faith and manners. Nevertheless, as that which giveth a true and faithful testimony of the first foundation, they are and may be esteemed a secondary rule, subordinate to the Spirit, from which they have all their excellency and certainty; for as by the inward testimony of the Spirit we do alone truly know them, so they testify that the Spirit is that guide by which the saints are led into all truth: therefore, according to the Scriptures, the Spirit is the first and principal Leader. And seeing we do therefore receive and believe the Scriptures, because they proceeded from the Spirit, therefore also the Spirit is more originally and principally the rule, according to that received maxim in the schools, *propter quod unumquodque est tale, illud ipsum est magis tale.* Englished thus: "That for which a thing is such, that thing itself is more such."

The Fourth Proposition

CONCERNING THE CONDITION OF MAN IN THE FALL

All Adam's posterity, or mankind, both Jews and Gentiles, as to the first Adam, or earthly man, is fallen, degenerated, and dead, deprived of the sensation or feeling of this inward testimony or seed of God, and is subject unto the power, nature, and seed of the Serpent, which he sows in men's hearts, while they abide in this natural and corrupted state; from whence it comes that not their words and deeds only, but all their imaginations are evil perpetually in the sight of God, as proceeding from this depraved and wicked seed. Man, therefore, as he is in this state, can know nothing aright; yea, his thoughts and conceptions concerning God and things spiritual, until he be disjoined from this evil seed, and united to the Divine Light, are unprofitable both to himself and others: hence are rejected the Socinian and Pelagian errors, in exalting a natural light; as also of the Papists, and most Protestants, who affirm that man, without the true grace of God, may be a true minister of the gospel. Nevertheless, this seed is not imputed to infants, until by transgression they actually join themselves therewith; for they are by nature the children of wrath, who walk according to the power of the prince of the air.

The Fifth and Sixth Proposition

CONCERNING THE UNIVERSAL REDEMPTION BY CHRIST, AND ALSO THE SAVING AND SPIRITUAL LIGHT, WHEREWITH EVERY MAN IS ENLIGHTENED

God, out of his infinite love, who delighteth not in the death of a sinner, but that all should live and be saved, hath so loved the world that he hath given his only Son a Light, that whosoever believeth in him should be saved; who enlighteneth every man that cometh into the world, and maketh manifest all things that are reprovable, and teacheth all temperance, righteousness, and godliness: and this Light enlighteneth the hearts of all in a day, in order to salvation, if not resisted: nor is it less universal than the seed of sin, being the purchase of his death, who tasted death for every man; "For as in Adam all die, even so in Christ shall all be made alive."

According to which principle (or hypothesis), all the objections against the universality of Christ's death are easily solved; neither is it needful to recur to the ministry of angels, and those other miraculous means which, they say, God makes use of, to manifest the doctrine and history of Christ's passion unto such, who, living in those places of the world where the outward preaching of the gospel is unknown, have well improved the first and common grace; for hence it well follows, that as some of the old philosophers might have been saved, so also may now some—who by providence are cast into those remote parts of the world where the knowledge of the history is wanting—be made partakers of the divine mystery, if they receive and resist not that grace, "a manifestation whereof is given to every man to profit withal." This certain doctrine then being received, to wit, that there is an evangelical and saving light and grace in all, the universality of the love and mercy of God toward mankind—both in the death of his beloved Son, the Lord Jesus Christ, and in the manifestation of the light in the heart—is established and confirmed against all the objections of such as deny it. Therefore "Christ hath tasted death for every man": not only for all kinds of men, as some vainly talk, but for every one, of all kinds; the benefit of whose offering is not only. extended to such, who have the distinct outward knowledge of his death and sufferings, as the same is declared in the Scriptures, but even unto those who are necessarily excluded from the benefit of this knowledge by some inevitable accident; which knowledge we willingly confess to be very profitable and comfortable, but not absolutely needful unto such, from whom God himself hath withheld it; yet they may be made partakers of the mystery of his death, though ignorant of this history, if they suffer his seed and light—enlightening their hearts—to take place; in which light communion with the Father and Son is enjoyed, so as of wicked men to become holy, and lovers of that power by whose inward and secret touches they feel themselves turned from the evil to the good, and learn to do to others as they would be done by; in which Christ himself affirms all to be included. As they then have falsely and erroneously taught who have denied Christ to have died for all men, so neither have they sufficiently taught the truth, who, affirming him to have died for all, have added the absolute necessity of the outward knowledge thereof in order to the obtaining its saving effect; among whom the Remonstrants of Holland have been chiefly wanting, and many other asserters of Universal Redemption, in that they have not placed the extent of this salvation in that divine and evangelical principle of light and life wherewith Christ hath enlightened every man that comes into the world, which is excellently and evidently held forth in these Scriptures: Gen. vi. 3; Deut. xxx. 14; John i. 7–9; Rom. x. 8; Titus ii. 11.

The Seventh Proposition

CONCERNING JUSTIFICATION

As many as resist not this light, but receive the same, in them is produced an holy, pure, and spiritual birth, bringing forth holiness, righteousness, purity, and all those other blessed fruits which are acceptable to God; by which holy birth, to wit, Jesus Christ formed within us, and working his works in us, as we are sanctified, so we are justified in the sight of God, according to the apostle's words, "But ye are washed, but ye are sanctified, but ye are justified, in the name of the Lord Jesus, and by the Spirit of our God." Therefore it is not by our works wrought in our will, nor yet by good works, considered as of themselves, but by Christ, who is both the gift and the giver, and the cause producing the effect in us; who, as he hath reconciled us while we were enemies, doth also in his wisdom save us, and justify us after this manner, as saith the same apostle elsewhere, "According to his mercy he saved us, by the washing of regeneration, and the renewing of the Holy Ghost."

The Eighth Proposition

CONCERNING PERFECTION

In whom this holy and pure birth is fully brought forth the body of death and sin comes to be crucified and removed, and their hearts united and subjected unto the truth, so as not to obey any suggestion or temptation of the evil one, but to be free from actual sinning and transgressing of the law of God, and in that respect perfect. Yet doth this perfection still admit of a growth; and there remaineth a possibility of sinning where the mind doth not most diligently attend unto the Lord.

The Ninth Proposition

CONCERNING PERSEVERANCE, AND THE POSSIBILITY OF FALLING FROM GRACE

Although this gift and inward grace of God be sufficient to work out salvation, yet in those in whom it is resisted it both may and doth become their condemnation. Moreover, in whom it hath wrought in part, to purify and sanctify them, in order to their further perfection, by disobedience such may fall from it, and turn it to wantonness, making shipwreck of faith; and "after having tasted of the heavenly gift, and been made partakers of the Holy Ghost, again fall away." Yet such an increase and stability in the truth may in this life be attained, from which there cannot be a total apostasy.

The Tenth Proposition

CONCERNING THE MINISTRY

As by this gift, or Light of God, all true knowledge in things spiritual is received and revealed; so by the same, as it is manifested and received in the heart, by the strength and power thereof, every true minister of the gospel is ordained, prepared, and supplied in the work of the ministry; and by the leading, moving, and drawing hereof ought every evangelist and Christian pastor to be led and ordered in his labor and work of the gospel, both as to the place where, as to the persons to whom, and as to the times when he is to minister. Moreover, those who have this authority may and ought to preach the gospel, though without human commission or literature; as, on the other hand, those who want the authority of this divine gift, however learned or authorized by the commission of men and churches, are to be esteemed but as deceivers, and not true ministers of the gospel. Also, who have received this holy and unspotted gift, as they have freely received, so are they freely to give, without hire or bargaining, far less to use it as a trade to get money by it; yet if God hath called any from their employments or trades, by which they acquire their livelihood, it may be lawful for such, according to the liberty which they feel given them in the Lord, to receive such temporals—to wit, what may be needful to them for meat and clothing—as are freely given them by those to whom they have communicated spirituals.

The Eleventh Proposition

CONCERNING WORSHIP

All true and acceptable worship to God is offered in the inward and immediate moving and drawing of his own Spirit, which is neither limited to places, times, or persons; for though we be to worship him always, in that we are to fear before him, yet as to the outward signification thereof in prayers, praises, or preachings, we ought not to do it where and when we will, but where and when we are moved thereunto by the secret inspirations of his Spirit in our hearts, which God heareth and accepteth of, and is never wanting to move us thereunto, when need is, of which he himself is the alone proper judge. All other worship then, both praises, prayers, and preachings, which man sets about in his own will, and at his own appointment, which he can both begin and end at his pleasure, do or leave undone, as himself sees meet, whether they be a prescribed form, as a liturgy, or prayers conceived extemporarily, by the natural strength and faculty of the mind, they are all but superstitious, will-worship, and abominable idolatry in the sight of God; which are to be denied, rejected, and separated from, in this day of his spiritual arising: however it might have pleased him—who winked at the times of ignorance, with respect to the simplicity and integrity of some, and of his own innocent seed, which lay as it were buried in the hearts of men, under the mass of superstition—to blow upon the dead and dry bones, and to raise some breathings, and to answer them, and that until the day should more clearly dawn and break forth.

The Twelfth Proposition

CONCERNING BAPTISM

As there is one Lord and one faith, so there is "one baptism; which is not the putting away the filth of the flesh, but the answer of a good conscience before God, by the resurrection of Jesus Christ." And this baptism is a pure and spiritual thing, to wit, the baptism of the Spirit and Fire, by which we are buried with him, that, being washed and purged from our sins, we may "walk in newness of life"; of which the

279

baptism of John was a figure, which was commanded for a time, and not to continue forever.

As to the baptism of infants, it is a mere human tradition, for which neither precept nor practice is to be found in all the Scripture.

The Thirteenth Proposition

CONCERNING THE COMMUNION, OR PARTICIPATION OF THE BODY AND BLOOD OF CHRIST

The communion of the body and blood of Christ is inward and spiritual, which is the participation of his flesh and blood, by which the inward man is daily nourished in the hearts of those in whom Christ dwells; of which things the breaking of bread by Christ with his disciples was a figure, which they even used in the Church for a time, who had received the substance, for the cause of the weak; even as "abstaining from things strangled, and from blood"; the washing one another's feet, and the anointing of the sick with oil; all which are commanded with no less authority and solemnity than the former; yet seeing they are but the shadows of better things, they cease in such as have obtained the substance.

The Fourteenth Proposition

CONCERNING THE POWER OF THE CIVIL MAGISTRATE, IN MATTERS PURELY RELIGIOUS, AND PERTAINING TO THE CONSCIENCE

Since God hath assumed to himself the power and dominion of the conscience, who alone can rightly instruct and govern it, therefore it is not lawful for any whatsoever, by virtue of any authority or principality they bear in the government of this world, to force the conscience of others; and therefore all killing, banishing, fining, imprisoning, and other such things, which men are afflicted with, for the alone exercise of their conscience, or difference in worship or opinion, proceedeth from the spirit of Cain, the murderer, and is contrary to the truth; provided always that no man, under the pretense of conscience, prejudice his neighbor in his life or estate, or do any thing destructive to, or inconsistent with, human society; in which case the law is for the transgressor, and justice to be administered upon all, without respect of persons.

The Fifteenth Proposition

CONCERNING SALUTATIONS AND RECREATIONS, ETC.

Seeing the chief end of all religion is to redeem man from the spirit and vain conversation of this world, and to lead into inward communion with God, before whom, if we fear always, we are accounted happy, therefore all the vain customs and habits thereof, both in word and deed, are to be rejected and forsaken by those who come to this fear; such as taking off the hat to a man, the bowings and cringings of the body, and such other salutations of that kind, with all the foolish and superstitious formalities attending them; all which man has invented in his degenerate state, to feed his pride in the vain pomp and glory of this world; as also the unprofitable plays, frivolous recreations, sportings, and gamings which are invented to pass away the precious time, and divert the mind from the witness of God in the heart, and from the living sense of his fear, and from that evangelical Spirit wherewith Christians ought to be leavened, and which leads into sobriety, gravity, and godly fear; in which, as we abide, the blessing of the Lord is felt to attend us in those actions in which we are necessarily engaged, in order to the taking care for the sustenance of the outward man.

Schaff, *Creeds,* III, 789–798

The New Hampshire Baptist Confession

Declaration of Faith

I. OF THE SCRIPTURES

We believe that the Holy Bible was written by men divinely inspired, and is a perfect treasure of heavenly instruction; that it has God for its author, salvation for its end, and truth without any mixture of error for its matter; that it reveals the principles by which God will judge us; and therefore is, and shall remain to the end of the world, the true center of Christian union, and the supreme standard by which all human conduct, creeds, and opinions should be tried.

II. OF THE TRUE GOD

We believe that there is one, and only one, living and true God, an infinite, intelligent Spirit, whose name is *Jehovah*, the Maker and Supreme Ruler of heaven and earth; inexpressibly glorious in holiness, and worthy of all possible honor, confidence, and love; that in the unity of the Godhead there are three persons, the Father, the Son, and the Holy Ghost; equal in every divine perfection, and executing distinct and harmonious offices in the great work of redemption.

III. OF THE FALL OF MAN

We believe that man was created in holiness, under the law of his Maker; but by voluntary transgression fell from that holy and happy state; in consequence of which all mankind are now sinners, not by constraint, but choice; being by nature utterly void of that holiness required by the law of God, positively inclined to evil; and therefore under just condemnation to eternal ruin, without defense or excuse.

IV. OF THE WAY OF SALVATION

We believe that the salvation of sinners is wholly of grace, through the mediatorial offices of the Son of God; who by the appointment of the Father, freely took upon him our nature, yet without sin; honored the divine law by his personal obedience, and by his death made a full atonement for our sins; that having risen from the dead, he is now enthroned in heaven; and uniting in his wonderful person the tenderest sympathies with divine perfections, he is every way qualified to be a suitable, a compassionate, and an all-sufficient Savior.

V. OF JUSTIFICATION

We believe that the great gospel blessing which Christ secures to such as believe in him is Justification; that Justification includes the pardon of sin, and the promise of eternal life on principles of righteousness; that it is bestowed, not in consideration of any works of righteousness which we have done, but solely through faith in the Redeemer's blood; by virtue of which faith his perfect righteousness is freely imputed to us of God; that it brings us into a state of most blessed peace and favor with God, and secures every other blessing needful for time and eternity.

VI. OF THE FREENESS OF SALVATION

We believe that the blessings of salvation are made free to all by the gospel; that it is the immediate duty of all to accept them by a cordial, penitent, and obedient faith; and that nothing prevents the salvation of the greatest sinner on earth but his own inherent depravity and voluntary rejection of the gospel; which rejection involves him in an aggravated condemnation.

VII. OF GRACE IN REGENERATION

We believe that, in order to be saved, sinners must be regenerated, or born again; that regeneration consists in giving a holy disposition to the mind; that it is effected in a manner above our comprehension by the power of the Holy Spirit, in connection with divine truth, so as to secure our voluntary obedience to the gospel; and that its proper evidence appears in the holy fruits of repentance, and faith, and newness of life.

VIII. OF REPENTANCE AND FAITH

We believe that Repentance and Faith are sacred duties, and also inseparable graces, wrought in our souls by the regenerating Spirit of God; whereby being deeply convinced of our guilt, danger, and helplessness, and of the way of salvation by Christ, we turn to God with unfeigned contrition, confession, and supplication for mercy; at the same time heartily receiving the Lord Jesus Christ as our Prophet, Priest, and King, and relying on him alone as the only and all-sufficient Savior.

IX. OF GOD'S PURPOSE OF GRACE

We believe that Election is the eternal purpose of God, according to which he graciously regenerates, sanctifies, and saves sinners; that being perfectly consistent with the free agency of man, it comprehends all the means in connection with the end; that it is a most glorious display of God's sovereign goodness, being infinitely free, wise, holy, and unchangeable; that it utterly excludes boasting, and promotes humility, love, prayer, praise, trust in God, and active imitation of his free mercy; that it encourages the use of means in the highest degree; that it may be ascertained by the effects in all who truly believe the gospel; that it is the foundation of Christian assurance; and that to ascertain it with regard to ourselves demands and deserves the utmost diligence.

X. OF SANCTIFICATION

We believe that Sanctification is the process by which, according to the will of God, we are made partakers of his holiness; that it is a progressive work; that it is begun in regeneration; and that it is carried on in the hearts of believers by the presence and power of the Holy Spirit, the Sealer and Comforter, in the continual use of the appointed means—especially the Word of God, self-examination, self-denial, watchfulness, and prayer.

XI. OF THE PERSEVERANCE OF SAINTS

We believe that such only are real believers as endure unto the end; that their persevering attachment to Christ is the grand mark which distinguishes them from superficial professors; that a special Providence watches over their welfare; and they are kept by the power of God through faith unto salvation.

XII. OF THE HARMONY OF THE LAW AND THE GOSPEL

We believe that the Law of God is the eternal and unchangeable rule of his moral government; that it is holy, just, and good; and that the inability which the Scriptures ascribe to fallen men to fulfill its precepts arises entirely from their love of sin; to deliver them from which, and to restore them through a Mediator to unfeigned obedience to the holy Law, is one great end of the Gospel, and of the means of grace connected with the establishment of the visible Church.

XIII. OF A GOSPEL CHURCH

We believe that a visible Church of Christ is a congregation of baptized believers, associated by covenant in the faith and fellowship of the gospel; observing the ordinances of Christ; governed by his laws, and exercising the gifts, rights, and privileges invested in them by his Word; that its only scriptural officers are Bishops, or Pastors, and Deacons, whose qualifications, claims, and duties are defined in the Epistles to Timothy and Titus.

XIV. OF BAPTISM AND THE LORD'S SUPPER

We believe that Christian Baptism is the immersion in water of a believer, into the name of the Father, and Son, and Holy Ghost; to show forth, in a solemn and beautiful emblem, our faith in the crucified, buried, and risen Savior, with its effect in our death to sin and resurrection to a new life; that it is prerequisite to the privileges of a

Church relation; and to the Lord's Supper, in which the members of the Church, by the sacred use of bread and wine, are to commemorate together the dying love of Christ; preceded always by solemn self-examination.

XV. Of the Christian Sabbath

We believe that the first day of the week is the Lord's Day, or Christian Sabbath; and is to be kept sacred to religious purposes, by abstaining from all secular labor and sinful recreation; by the devout observance of all the means of grace, both private and public; and by preparation for that rest that remaineth for the people of God.

XVI. Of Civil Government

We believe that civil government is of divine appointment, for the interests and good order of human society; and that magistrates are to be prayed for, conscientiously honored and obeyed; except only in things opposed to the will of our Lord Jesus Christ, who is the only Lord of the conscience, and the Prince of the kings of the earth.

XVII. Of the Righteous and the Wicked

We believe that there is a radical and essential difference between the righteous and the wicked; that such only as through faith are justified in the name of the Lord Jesus, and sanctified by the Spirit of our God, are truly righteous in his esteem; while all such as continue in impenitence and unbelief are in his sight wicked, and under the curse; and this distinction holds among men both in and after death.

XVIII. Of the World to Come

We believe that the end of the world is approaching; that at the last day Christ will descend from heaven, and raise the dead from the grave to final retribution; that a solemn separation will then take place; that the wicked will be adjudged to endless punishment, and the righteous to endless joy; and that this judgment will fix forever the final state of men in heaven or hell, on principles of righteousness.

Schaff, *Creeds*, III, 742–748.

The Theological Declaration of Barmen

I. An Appeal to the Evangelical Congregations and Christians in Germany

The Confessional Synod of the German Evangelical Church met in Barmen, May 29–31, 1934. Here representatives from all the German Confessional Churches met with one accord in a confession of the one Lord of the one, holy, apostolic Church. In fidelity to their Confession of Faith, members of Lutheran, Reformed, and United Churches sought a common message for the need and temptation of the Church in our day. With gratitude to God they are convinced that they have been given a common word to utter. It was not their intention to found a new Church or to form a union. For nothing was farther from their minds than the abolition of the confessional status of our Churches. Their intention was, rather, to withstand in faith and unanimity the destruction of the Confession of Faith, and thus of the Evangelical Church in Germany. In opposition to attempts to establish the unity of the German Evangelical Church by means of false doctrine, by the use of force and insincere practices, the Confessional Synod insists that the unity of the Evangelical Churches in Germany can come only from the Word of God in faith through the Holy Spirit. Thus alone is the Church renewed.

Therefore the Confessional Synod calls upon the congregations to range themselves behind it in prayer, and steadfastly to gather around those pastors and teachers who are loyal to the Confessions.

Be not deceived by loose talk, as if we meant to oppose the unity of the German nation! Do not listen to the seducers who pervert our intentions, as if we wanted to break up the unity of the German Evangelical Church or to forsake the Confessions of the Fathers!

Try the spirits whether they are of God! Prove also the words of the Confessional Synod of the German Evangelical Church to see whether they agree with Holy Scripture and with the Confessions of the Fathers. If you find that we are speaking contrary to Scripture, then do not listen to us! But if you find that we are taking our stand upon Scripture, then let no fear or temptation keep you from treading with us the path of faith and obedience to the Word of God, in order that God's people be of one mind upon earth and that we in faith experience what he himself has said: "I will never leave you, nor forsake you." Therefore, "Fear not, little flock, for it is your Father's good pleasure to give you the kingdom."

II. Theological Declaration Concerning the Present Situation of the German Evangelical Church

According to the opening words of its constitution of July 11, 1933, the German Evangelical Church is a federation of Confessional Churches that grew out of the Reformation and that enjoy equal rights. The theological basis for the unification of these Churches is laid down in Article 1 and Article 2 (1) of the constitution of the German Evangelical Church that was recognized by the Reich Government on July 14, 1933:

> Article 1. The inviolable foundation of the German Evangelical Church is the gospel of Jesus Christ as it is attested for us in Holy Scripture and brought to light again in the Confessions of the Reformation. The full powers that the Church needs for its mission are hereby determined and limited.
>
> Article 2 (1). The German Evangelical Church is divided into member Churches (*Landeskirchen*).

We, the representatives of Lutheran, Reformed, and United Churches, of free synods, Church assemblies, and parish organizations united in the Confessional Synod of the German Evangelical Church, declare that we stand together on the ground of the German Evangelical Church as a federation of German Confessional Churches. We are bound together by the confession of the one Lord of the one, holy, catholic, and apostolic Church.

We publicly declare before all evangelical Churches in Germany that what they hold in common in this Confession is grievously imperiled, and with it the unity of the German Evangelical Church. It is threatened by the teaching methods and actions of the ruling Church party of the "German Christians" and of the Church administration carried on by them. These have become more and more apparent during the first year of the existence of the German Evangelical Church. This threat consists in the fact that the theological basis, in which the German Evangelical Church is united, has been continually and systematically thwarted and rendered ineffective by alien principles, on the part of the leaders and spokesmen of the "German Christians" as well as on the part of the Church administration. When these principles are held to be valid, then, according to all the Confessions in force among us, the Church ceases to be the Church and the German Evangelical Church, as a federation of Confessional Churches, becomes intrinsically impossible.

As members of Lutheran, Reformed, and United Churches we may and must speak with one voice in this matter today. Precisely because we want to be and to remain faithful to our various Confessions, we may not keep silent, since we believe that we have been given a common message to utter in a time of common need and temptation. We commend to God what this may mean for the interrelations of the Confessional Churches.

In view of the errors of the "German Christians" of the present Reich Church government which are devastating the Church and are also thereby breaking up the unity of the German Evangelical Church, we confess the following evangelical truths:

1. "I am the way, and the truth, and the life; no one comes to the Father, but by me" (John 14:6). "Truly, truly, I say to you, he who does not enter the sheepfold by the door but climbs in by another way, that man is a thief and a robber. . . . I am the door; if anyone enters by me, he will be saved" (John 10:1, 9).

Jesus Christ, as he is attested for us in Holy Scripture, is the one Word of God which we have to hear and which we have to trust and obey in life and in death.

We reject the false doctrine, as though the Church could and would have to acknowledge as a source of its proclamation, apart from and besides this one Word of God, still other events and powers, figures and truths, as God's revelation.

2. "Christ Jesus, whom God made our wisdom, our righteousness and sanctification and redemption" (I Cor. 1:30).

As Jesus Christ is God's assurance of the forgiveness of all our sins, so in the same way and with the same seriousness he is also God's mighty claim upon our whole life. Through him befalls us a joyful deliverance from the godless fetters of this world for a free, grateful service to his creatures.

We reject the false doctrine, as though there were areas of our life in which we would not belong to Jesus Christ, but to other lords—areas in which we would not need justification and sanctification through him.

3. "Rather, speaking the truth in love, we are to grow up in every way into him who is the head, into Christ, from whom the whole body [is] joined and knit together" (Eph. 4:15, 16).

The Christian Church is the congregation of the brethren in which Jesus Christ acts presently as the Lord in Word and sacrament through the Holy Spirit. As the Church of pardoned sinners, it has to testify in the midst of a sinful world, with its faith as with its obedience, with its message as with its order, that it is solely his property, and that it lives and wants to live solely from his comfort and from his direction in the expectation of his appearance.

We reject the false doctrine, as though the Church were permitted to abandon the form of its message and order to its own pleasure or to changes in prevailing ideological and political convictions.

4. "You know that the rulers of the Gentiles lord it over them, and their great men exercise authority over them. It shall not be so among you; but whoever would be great among you must be your servant" (Matt. 20:25, 26).

The various offices in the Church do not establish a dominion of some over the others; on the contrary, they are for the exercise of the ministry entrusted to and enjoined upon the whole congregation.

We reject the false doctrine, as though the Church, apart from this ministry, could and were permitted to give to itself, or allow to be given to it, special leaders vested with ruling powers.

5. "Fear God. Honor the emperor" (I Peter 2:17).

Scripture tells us that, in the as yet unredeemed world in which the Church also exists, the State has by divine appointment the task of providing for justice and peace. [It fulfills this task] by means of the threat and exercise of force, according to the measure of human judgment and human ability. The Church acknowledges the benefit of this divine appointment in gratitude and reverence before him. It calls to mind the Kingdom of God, God's commandment and righteousness, and thereby the responsibility both of rulers and of the ruled. It trusts and obeys the power of the Word by which God upholds all things.

We reject the false doctrine, as though the State, over and beyond its special commission, should and could become the single and totalitarian order of human life, thus fulfilling the Church's vocation as well.

We reject the false doctrine, as though the Church, over and beyond its special commission, should and could appropriate the characteristics, the tasks, and the dignity of the State, thus itself becoming an organ of the State.

6. "Lo, I am with you always, to the close of the age" (Matt. 28:20). "The word of God is not fettered" (I Tim. 2:9).

The Church's commission, upon which its freedom is founded, consists in delivering the message of the free grace of God to all people in Christ's stead, and therefore in the ministry of his own Word and work through sermon and sacrament.

We reject the false doctrine, as though the Church in human arrogance could place the Word and work of the Lord in the service of any arbitrarily chosen desires, purposes, and plans.

The Confessional Synod of the German Evangelical Church declares that it sees in the acknowledgment of these truths and in the rejection of these errors the indispensable theological basis of the German

Evangelical Church as a federation of Confessional Churches. It invites all who are able to accept its declaration to be mindful of these theological principles in their decisions in Church politics. It entreats all whom it concerns to return to the unity of faith, love, and hope.

Reprinted from Arthur C. Cochrane,
The Church's Confession under Hitler
(Philadelphia: Westminster Press, 1962), pp. 237–242.
Used by permission.

Confession of Faith of the Huria Kristen Batak Protestant (Batak, Indonesia)

1. This Confession of Faith of the H.K.B.P. is the continuation of the confessions (creeds) already existing, namely, the three confessions of faith (creeds) which were already known to our Christian forefathers and are called: (1) The Apostles' Creed; (2) The Nicene Creed; (3) The Athanasian Creed.

2. This Confession of Faith is the summary of what we believe and hope in this life and the life to come.

3. This Confession of Faith is the basis of the H.K.B.P. in preaching, in teaching and in public life.

4. This Confession of Faith is the basis of the H.K.B.P. on which to reject every false doctrine and heresy that is contrary to God's Word.

ARTICLE 1

We believe and confess: There is a God—eternal, almighty, unchangeable, omniscient, inscrutable, righteous, gracious, all-bountiful. The earth and all that is on it, is His; He is true, all holy, full of love.

In adopting this doctrine we reject the custom of calling God grandfather ("Ompung"), and the idea that God is a gracious God only, as well as the idea that blessing may be expected from the spirits of our ancestors. We also give up striving for a good time, and reject all those who listen to fortune-tellers and read their fate in the lines of their hands.

In adopting this doctrine we also reject the heresy of considering God's power to be greater than His holiness and love.

290

ARTICLE 2. THE TRINITY OF GOD

We believe and confess: There is one God, and at the same time He is a Trinity, namely, God the Father, God the Son, and God the Holy Spirit.

The Father has begotten His Son of His own being, for ever and ever, that is: Just as the Father is eternal, the Son also is eternal. Likewise the Holy Spirit—proceeding from the Father and the Son—is eternal.

In adopting this doctrine we reject any interpretation of the Trinity of God (Maha Esa) to the effect that the Son and the Spirit are subordinated to the Father.

We also reject the false doctrine interpreting the Trinity as God the Father, His Son, the Lord Jesus Christ, and the Mother: the Holy Spirit.

ARTICLE 3. THE SPECIAL ACTS OF THE TRIUNE GOD

We believe and confess:

A. God the Father is the Maker, the Provider and the Lord of all things visible and invisible.

According to this doctrine we reject any fatalism (Takdir and the like).

B. God the Son, Who was incarnate, born of the Virgin Mary, conceived by the Holy Spirit, Who is called Jesus. Two natures are found in Him, namely, God and man at the same time in one person, which cannot be separated. Jesus Christ was very God, and at the same time He is very man. He has suffered under the judgment of Pontius Pilate, was crucified on the cross in order to deliver us from sin, from death and from the rule of the Devil. He is the abundance of all expiatory sacrifices to God because of all man's sin. He descended into hell after being buried; the third day He rose again, He ascended into heaven, sitting on the right hand of God the Father Who is glorious for ever. He is our intercessor in Heaven and Lord of all, until He will come again to judge the quick and the dead.

According to this doctrine we reject the Roman Catholic doctrines such as

1. the doctrine teaching that Mary, the mother of the Lord Jesus or, as they call her, the Glorified, may intercede for us with God;

2. the doctrine teaching that any pastor (priest) may sacrifice Christ in the Mass;

3. the false doctrine that the Roman Pope is the Vicar of Christ on earth.

4. we reject the human conception teaching that the Lord Jesus is comparable to the prophets of the world.

C. God the Holy Spirit has called the Church and has taught it and preserved it in true faith and holiness in the Gospel, to the honor of God.

According to this doctrine we reject the doctrine teaching that the Holy Spirit can descend upon somebody through his own preparation, beyond the Gospel.

Furthermore, we reject the doctrine teaching that all medicines are unnecessary, because physical illnesses may be properly cured only by prayer to the Holy Spirit; as well as the false prophecies made in the name of the Holy Spirit, and the dissolute life of people who say that they are established in the name of the Holy Spirit.

All these false doctrines we reject because they are a misuse of the name of the Holy Spirit.

ARTICLE 4. THE WORD OF GOD (THE HOLY SCRIPTURES)

We believe and confess: The words written in the Bible, in the Old and New Testaments, are certainly words of God, "For the prophecy came not in old time by the will of man" (II Peter 1:21). "All Scripture is given by inspiration of God, and is profitable for doctrine, for reproof, for correction, for instruction in righteousness: That the man of God may be perfect, thoroughly furnished unto all good works" (II Timothy 3:16–17).

According to this doctrine we emphasize: The Holy Scripture is completely sufficient to reveal God's being and His will, and the Holy Scripture is also completely sufficient to instruct what to believe in order to gain eternal life. The Holy Scripture is the beginning and the end of all thoughts, wisdom and activity of the Church and the believers.

According to this doctrine we reject any science and wisdom of man differing from the Holy Scriptures.

ARTICLE 5

The originator of sin is the Devil; it is his will that all men become sinners and turn away from God.

Thus, although the first men (Adam and Eve) were perfect and able to act in conformity with God's will, they nevertheless infringed the commandment God had given them and turned away from God because of the seduction by the Devil. Consequently, the sin is the infringement of God's commandment.

ARTICLE 6

We believe and confess: Since Adam and Eve had fallen into sin, sin has been passed on to all their descendants. Therefore all men are conceived in sin and are enslaved by the sin of trespassing against God's commandments. Punishment and eternal death are the result of sin.

According to this doctrine we reject the false thought that newborn children are without sin, as well as the false thought teaching that sin can only be the result of poverty, penury or distress, and that, consequently, such sin cannot be taken for sin.

We also reject the doctrine teaching that the heart of man at the time of his birth is pure like blank paper.

ARTICLE 7. REDEMPTION FROM SIN

We believe and confess: No man gains redemption from sin by means of good works, or through his own power. Only the grace of God through the redemption of Jesus Christ brings us salvation. The only way to gain salvation is by faith and the working of the Holy Spirit, by which the believer receives remission of sin which is won by Jesus Christ through His death.

Such faith is also taken by God for true righteousness.

ARTICLE 8. THE CHURCH

A. We believe and confess: The Church is the communion of believers in Jesus Christ, who are called, gathered, sanctified and preserved by God through the Holy Spirit.

According to this doctrine we reject the doctrine teaching the following:

1. That the Church (communion) is established by men through their own will, and the followers of that doctrine for that reason separate from our Church, not because in our Church there is any false doctrine that does not harmonize with God's Word.

2. Likewise we reject the false thought that only the leaders and only the assemblies or the members can exert full authority over the Church; for Christ only is the Lord of the Church, and the Church has to follow only such orders that harmonize with His word. In the Church there is no democracy, but Christocracy.

3. Likewise we oppose the idea that the Church should become a State Church, since the task of the State is different from the service of the Church.

4. We also oppose the idea that the Church should be based upon the Adat (nationalities*?) and bound to it, as well as the false thought that expects organization to impart life to the Church.

B. We believe and confess: The Church is holy. The Church is holy not because its members as such are holy, but because its head, Jesus Christ, is holy.

Thus, Christ has sanctified the Church, and therefore the members, too, are considered holy by God. Because of the holiness of the Church they are also considered a holy people, a temple of the Holy Spirit and habitation of God.

According to this doctrine we reject the doctrine teaching that man can gain his holiness through his work, as well as pessimism and separation on the basis of the perception that there is still sin among the Church members.

C. We believe and confess: The Church is a congregation. The congregation is the assembly of all saints who have a share in Jesus Christ and all His gifts, namely: the Gospel, the Holy Spirit, love, and hope. They are of every country and people, every tribe and race and every language in their various ceremonies and orders.

According to this doctrine we reject the interpretation considering the Church a national Church (intended for one people), and the idea of isolating one Church from another one.

D. We believe and confess: There is one Church. The basis is Ephesians 4:4; I Cor. 12:20. There is one body, that is the Church, and even though there are many members, there is but one body.

The unity of the Church is different from the secular unity, because it is a spiritual unity.

According to this doctrine we reject any separations of churches that are not based on differences of faith, but only on external reasons.

Features of the true Church:

We believe and confess:

1. The pure preaching of the Gospel;

2. The proper administering of the Sacraments ordered by the Lord Jesus;

3. The proper exercise of discipline in order to combat sin are the features of the true Church.

ARTICLE 9. THE SERVANTS OF THE CHURCH

We believe and confess: Every Christian is called to be a witness for Christ and a worker in the Church. God has called the servants

---

* In other translations, *Adat* is rendered as "custom." Cf. Vajta, V. and Weiss-gerber, H., *The Church and the Confessions* (Philadelphia: Fortress Press, 1963), p. 142.

through the Church according to the services of the Church and to the three offices of Christ, namely: prophet, priest, and king.

These offices the Church has to fulfill.

The service of the Church comprehends:

1. The preaching of the Gospel to the Church members and outside of the Church;

2. The administering of the two Sacraments, namely: the Holy Baptism and the Holy Communion;

3. The pastoral care of souls;

4. The preserving of the pure doctrine, the exercise of proper discipline and the opposing of false doctrines;

5. The doing of diaconal work.

To these services God has called in the Church apostles, prophets, evangelists, pastors, and teachers.

According to this doctrine we reject the idea of denying and refusing the service of the servants on the basis of one's own opinion, unless on the basis of machinations which do not harmonize with their service.

According to this doctrine we also oppose anyone in the congregation rising to preach and to teach and to administer the Sacraments without being called to these services by the Church.

ARTICLE 10. THE HOLY SACRAMENTS

We believe and confess: There are two Sacraments ordered by the Lord Jesus, namely: the Holy Baptism and the Holy Communion. The Lord Jesus Christ has ordered them for His congregation in order to grant His invisible grace, namely: remission of sin, redemption, life and glory, which are to be won by faith, through visible signs.

According to this doctrine we reject the Roman Catholic doctrine teaching that there are seven Sacraments.

A. Holy Baptism. We believe and confess: The Holy Baptism is a means of God's grace toward men, for by means of Baptism the believer is granted remission of sin, regeneration, redemption from death and Devil, and also life everlasting.

According to this doctrine we confess that also children should be baptized, since through Baptism they will be received into the communion of those who are saved by Christ. The Lord Jesus also accepted children.

It is not necessary that the person to be baptized be immersed.

B. Holy Communion. We believe and confess: The Holy Communion is the eating of the bread by means of which we are given the Body of our Lord Jesus Christ, and the drinking of the wine by means of which we are given the Blood of our Lord Jesus Christ, whereby we receive redemption from sin, and life, and glory.

According to this doctrine we reject the false doctrine teaching that only the bread without the wine should be given to the members of the Church. For the Lord Jesus himself, when he instituted the Lord's Supper, has spoken the words: "Drink ye all of it." And the first Church has acted in accordance with this.

Also the mass is not in accordance with the Holy Scriptures, when one says that our Lord is sacrificed again each time in the mass. Consequently, we are against this heresy.

ARTICLE 11. THE CHURCH ORDER

We confess: In the Church there shall be a Church order which is based upon the Holy Scriptures. For the Church order is something to give order and peace to the Church. Also in the Church the Church festivals are celebrated, namely: the Birth of Jesus Christ, Good Friday, the Resurrection and Ascension of the Lord, and the pouring out of the Holy Spirit. Nevertheless everyone should remember that no one can win remission of sins by observation of all these festivals.

ARTICLE 12. THE SECULAR GOVERNMENT

We confess: That the authority who has power is ordained by God. That means an authority who opposes the evil and does right in order to bring peace and certainty to the believers, as it is written in Romans 13 and I Timothy 2:2. Nevertheless one should also remember what is written in Acts 5:29: "We ought to obey God rather than man."

According to this doctrine we confess: We ought to pray for the authority, that it may do right, and the Church shall raise its voice toward the authority.

According to this doctrine we also reject the idea that the Church should become a State Church, for the State is a State, and the Church is a Church.

Whenever it is necessary before the judge, a Christian is permitted to take an oath for truthfulness. The same may be done at the time of induction into an office or a responsibility.

ARTICLE 13. SUNDAY

We consider Sunday holy. It is the Day of the Lord, which is the first day of creation, the day of Resurrection of the Lord, and which has been celebrated by the Church from the very beginning.

We refuse to return to the Jewish Sabbath, for we are Christians.

According to this doctrine we reject the false doctrine which declares Saturday to be the Holy Sabbath Day.

ARTICLE 14. FOOD

We believe and confess: Every creature of God is good, and one should not make any difference between various kinds of food, if it is received with thanksgiving and is sanctified by God's Word and by prayer.

No man can gain holiness by abstaining from certain foods, for holiness is received from God by faith. For this reason the apostles opposed the Jewish food laws. For the Gospel should not be perverted by abstaining from certain foods and by any habit or tradition.

According to this doctrine we reject any heresy teaching something different.

ARTICLE 15. FAITH AND GOOD WORKS

We believe and confess: Good works are the fruits of faith. Whosoever hopes to gain righteousness, life, comfort, or glory by doing good works is mistaken. The Lord Jesus Christ alone can grant remission of sins and can bring man back to God.

We have to follow the ten commandments. However, we live only by faith, not by doing good works.

The Holy Spirit moves man to do good works. (If not urged by the Spirit, good works will become sin.)

ARTICLE 16. THE FUNERAL

We believe and confess: Men are destined to die, but after that there will be the judgment. Then they rest from their work. Jesus Christ is the Lord of the quick and the dead. So, when conducting a funeral we think of the end of our lives, for the strengthening of our hope for the communion of the believers with God. This we do in order that we may be strengthened in our struggles in this life.

According to this doctrine we reject: The heathenish concept that the souls of the dead have influence on the living; as well as the false doctrine teaching that the soul of a dead person remains in the grave with the body. We also reject the Roman Catholic doctrine teaching that there is a purgatory which the dead must experience in order to purify their souls and to win eternal life, furthermore, that one may conduct a mass or prayers for the dead, praying to the souls of the saints and the hope that the power or the holiness of the dead may enter into their graves, their shrouds or any things or even into their bones and may be passed on in this way (relics).

ARTICLE 17. THE ANGELS

We believe and confess: The angels are created by God to serve Him, they are ministering spirits sent by God to protect the heirs of salvation.

ARTICLE 18. THE LAST JUDGMENT

We believe and confess: Our Lord Jesus Christ will come again on Judgment Day to awake the dead, and to judge men. Then He will lead the believers to everlasting life. The unbelievers, however, will go to everlasting torment.

The inheritance of the believers with God will last throughout eternity.

According to this doctrine we reject the heresy teaching that:

A. the time of Christ's coming again may be computed;

B. after death there is still a period of grace.

We confirm: that the coming again of our Lord will be unexpected. Consequently, we should be ready at any time, as He has warned us.

Missionary Research Library, 3041 Broadway,
New York, New York, 10027, 1957.

Statement of Faith of the United Church of Christ

We believe in God, the Eternal Spirit, Father of our Lord Jesus Christ and our Father, and to His deeds we testify:

He calls the worlds into being, creates man in his own image and sets before him the ways of life and death.

He seeks in holy love to save all people from aimlessness and sin.

He judges men and nations by his righteous will declared through prophets and apostles.

In Jesus Christ, the man of Nazareth, our crucified and risen Lord, he has come to us and shared our common lot, conquering sin and death and reconciling the world to himself.

He bestows upon us his Holy Spirit, creating and renewing the Church of Jesus Christ, binding in covenant faithful people of all ages, tongues, and races.

He calls us into his Church to accept the cost and joy of discipleship, to be his servants in the service of men, to proclaim the gospel to all the world and resist the powers of evil, to share in Christ's baptism and eat at his table, to join him in his passion and victory.

He promises to all who trust him forgiveness of sins and fullness of grace, courage in the struggle for justice and peace, his presence in trial and rejoicing, and eternal life in his kingdom which has no end.

Blessing and honor, glory and power be unto him. Amen.

The Christian Century, vol. LXXVI, 29
(July 22, 1959), p. 846.

INDEX

INDEX

Loved One, The (Waugh), 147, 158n
Lord's Prayer, 117
Lord's Supper, sacrament of the, 220–224
different views, 220–224
Love
agape, 100–102
children require, 100
divine, 98–102
eros, 101
God is absolute love, 62, 101–102
of neighbor, 137
reality of, 46
revelation in Christ's Cross, 181–183
righteousness and, 98–102
Lowrie, Walter, 75n
Luther, Martin, 19, 30n, 32, 42, 75n, 103n, 116, 122n, 153, 228n, 235
on authority of Holy Scriptures, 68
on confession of sin, 142
Diet of Worms, 13–14, 30n
explanation of the Apostles' Creed, 82, 167, 189
on the Holy Spirit, 189–190
hymns, 176
on the Lord's Supper, 224
on the millennium, 236
on the philosophical approach to God, 81
on the political use of law, 90
on prayer, 119
proclamation of Scriptures, 212–214
rejected authority of direct revelation, 23–24
on religious zeal, 42
on the sovereignty of God, 53
on the unity of the church, 202
Lutheran Christians, 217
Lutherans, 18, 141, 208, 210, 217, 223
number of, 16
The Service of, 142, 158n, 188n, 227n

Man
belief in innate goodness of, 2
created in the image of God, 125
doctrine of, 123–158
result of sin, 139–158
fallibility of, 27–29, 30
humanity of, 126–128
relationship to God, 124
as sinner, 128–139
Man Nobody Knows, The, 60
Marcion, Christian gnostic, 69
Marks of the Protestant religion, 16–30
Marx, Karl, 5
Marxism, 5, 133
Meaninglessness of life, 159
result of sin, 144–149, 153
Mennonites, 16, 207, 208

Merrill, William Pierson, 187
Methodists, 28, 208, 217
doctrines of, 22, 30n
number of, 16
Millennium, 235–237
definition, 235
Miller, Arthur, 157
Ministry, 225–226
ordination of ministers, 225
Miracle, 120–122
definitions, 120
of Pentecost, 120–121
Protestant view, 120–122
Missionary movement, 15
Missionary Research Library, 298n
Modern Protestantism, 72, 85
Modernism, 231
Mohammed, 40
Money, making a god of it, 1, 129
Moody, Dwight L., 199
Moravian Brethren, 113
Moslem faith, 9, 42
Münzer, Thomas, 23–24
Music, religious, 59–60
Mysticism, 41–42, 83–84

National Council of the Churches of Christ in the United States of America, 208
"Natural" catastrophes and sin, 150–152
Naturalism, 154–155
Nature
pantheism, 83–84, 105–109
worship of, 109
Nazism, 228
Neander, Joachim, 80
Neo-Orthodoxy, 28
Netherlands, Protestantism in, 15
New Hampshire Baptist Confession, 281–285
New Testament, 70–75
Nicene Creed, 32, 61
text, 239–240
Niebuhr, Helmut R., 227n
Niemoeller, Martin, 216
Nietzsche, Friedrich, 4–5, 6, 128, 158n
No Exit (Sartre), 157
Norway, Protestantism in, 15

Oedipus, King, 116, 156
Old Testament, 70–75
books of, 68
contemporary neglect of, 72
law, 40
testifies of Christ, 70
Ordination of ministers, 225
Organization of the church, 205–207
Original sin, 134–137

305